D0939250

THE COMPLETE IDIOT'S GUIDE® TO

Christian Mysteries

by Ron Benrey

ALPHA

A member of Penguin Group (USA) Inc.

I dedicate this book to readers who seek to learn more about Jesus of Nazareth, both Christians and "soon to be Christians." May you succeed—and strengthen your faith.

ALPHA BOOKS

Published by the Penguin Group

Penguin Group (USA) Inc., 375 Hudson Street, New York, New York 10014, USA

Penguin Group (Canada), 90 Eglinton Avenue East, Suite 700, Toronto, Ontario M4P 2Y3, Canada (a division of Pearson Penguin Canada Inc.)

Penguin Books Ltd., 80 Strand, London WC2R 0RL, England

Penguin Ireland, 25 St. Stephen's Green, Dublin 2, Ireland (a division of Penguin Books Ltd.)

Penguin Group (Australia), 250 Camberwell Road, Camberwell, Victoria 3124, Australia (a division of Pearson Australia Group Pty. Ltd.)

Penguin Books India Pvt. Ltd., 11 Community Centre, Panchsheel Park, New Delhi—110 017, India

Penguin Group (NZ), 67 Apollo Drive, Rosedale, North Shore, Auckland 1311, New Zealand (a division of Pearson New Zealand Ltd.)

Penguin Books (South Africa) (Pty.) Ltd., 24 Sturdee Avenue, Rosebank, Johannesburg 2196, South Africa

Penguin Books Ltd., Registered Offices: 80 Strand, London WC2R 0RL, England

Copyright © 2008 by Ron Benrey

International Standard Book Number: 978-159257-762-0
Library of Congress Catalog Card Number: 2008920990

10 09 08   8 7 6 5 4 3 2 1

Interpretation of the printing code: The rightmost number of the first series of numbers is the year of the book's printing; the rightmost number of the second series of numbers is the number of the book's printing. For example, a printing code of 08-1 shows that the first printing occurred in 2008.

Printed in the United States of America

Note: This publication contains the opinions and ideas of its author. It is intended to provide helpful and informative material on the subject matter covered. It is sold with the understanding that the author and publisher are not engaged in rendering professional services in the book. If the reader requires personal assistance or advice, a competent professional should be consulted.

The author and publisher specifically disclaim any responsibility for any liability, loss, or risk, personal or otherwise, which is incurred as a consequence, directly or indirectly, of the use and application of any of the contents of this book.

Most Alpha books are available at special quantity discounts for bulk purchases for sales promotions, premiums, fundraising, or educational use. Special books, or book excerpts, can also be created to fit specific needs.

For details, write: Special Markets, Alpha Books, 375 Hudson Street, New York, NY 10014.

Publisher: *Marie Butler-Knight*
Editorial Director: *Mike Sanders*
Senior Managing Editor: *Billy Fields*
Executive Editor: *Randy Ladenheim-Gil*
Development Editor: *Lynn Northrup*
Production Editor: *Megan Douglass*

Copy Editor: *Emily Garner*
Cover Designer: *Kurt Owens*
Book Designer: *Trina Wurst*
Indexer: *Joan Green*
Layout: *Ayanna Lacey*
Proofreader: *Mary Hunt*

Contents at a Glance

Contents

11   The Mystery of Jesus' Descent into Hell   121

12   The Mystery of Jesus' Ascension   129

13   The Mystery of the Dead Messiah   137

Introduction

Many of Christianity's essential teachings are ultimately mysteries that our limited minds will never fully comprehend. We can think about these doctrines, we can talk about them, we can argue about them, but we'll never reach the point where we truly understand them.

The existence of Christian mysteries shouldn't surprise anyone. As the prophet Isaiah wrote more than 700 years before Jesus Christ lived: "For my thoughts are not your thoughts, nor are your ways my ways, says the LORD. For as the heavens are higher than the earth, so are my ways higher than your ways and my thoughts than your thoughts." (Isaiah 55:8–9, NRSV)

The toughest, most mind-bending Christian mystery of all is Jesus Himself. At first glance, understanding Jesus doesn't seem like an especially difficult chore. The basics of His story are easy to grasp:

- Jesus of Nazareth lived 2,000 years ago and began a 3-year ministry at age 30.
- He was an itinerant preacher and healer in Judea, Galilee, and Samaria, three minor—though troubled—provinces of the Roman Empire.
- His followers assert that he said many notable things, did many remarkable things, and made several astonishing claims—all of which managed to put Jesus in peril with the local authorities.
- He was killed in an especially degrading way by the Romans.

But then, instead of disappearing from history and being forgotten by everyone, a seemingly impossible thing happened: Jesus was resurrected by God in a body that had incredible properties and was subsequently seen by several hundred people. Forty days later he left Earth in an equally perplexing manner, after promising to return.

His followers see these mystifying events as evidence that validates their most extraordinary assertions of all:

- The Jesus who walked the dusty roads of ancient Israel is still alive today—in Heaven, in His glorified body.
- Then and now he is both true God and true man at the same time.
- He was born of a virgin and is the Son of God.
- Jesus is the world's Savior who made possible sinful humanity's reconciliation with God.

◆ Jesus' death on the Cross revealed the depth of God's love for us and crushed the powers of sin and death.

Trying to make sense of what Jesus said, did, and accomplished has occupied legions of theologians and scholars for nearly two millennia. Rather than produce a tidy explanation of Jesus Christ, their efforts have led to many of the leading Christian mysteries we'll examine in the chapters that follow.

But didn't I just say that our feeble intellects can't understand Christianity's mysteries?

Well, not quite. As you'll see, there's much about the toughest doctrines that Christians can comprehend with a little effort. The majority of Christianity's mysteries consist of genuinely mysterious "cores" surrounded by teachings and ideas that *can* be understood. And so, we don't have to switch off our brains whenever we meet a Christian mystery face to face.

By the time you finish this book, you'll have a much richer appreciation of two dozen of Christianity's most challenging teachings and doctrines—including the industrial-strength Christian mindbenders: the Trinity, the Incarnation, the Atonement, Jesus' dual natures, and the Resurrection.

Now, I readily admit Christianity's chief mysteries will retain their power to confound you after you read this book, because not even a *Complete Idiot's Guide* can explain the inexplicable. My goal is to give you what I've dubbed a "comfortable understanding" of the most mysterious Christian teachings, concepts, and historical events. Specifically, you will know (and will be able to better explain to others):

◆ The fundamental details of the most mysterious Christian teachings

◆ Why these doctrines are considered essential to Christianity

◆ Which aspects of the doctrines are valid mysteries—and which are merely tricky concepts to grasp

As we study each mystery, we'll also look briefly at the opposing notions—the *heresies*—that had to be overcome to establish these key doctrines as orthodox ("right thinking") teachings. Many of these ancient, arguably flawed, views are alive and well today, still causing confusion—and dissention—among believers.

As you'll discover, one reason that there are so many Christian denominations is that sincere people can easily disagree about the interpretation of Scripture and the appropriate content of Christian doctrine. Throughout this book I've presented the most widely held viewpoints: core Christian teachings that are accepted by the bulk of the world's Christians and theologians. I've used different labels for these doctrines, including *mainstream teaching*, *widely held belief*, and *majority viewpoint*.

Here's more good news: I've made this book easy to read and follow—with a minimum of "Christian-ese" and complex theological language and a maximum of simple analogies and straightforward discussion. You'll find that the Christian mysteries become less murky when you tackle them step by step.Naturally, I've included verses of Scripture when appropriate to set the stage. I took them from six popular Bible translations: the New International Version (NIV), the Revised Standard Version (RSV), the New Revised Standard Version (NRSV), the Holman Christian Standard Bible (HCSB), the King James Version (KJV), and The Message (TMSG). I've used the traditional method of citing Bible verses. For example: (Matthew 22:36–38, NIV) is Chapter 22, Verses 36 through 38 of The Gospel According to Matthew as rendered in the New International Version.

The three verses from Matthew that I used as an example above are worth reading now: … a lawyer, asked him [Jesus] a question to test him. "Teacher, which commandment in the law is the greatest?" He said to him, "'You shall love the Lord your God with all your heart, and with all your soul, and with all your mind.' This is the greatest and first commandment."

The point is that our minds have a vital role to play in our Christian walk. One way we love God is by gaining a greater understanding of Christianity. So sit back and join me on a fascinating journey as we explore Christianity's most bewildering—and exciting—mysteries.

What You'll Learn in This Book

Part 1, "The Christian Mindbenders," leads off your study of Christianity's mysteries with the toughest of the tough teachings, starting with the doctrines of the Incarnation and the Trinity. When you finish this section you'll know much more about the key teachings of mainstream Christianity—the core doctrines that are accepted and taught by the majority of Christian denominations in North America, Europe, and Australia/New Zealand.

Part 2, "Other Mysteries About Jesus," investigates several truly mysterious aspects of Jesus Christ's life and death, including some of the most fascinating—and surprising—beliefs about Jesus. Because most of these teachings are so familiar—the Virgin Birth and the claim that Jesus was the Messiah, for example—Christians tend to overlook the true mysteries buried inside.

Part 3, "The Mysteries of Jesus' Ministry," takes a closer look at many of the astounding things Jesus said and did during his brief ministry in ancient Israel. The powers he displayed have mysterious aspects—so do his "hard sayings" and difficult teachings. Learning more about these things will give you new insights into what Jesus sought to accomplish.

Part 4, "Other Mysteries of Christianity," examines several tough teachings, conundrums, and enigmas that have baffled Christians since the dawn of Christianity. At first glance, some of them may not strike you as true Christian mysteries. But try to explain them to someone else, and the depth of their difficulty quickly becomes clear. It's no accident that certain of these mysteries are routinely cited by nonbelievers as evidence that Christianity is not true.

Extras

I've included a number of different sidebars throughout the chapters that supplement the chief explanations and teaching. They are identified by the following labels:

Walking with the Wise

To help explain tough teachings and complex doctrines, I include intriguing—and pertinent—quotations from the early "Church fathers," key figures from Christianity's history, well-known Christian apologists and theologians, and others.

Take Warning!

One reason Christianity is confusing is the mass of *mis*information out there. These sidebars highlight common false doctrines, popular myths, and recurrent heresies that muddle Christianity

Scripture Says

These relevant passages from Scripture give you additional insight into the mind-bending Christian concepts.

Get Wisdom

These sidebars provide historical details and background information that you may find interesting, enlightening, or even humorous.

def•i•ni•tion

These sidebars provide definitions of key words that help you make sense of Christianity's tough teachings and difficult doctrines.

Acknowledgements

Many thanks to the professional and supportive editorial team at Alpha Books, including Randy Ladenheim-Gil, Executive Editor; Lynn Northrup, Development Editor; Megan Douglass, Production Editor; and Emily Garner, Copy Editor. They made writing this book a pleasure. And a big thank you to my literary agent, Marilyn Allen.

Special Thanks to the Technical Editor

Dr. Angela Hunt, who holds Master of Biblical Sciences and Doctor of Biblical Sciences degrees, served as Technical Editor of this book. She verified the accuracy of my manuscript. Incidentally, you may know Angela as a best-selling author of Christian fiction (her novels have sold more than 3 million copies worldwide). I want to thank Angela for the care she took, for the excellent suggestions she made, and for her friendly support throughout the development process.

Trademarks

All terms mentioned in this book that are known to be or are suspected of being trademarks or service marks have been appropriately capitalized. Alpha Books and Penguin Group (USA) Inc. cannot attest to the accuracy of this information. Use of a term in this book should not be regarded as affecting the validity of any trademark or service mark.

Scripture quotations marked HCSB have been taken from the *Holman Christian Standard Bible®*, Copyright © 1999, 2000, 2002, 2003 by Holman Bible Publishers. Used by permission.

Scripture quotations marked NIV have been taken from the *HOLY BIBLE, NEW INTERNATIONAL VERSION®*. Copyright © 1973, 1978, 1984 International Bible Society. Used by permission of Zondervan. All rights reserved.

Scripture quotations marked NRSV have been taken from the *New Revised Standard Version Bible*, copyright 1989, Division of Christian Education of the National Council of the Churches of Christ in the United States of America. Used by permission. All rights reserved.

Scripture quotations marked RSV have been taken from the *Revised Standard Version of the Bible*, copyright 1952 [2nd edition, 1971] by the Division of Christian Education of the National Council of the Churches of Christ in the United States of America. Used by permission. All rights reserved.

Part  The Christian Mindbenders

We begin with the most mysterious of Christianity's mysteries. Part 1 of this book is chock full of Christianity's toughest teachings—doctrines that have kept the brightest theologians debating for centuries.

The mind-bending medley leads off with the Incarnation that somehow made Jesus of Nazareth fully God and fully human and continues with the "illogical" Trinity of Father, Son, and Holy Spirit—the doctrine that most believers consider to be the most bewildering in Christendom.

I begin at the deep end of the Christian conundrum pool because these teachings are the foundation stones of mainstream Christian theology, the core doctrines that explain Jesus Christ. Master these mysteries and you'll have taken a giant leap on your journey to understanding Christianity.

Christianity—a Faith Full of Mysteries

In This Chapter

- ◆ Christianity: a hard-to-understand religion
- ◆ What we mean by *Christian mysteries*
- ◆ Why nonbelievers see Christianity as "foolish"
- ◆ Your responsibilities as a thinking Christian
- ◆ Knowledge will help you make disciples
- ◆ Proven strategies for tackling the Christian mysteries

Christianity is full of mind-bending teachings that we won't fully understand this side of heaven; for example, the Trinity, the Incarnation, and the Atonement. Christians know that they are true, but we also confess that we can't imagine how such things are possible. A Christian tenet that simultaneously creates this strange combination of certainty and bewilderment is called a *Christian mystery*.

There are lots of Christian mysteries. Taken together, they can make Christianity more difficult to understand than other world religions. In this first chapter, I'll talk about why this is so—and how you should respond to the challenge.

Christianity Can Be Mysterious

Christianity is a difficult religion to grab hold of. Oh, the basic idea is easy enough to grasp: as C. S. Lewis wrote in *Mere Christianity* (see Appendix B), "The central Christian belief is that Christ's death has somehow put us right with God and given us a fresh start."

So far, so good. But then, we're taught that ...

- The *one* God consists of *three* "Persons": Father, Son, and Holy Spirit.

- Jesus is both fully God and fully man—*at the same time*.

- Jesus told his disciples to love their enemies (see Luke 6:27), but to *hate* their father, mother, wife, children, brothers, and sisters (see Luke 14:26).

- Jesus died, was somehow resurrected in a glorified body, and then ascended to Heaven—in his new, improved body.

- Jesus was crucified almost 2,000 years ago—yet this very same Jesus is alive today and available for a personal relationship with any believer who wants one.

These are some of Christianity's mysteries—doctrines that can never be fully explained. Consequently, we'll never fully understand the workings of a Christian mystery. If we could, it wouldn't be a true mystery.

The Meaning of Mystery

Mystery comes from the Greek word *mysterion*, which in turn comes from *myein*, a Greek word meaning to shut, or to close. A theological mystery is a revealed truth that's too complex to be unraveled by our limited minds. It's also too full of meaning to be expressed by mere language. The Apostle Paul had both these characteristics in mind when he wrote about the "mystery of God" (see 1 Corinthians 2:1), the "mystery of Christ" (see Ephesians 3:4), and the "mystery of the gospel" (see Ephesians 6:9).

> **Scripture Says**
>
> Pray also for me, so that when I speak, a message may be given to me to make known with boldness the mystery of the gospel .... (Ephesians 6:19, NRSV)

Some Christian denominations use the term *sacred mystery* to identify the Lord's Supper (Communion), baptism, and other sacraments that have been instituted by Jesus. I've limited the use of "mystery" in this book to tough teachings that are shared by most denominations.

Mysteries Are Not Illogical

It's often said that the more you study a mystery, the more you realize how little you know about it. While this is true, keep in mind that mysteries are *beyond*—not *opposed* to—our powers of reason. As John Wesley, the founder of Methodism, said, "Show me a worm that can comprehend a man and I will show you a man that can comprehend God." In other words, the mindbenders are not illogical or even unreasonable. They are merely too profound for our limited minds to encompass.

Equally important, although Christianity's mysteries can never be fully explained, there's much about each mystery that we can understand. We may not be able to fathom the *why's* or the *how's* of a tough teaching, but we usually can grasp the facts and the reasons why Christians have long considered the doctrine significant and worthy of belief.

Foolishness?

Given the abundance of mysteries in Christianity—mind-bending doctrines that are impossible to fully understand—it's no wonder that many non-Christians consider Christianity to be irrational. That's actually a fairly tame criticism considering that the Apostle Paul wrote that the Christian gospel is *foolishness* to nonbelievers: "For the message about the cross is foolishness to those who are perishing, but to us who are being saved it is the power of God." (1 Corinthians 1:18, NIV) "The man without the Spirit does not accept the things that come from the Spirit of God, for they are foolishness to him, and he cannot understand them, because they are spiritually discerned." (1 Corinthians 2:14, NIV)

Some Christians are uncomfortable with Paul's choice of words. "Foolishness" seems too disparaging, too irreverent a label for the gospel of Jesus Christ. Perhaps the Bible translators got it wrong.

In fact, the translators got it exactly right. Paul, who proclaimed the gospel to thousands of nonbelievers during the first century, used a Greek word which means silliness, absurdity—in short, foolishness. He understood something that many twenty-first century Christians ignore: seen from the outside, much of Christianity looks preposterous.

Try to imagine Paul preaching in ancient Asia Minor, working hard to convince a pagan audience that a failed Jewish messiah—a man crucified by the Romans—was actually the Son of God, because somehow the God of the Universe became incarnate in "sinful human flesh." We can almost hear the hecklers in Paul's audience jeering: "Tell us, Paul, how did the God of the Universe squeeze himself into a baby?" And, "Who ran the Universe when the Baby Jesus was asleep?" Or, "Where was God 'hiding' while Jesus was growing up?"

Tuned-Out Believers

It's just as easy today for twenty-first century nonbelievers to come up with similar "logical" questions that seem to debunk the Incarnation and Christianity's other mysteries. Unfortunately, few believers today are as well equipped as Paul to provide levelheaded answers that make Christianity seem less foolish.

Congratulate yourself for wanting to be an exception to the rule. Tens of millions of your fellow Christians don't care that they can't understand (or explain) the tough teachings that are the foundation stones of Christianity. Because they find these beliefs overwhelmingly mysterious, they tune out and ignore the accessible truths inside each mystery.

Should You and I Care?

Are they right? Should believers plumb Christianity's mysteries or should we leave the tough teachings for trained theologians and center our efforts on being "good Christians"? Many sincere believers prefer to avoid the mysteries; they have reasons to justify why ignorance is bliss:

> ### Walking with the Wise
>
> Albert Einstein, the famed twentieth-century physicist, wrote, "The most beautiful thing we can experience is the mysterious." That is certainly true of Christianity's chief mysteries. They are beautiful concepts that have inspired believers for upward of 2,000 years.

- "I'm a 'heart Christian,' not a 'head Christian.' I just want to know and love Jesus and live a Christian life. I don't need to understand the mysteries of Christianity."

- "I honor what Paul wrote: 'Knowledge puffs up, but love builds up. The man who thinks he knows something does not yet know as he ought to know. But the man who loves God is known by God.'" (1 Corinthians 8:1–3, NIV)

◆ "All that matters to me is that I'm saved. Why should I care about the minor technical details?"

◆ "There's no need to study Christianity's mysteries. The Holy Spirit teaches me everything I have to know about God."

◆ "I studied *theology* once and I discovered that all theologians do is split hairs. Who cares how many angels can sit on the point of a pin?"

◆ "The stuff I'll learn won't be useful. What difference will the explanations make in my daily life? Or with my relationship with God?"

◆ "Delving into the mysteries will probably do damage by confusing me even more. What really counts is my sincerity as a believer."

◆ "If I try to understand the tough teachings, it means that I'm not exerting my faith that they are true."

def•i•ni•tion

The literal meaning of **theology** is "words about God"—a handy summation. Theology has also become the field of study that examines God's interactions with His creation and the claims of the Bible.

Sorry—Those Excuses Make No Sense

The last reason on the list is particularly silly. It suggests that the less someone knows about Christianity, the more faith he or she has—a wholly goofy concept. In fact, the reverse is usually true. The more understanding Christians have, the more they grow in Christian faith and discernment. Because many of the toughest teachings involve the nature of God—and his redemptive purposes—knowledge about them is an irreplaceable source of spiritual nourishment for believers.

But the other "excuses" for avoiding the Christian mysteries also break down with a little thought. They ignore the fact that Christianity is a religion that claims that God entered history at a specific time and place, and that He changed the very nature of things. Sincere Christians need to test these claims for themselves, not merely "suspend disbelief" and accept them at face value. It's lazy thinking to invoke the concept of "mystery" as a free pass, as an escape hatch from the obligation to learn the difficult precepts of our faith.

This doesn't mean that we have to become experts in Christian theology. Rather we need the sort of practical knowledge that makes us comfortable enough to talk about Christianity's mysteries with other people. For therein lies one of the most important reasons to understand these teachings: several of our chief responsibilities as Christians require that we understand the complexities of Christianity well enough to explain them to other people.

Get Wisdom

Here's how to respond if anyone brings up the antique (though common) argument that theologians try to count the number of angels sitting on the point of a pin: in 1638, William Chillingworth, author of "Religion of Protestants," rebutted a Jesuit who challenged the quality of education given to Protestant ministers: "… men might be learned even though they dispute not eternally … whether a million of angels may not sit upon a needle's point." Chillingworth was apparently referring to a debating exercise used to train Jesuits, not a real topic of theological research. The point is, Christian theology deals with issues of genuine concern to believers—not trivial matters.

We're Told to Make Disciples

The *Great Commission* is straightforward instruction that applies to every Christian: "Go therefore and make disciples of all nations, baptizing them in the name of the Father and of the Son and of the Holy Spirit, and teaching them to obey everything that I have commanded you …." (Matthew 28:19–20, NRSV)

We can't fulfill our responsibility to make disciples unless we have the ability to explain—and defend—the tough teachings. This is especially true when we try to witness to adults, who start out skeptical of the "foolish doctrines." Grownups tend to be hard-nosed; they expect more than, "Gee, I don't know how the Trinity works; it's a *mystery*." At the very least, they want to know what it "means" and why Christians consider the doctrine essential.

The difficulties of explaining Christianity to adults is a likely reason why there are surprisingly few late-blooming Christians in North America's churches. As any youth pastor will proudly tell you, the vast majority of Christians commit themselves to Christ as a child or a teenager. Depending on whose survey data you prefer, the statistics range from two-thirds of all Christians to upward of 90 percent.

Because "less-irrational" religions have a significantly greater proportion of adult converts, we can conclude that the foolishness of Christianity is a genuine stumbling block for many adults—an obstacle that could be overcome if more believers had the knowledge to explain Christianity's mysteries.

We Need to Encourage by Sound Doctrine

Paul was thinking about a church leader when he wrote, "He must hold firmly to the trustworthy message as it has been taught, so that he can encourage others by sound doctrine and refute those who oppose it." (See Titus 1:9, NIV.) But the wisdom behind this requirement applies to all Christians.

We all share the responsibility to proclaim the "trustworthy message," to encourage with "sound doctrine," and—when necessary—to rebut the teachers of false doctrine. Clearly we can't do any of these things without a comfortable understanding of Christianity—from the simple teachings to the mysteries. If we don't know what's true, how can we recognize what's false? A real danger of not being able to spot untruth is that we become susceptible to false teachings ourselves.

We're All Called to be Apologists

No, that doesn't mean we're supposed to keep saying, "I'm sorry." We become *apologists* whenever we seek to prove that Christian doctrine makes sense or that Christianity promotes worthy values. The scholarly field of *apologetics* is considered a branch of theology, but don't let that tricky label throw you. The Apostle Peter didn't expect you to become a theologian when he wrote, "Always be prepared to give an answer to everyone who asks you to give the reason for the hope that you have. But do this with gentleness and respect …." (1 Peter 3:15, NIV)

def•i•ni•tion

In Ancient Greece, the prosecutor at a trial delivered an accusatory speech called a *kategoria*. In response, the defendant offered an **apologia**—a statement that rebutted the prosecutor's charges. The word "apologia" appears several times in the New Testament, most notably in 1 Peter 3:15. Different Bibles provide different translations, for example: "give the reason" (NIV); "make your defense" (NRSV); "be ready to speak up" (TMSG); and "give an answer" (KJV). **Apologetics** is the branch of theology concerned with explaining and defending the Christian faith. An **apologist** is a person who seeks to explain or defend Christianity.

Apologetics need not be highly technical and dripping with theological language. You can prove this point by browsing through a well-stocked online bookstore. You'll find hundreds of books for everyday readers that defend the underpinnings of Christianity, restate complex Christian doctrines in simple language, and seek to persuade skeptics and doubters that Christian teachings are not foolishness.

These days, Christian apologetics serves two major functions: giving nonbelievers reasons to become Christian and reinforcing the faith of believing Christians. But the earliest apologists—many of them church fathers who lived in the first century—wrote *apologias* designed to prove that the emerging faith of Christianity (and the fast-growing band of Christians) did not threaten Rome. The power of these treatises to change minds was literally a matter of life and death for tens of thousands of new believers.

Your *apologias* will probably be verbal rather than written, and may have more modest purposes. But your defenses of Christianity can still be essential for nonbelieving friends and family members who argue that Christianity is irrational. It could be your clarification of a Christian mystery that invites a change of mind and a charge of heart. This is why "always be prepared" is a requirement, not a gentle suggestion. As Christians, we've been assigned the duty to communicate as much of what we believe as possible.

Incidentally, the second half of Peter's guidance—explain your reasons "with gentleness and respect …" is an essential aspect of apologetics. No one pays attention to an explanation that screams: "You're stupid for not knowing this!" The best apologetics are wholly without insult and often genuinely entertaining.

Get Wisdom

Most religions have some apologetics, but none has more than Christianity. Use an Internet search engine to search for "Christian apologetics," "Jewish apologetics," "Hindu apologetics," "Buddhist apologetics" and any other religion you care to try. "Christian apologetics" will point you to hundreds of thousands of websites, the others only a few hundred each. This is more evidence, if you need any, that Christianity can be a challenge to understand.

Strategies for Tackling Christianity's Mysteries

Some of Christianity's greatest mysteries were recognized during the first century. Others surfaced during the subsequent 300 years. Because they've been part of the faith for upward of two millennia, countless believers have struggled with them. We can learn from their successes and mistakes.

Keep Your Eye on the Essentials

Christianity's mysteries may be mind-bending, but as I said earlier, the basics of our faith are easy to grasp. The essential Christian teachings tell the story of a Creator God who really exists, a God who loves and forgives, a God who chose to enter his creation and repair it, a God who devised an unexpected way to rescue fallen humanity from the consequences of sin. The New Testament sets forth a straightforward route to salvation: "… if you confess with your lips, 'Jesus is Lord,' and believe in your heart that God raised him from the dead, you will be saved." (Romans 10:9, NIV)

Most of Christianity's deepest mysteries are additional teachings that explain more about God and his plan for salvation. They're important—and worth studying—but don't be discouraged when you find it difficult to understand them. Every thinking Christian who's lived during the past 1,500 years has experienced the same difficulties. Let the essentials serve as the anchors of your faith.

Focus on *Mere Christianity*

Chances are, many of the budding evangelists you know have two goals in mind when they witness to nonbelievers. On the one hand, they want to explain Christianity; on the other hand, they want to communicate the benefits of your specific Christian denomination. You'll see this same double-barreled approach at work in many "explanations" of Christianity's mysteries.

Regrettably, a determined denominational spin on a tough teaching can add to the complexity and confusion. Whenever possible, identify the sources of the explanatory materials you find on the Internet and in books. Denominationally focused resources are often written from a specific theological point of view and may not represent a majority perspective. They may also add nuances and details that go beyond the original mystery.

Get Wisdom

Christianity comes in many different "flavors." The World Christian Database created by the Center for the Global Study of Christianity at Gordon-Conwell Theological Seminary lists 9,000 Christian denominations. Other estimates put the worldwide total between 30,000 and 40,000.

Richard Baxter, a fifteenth-century English clergyman, coined the term *mere Christianity* to describe the core beliefs of our faith that are shared by most Christians. C. S. Lewis borrowed the title for his apologetic masterpiece—a slim volume that sought to explain Christian doctrine in a way that would be acceptable to all of the major denominations. In this book, I've tried to do the same thing by choosing tenets and teachings that nearly all Christians accept, even if they don't fully understand the mysteries they raise.

Don't Take the Easy Way Out

A simple way to make a knotty problem disappear is to say, "I don't agree that the problem exists." At one time or another, that approach has been applied to all of Christianity's mysteries. The upshot is that the majority of Christian *heresies* concern the tough teachings.

def•i•ni•tion

A **heresy** is a religious belief at odds with the "orthodox" (right-thinking) position.

Consider the dual natures of Jesus—he is fully God and fully human. We can quickly resolve this mystery by denying that Jesus has dual natures. And so, the ancient heresy of Docetism argued that Jesus' physical body was some sort of illusion—that he merely *seemed* to be human.

Many Christians think that the last of the heresies vanished during the Middle Ages. Actually, many of the old-timers are alive and well today. Modalism—which dates back more than 1,800 years—is a perennially popular way to "explain" the Trinity. This is the wrong idea that Father, Son, and Holy Spirit are merely three different *modes* (or aspects) of the one God. Imagine God putting on three different masks, so that he sometimes looks like the Father, sometimes like the Son, and sometimes like the Holy Spirit. In essence, modalism short-circuits the tough teaching that somehow the Godhead has three distinct "Persons."

The lesson here for anyone who seeks a better understanding of Christianity's mysteries is to be skeptical of simple answers. Simply put, there aren't any.

Don't Rebel Against Inevitable Complexity

When the Apostle Peter wrote about the Apostle Paul's letters, he noted (as have unnumbered other Christians after him), "There are some things in them hard to understand." (2 Peter 3:16, NRSV)

It shouldn't surprise anyone that many aspects of Christianity are complicated—and some are beyond our powers of understanding. To quote C. S. Lewis and *Mere Christianity:* "But as soon as you look at any real Christian writings, you find that they ... say that Christ is the Son of God (whatever that means). They say that those who give Him their confidence can also become Sons of God (whatever that means). They say that His death saved us from our sins (whatever that means). There is no good complaining that these statements [about Christianity] are difficult. Christianity claims to be telling us about another world, about something behind the world we can touch and hear and see. You may think the claim false, but if it were true, what it tells us would be bound to be difficult—at least as difficult as modern Physics, and for the same reason."

What Lewis is saying is that key teachings of Christianity are mind-bending because they explain aspects of an unseen world, a highly complex topic. The physical sciences like physics, chemistry, astronomy, and geometry each deal with facets of the world around us—we all know how difficult to master they are. Looked at the other way around, if Christianity were simple, if it had no impossible-to-understand mysteries, we could be confident that it *isn't* true.

Ask Yourself If Christianity's Mysteries *Feel* True

Many, perhaps most, Christians sense that Christianity's mysteries are true—without the benefits of "logical explanations." This experience has been called the inward witness of the Holy Spirit; itself a Christian mystery in its own right. The inward witness rarely involves a spoken voice or recognizable words, although some Christians report having heard the Holy Spirit. Typically, a believer experiences a hard-to-describe gut feeling that imparts a sense of understanding.

Spirit-taught truth leads to understanding of the truth revealed by God—not mere hand-waving. If a Christian mystery remains wholly mysterious, with not even a glimmer of comprehension, no enlightenment has taken place.

Seek Useful Analogies

Analogies make it easier for many people to understand, and explain, difficult concepts. I'm confident that you learned that an atom is analogous to our solar system, with electrons (the "planets") whirling around the nucleus (the "Sun"). Not surprisingly, the Bible is chock full of analogies. Jesus analogizing himself to a vine is certainly one of the best known—and most fruitful.

The thing to never forget is that analogies can only go so far. They break down when you push them beyond their usefulness. We all recognize that Jesus is not a member of the species *vitis vinifera* and that we don't need a limestone-rich soil to thrive.

Good analogies can be powerful learning tools, because comparing something unfamiliar to something familiar makes the "target concept" seem possible. That's why I'll present an unusual analogy in Chapter 2. Even though it must eventually fail—no finite analogy can fully represent our infinite God—it has helped me dig deeper into one of Christianity's most bewildering mysteries.

Avoid "Logical Explanations"

You may occasionally run across supposedly "logical explanations" of the Incarnation, the Reincarnation, the Trinity, and other tough teachings. The problem with them was identified by Thomas Aquinas, the famed Italian theologian, during the thirteenth century: because Christianity's mysteries outstrip the power of human beings to understand them, human minds don't have the ability to invent comprehensive explanations. At best, these "logical explanations" are merely partial clarifications.

Thomas also pondered the other side of the coin. He pointed out that the limitations of the human mind mean that no skeptic or doubter can ever invent a successful "proof" that refutes a Christian mystery, because finite human minds can't produce proofs (or refutations) about infinite concepts. Remember that simple truism whenever you're offered a "compelling argument" that a Christian mystery is false.

Thomas went a step further. He argued against trying to "prove" your faith to others for the same reason: you'll never come up with an all-inclusive proof. He pointed out that Peter urged us to be ready with a reason or an answer—not to attempt some sort of rational proof.

The Least You Need to Know

- Christianity has many mind-bending teachings that explain different aspects of an unseen world—they are inevitably complex.

- You'll never fully comprehend Christianity's mysteries, but you can grasp a surprising amount of detail about each.

- Knowing the "facts" of each tough teaching—and the reasons why Christians consider them important—will strengthen your faith and help you disciple others.

◆ You have a responsibility to be a Christian apologist, a responsibility that requires you to learn the basics of your faith—including the "basics" of Christianity's mysteries.

◆ Analogies can be helpful learning aids—but remember that all analogies have limits and can never fully represent a Christian mystery.

◆ Be skeptical when you are offered a "simple explanation" of a tough teaching— many are based on ancient heresies.

Chapter 2

The Mystery of the Incarnation

In This Chapter

- The incredible happened when Jesus was born
- Why the Incarnation is Christianity's central miracle
- Jesus is both fully divine and fully human
- How can Heaven and Earth intersect?
- Only Jesus can reconcile God and mankind
- The "creator's-eye" view of the Incarnation

According to Christians, the single most remarkable event in the history of the world happened approximately 2,000 years ago in a small village in the ancient Roman province of Judea. Somehow, the God who created the universe perfectly united himself with humanity so that Jesus of Nazareth was both truly God and truly man—and will remain so for all eternity.

We'll look at the fundamental mystery of the Incarnation in this chapter: the notion that God the Son put on flesh and moved "into our neighborhood" for approximately 33 years. In Chapter 4, we'll look at the mystery of Jesus' two natures, including how Jesus could be truly God and truly man at the same time.

The Miracle of Miracles

It's easy to define the Incarnation in a single sentence:

The second Person of the timeless Trinity—the eternal Word—came to Earth at a specific point in time, took human form, and dwelt among us—but did not stop being God.

Get Wisdom _____

The word "Incarnation" was adopted during the twelfth century. It comes from a Norman-French word, based on *Incarnatio,* a Latin word coined in the fourth century, which translates the Greek *sarkosis,* which came from *sarx* (flesh) used in the phrase *"kai ho Logos sarx egeneto"* ("And the Word became flesh"), the well-known phrase from John 1:14.

This is a truly astonishing statement. It's no wonder that early leaders of Christianity needed upward of 400 years to work out the language to describe the concept of the Incarnation and to resolve the many arguments that arose about Jesus' dual natures and the relationship between them.

However, because most contemporary Christians are familiar with the idea, the Incarnation has lost much of its power to awe believers. We simply don't appreciate how remarkable an event it was.

If the Incarnation took place the way Christians claim, it was certainly the most astonishing miracle—and the most significant event—to occur in the entire history of the world. Nothing more noteworthy has happened before or since. And the Incarnation is truly mysterious; a festival of tough teachings we'll never fully understand. Merely describing the details of the Incarnation forces me to use "somehow" in nearly every sentence:

◆ Somehow Heaven and Earth intersected in the person of Jeshua Ben Joseph, of Nazareth, also known as Jesus.

◆ The God who sustains the universe and is present at every point in it somehow united perfectly with every aspect of a human born some 2,000 years ago—including body, soul, and spirit.

- Jesus' humanity and divinity somehow function together side-by-side—his humanity does not diminish his divinity.

- God the Son didn't merely take on the appearance of a man, or merely enter into the body of a man—rather divinity and humanity somehow bonded together, leaving Jesus fully human despite his divinity. "For in Christ all the fullness of the Deity lives in bodily form ...." (Colossians 2:9, NIV)

> **Walking with the Wise**
>
> St. Bernard of Clairvaux wrote in a famous passage quoted by Martin Luther that "the Incarnation involves three miracles, not one. First, that God and man could be united in this promised Child. Second, that a virgin could be a Mother. And the third and greatest miracle—that Mary (and the rest of mankind) should believe it."

- In Jesus, the God who created us somehow experienced much of what mankind experiences—from wet diapers, to joy, to hunger, to temptation, to anguish, to disappointment, to death.

- The Incarnation is forever; after his birth, Jesus never shed his glorified Resurrection body, stopped being a man, or stopped being God the Son.

Proclaiming Jesus' Divinity

Chances are your introduction to the concept that Jesus was divine came from a Gospel verse such as:

- John 14:9, NIV, where Jesus says, "Anyone who has seen me has seen the Father."

- John 8:58, NIV: "I tell you the truth," Jesus answered, "before Abraham was born, I am!" (This was such a shocking invocation of the Old-Testament name of God that the people who heard Jesus say this were ready to stone him for blasphemy.)

- Matthew 28:18, NIV: "Then Jesus came to them and said, 'All authority in heaven and on earth has been given to me.'"

- The approximately two dozen times in the Gospel that Jesus is described as "the Son of God."

Surprisingly, the earliest Christians proclaimed Jesus' divinity long before any of the Gospels were written. Consider the words that Paul wrote to the church at Thessalonica: "For God did not appoint us to suffer wrath but to receive salvation through our Lord Jesus Christ. He died for us so that, whether we are awake or asleep, we may live together with him." (1 Thessalonians 5:9, NIV)

Take Warning!

Keep in mind that when mainstream Christians claim that the Incarnation united deity and humanity in Jesus, the humanity in question is not the sinful humanity possessed by other human beings. Jesus incorporates the perfect sinless humanity that human beings enjoyed before the fall. Paul expresses this idea in Romans 8:3, NIV: "God [sent] his own Son in the likeness of sinful man to be a sin offering." "Likeness" implies that Jesus shares all the attributes of sinful humanity except sin itself.

Paul's first letter to the Thessalonians is considered by many Biblical scholars to be the oldest known Christian document, and the first of Paul's letters that are included in the New Testament. Paul probably wrote it in A.D. 52, more than a decade before the earliest Gospels were written. He presents the idea of Jesus' divinity as a well-established teaching, which suggests that many first-century Christians had come to believe, within a startlingly short time after his death and Resurrection, that Jesus was God incarnate.

Four things are remarkable about Paul's words:

- Paul and the early Christians—most of whom were Jewish—had previously reserved the name "Lord" for God alone—and would have needed a profound reason to apply the term to a man.

- They believed that only God can offer salvation to mankind.

- They believed that "anyone who is hung on a tree is under God's curse." (Deuteronomy 21:23, NIV)

- They recognized that their new beliefs about Jesus challenged the Roman Empire, where Caesar (not Jesus) was held to be "Lord"—and that proclaiming Jesus' Lordship was a dangerous thing to do.

Simply put, Paul and the church members who read his letter fully appreciated the potentially incendiary nature of Paul's words. The fact that Paul wrote them testifies to the strength of early Christian beliefs that Jesus was fully God.

On the other hand, the early beliefs about Jesus' divinity were not held unanimously. Some first-century Christians simply couldn't accept that Jesus could be both fully God and fully human. Many, of course, argued against there being "more than one God." They asked, if the Father is God how can Jesus also be God? (See Chapter 3 on the mystery of the Trinity.)

As Christianity grew and expanded during the first, second, third, and fourth centuries many of the most challenging *Christological* controversies to emerge concerned Jesus' divinity and the relationship of his divine and human natures. I'll talk about a few of them later in this chapter.

> **Scripture Says**
>
> Perhaps the most oft-cited Old-Testament prediction that lends credence to Jesus' divinity comes from the *Book of Isaiah.* "Therefore the Lord himself will give you a sign. Look, the young woman is with child and shall bear a son, and shall name him Immanuel" (*God with us*). (Isaiah 7:14, NRSV) Some Bible versions translate "young woman" as "virgin."

def•i•ni•tion

Christology is the branch of Christian theology that addresses the person and work of Jesus Christ. One can focus on Jesus' work as a prophet, healer, rabbi, miracle worker, Messiah, high priest, and master of his disciples without insisting that he is also the Incarnate God. This is said to be *low Christology*. By contrast, talking about Jesus as Lord, Son of God, God, and Savior emphasizes his divinity. This is said to be *high Christology*.

Why Must Jesus Be Fully Divine?

First, though, let me tackle an obvious question: is it important that Jesus be God Incarnate? The answer is yes, for reasons I've touched on plus a few new considerations:

◆ Many verses in the Bible point directly to Jesus' divinity.

◆ The earliest theologians pointed out that Jesus can't be the Savior of the world unless he is God Incarnate (simply put, a mere creature doesn't have the power to save other creatures).

◆ A mere creature can't answer prayer. Aside from the point that praying to a creature is idolatry, Christians have observed that Jesus has the power to answer prayer.

◆ Theologians also note that only a divine Jesus can become an effective mediator or intercessor between humankind and the Father—a "defense counsel" who pleads our case and ultimately reconciles man to God.

◆ God intended Jesus to be a *revelation* of Himself, which also requires Jesus to be fully God.

God! Not Merely Godly

Many non-Christians are perfectly willing to accept that Jesus who walked the dusty roads of Judea, Galilee, and Samaria was a great teacher, a man who embodied great quantities of goodness, love, wisdom, and other qualities that made him seem "godly" to the people he met.

Christians who understand the purpose of the Incarnation counter that it wasn't enough for Jesus to resemble God and echo God's attributes of forgiveness, compassion, ability to heal—Jesus needed to be a God/man who *possessed* the actual attributes, could provide salvation, and could restore humanity's broken relationship with God.

What About Jesus' Humanity?

Nothing in the Gospel accounts suggests that anyone who knew Jesus before his crucifixion doubted his full humanity. He was born a baby and grew up like every other human being. He spoke, ate, cried, became tired, argued with his family, and eventually bled and died, all like a perfectly routine human being. Of course, his apostles witnessed many examples of Jesus' extraordinary nonroutine behavior (from turning water into wine, to healing the blind, to curing lepers, to walking on water, to raising Lazarus) but watching Jesus perform miracles didn't seem to make him look less a man.

In time, though, assertions that Jesus wasn't fully human eventually did arise— not as many as those challenging his divinity, but enough to create a few interesting heresies.

Why Must Jesus Be Fully Human?

This can be a tricky question to answer. It's fairly easy to grasp that Jesus needed divine attributes to be an effective savior of humanity or the mediator that reconciles sinful mankind with God. But why should we argue if someone challenges Jesus' human nature? In fact, there are important reasons to insist that Jesus was fully human:

◆ Scripture describes Jesus as fully human, as a *man* who was tempted by Satan, experienced a broad spectrum of human desires and emotions, and could suffer mental and physical anguish.

◆ Jesus told the Apostles that he must suffer and be killed (see Matthew 16:21)— which only makes sense if he was fully human.

◆ Many theologians have noted that Jesus needs to be a man to be able to obey God the Father in the way that Adam, the first man, did not. (See Chapter 6 on the mystery of Jesus' Atonement.)

Why the Incarnation Is Considered Vital to Christianity

Christianity would be a lot simpler to understand and explain without the doctrine of the Incarnation—but it would no longer be Christianity.

Christianity's ultimate claim about the Incarnation is that the God who created everything entered history at a specific time and a specific place, for a specific purpose. "God with us" was the first phase of an extraordinary rescue operation designed to restore fallen humanity (and ultimately the fallen creation).

For reasons we'll never fully understand, God's plan of salvation required the Second Person of the Trinity to interact with humankind in a form that they could see, touch, and eventually kill.

Christians also view the event of the Incarnation as nothing less than God's decision to enter time and space to share life with humanity. Because of the Incarnation, mankind has gained the ability to enter a personal relationship, through Jesus, with the God who created the universe.

Are You Baffled Yet?

As we've seen, there are lots of "somehows" to consider when we talk about the mechanics of the Incarnation. But the central mystery of the Incarnation has to do with the idea that the *transcendent* God of the Universe—a spirit beyond our

def•i•ni•tion

Two important words to know when you talk about God are **transcendent** and **immanent**. Transcendent is outside of anything we can know directly or understand; beyond time and space. Immanent is close to us and accessible; inside our time and space.

conception and understanding—made himself *immanent* and available to mankind. That this happened flies in the face of human reason. And yet, the Incarnation is so bound up with who and what Jesus is that we have to look past the "somehows" and the central mystery to focus on what Christians claim God actually did and what Jesus accomplished.

To say the Incarnation represents condescension by God is a major understatement. This makes the Incarnation difficult to accept, even when we're taught that God's love motivated him to become flesh.

If you try to explain the Incarnation to other people (especially nonbelievers), expect to hear several questions that have been asked for 2,000 years:

- ◆ Why would God decide to climb "inside" Jesus?

- ◆ Who sustained the universe when Jesus was a baby?

- ◆ Didn't the Incarnation limit God's powers, including his omnipotence (unlimited power), omnipresence (unlimited by the restraints of time or place), and omniscience (infinite knowledge of everything)?

- ◆ Why didn't God simply appear on Earth; after all, aren't there several theophanies—appearances of God to people—recorded in the Old and New Testaments?

Walking with the Wise

One especially vivid analogy of the "feeling" of Incarnation from God' perspective can be found in *Mere Christianity*, by C. S. Lewis (see Appendix B): "If you want to get the hang of it [the Incarnation], think how you would like to become a slug or a crab."

These mistaken views involve several common misconceptions about the Incarnation. Christians don't teach that God "climbed inside" Jesus. Rather, we insist that the Son of God bonded with humanity to create a unique being—a God-man who is fully divine and fully human.

Christians repeatedly point out that God didn't change into a man and stop being God. God's nature was not compromised by the Incarnation, even though the Jesus who interacted with his disciples had distinct limitations compared to God the Son. One of the most significant of these is that Jesus' fully human body could die.

Lastly, Christians assert that God did more than merely "appear" on Earth during the Incarnation. Jesus was the "intersection" of Heaven and Earth, a God/man who had the unique capacity to reconcile God and mankind.

Heresies That Challenged the Incarnation

Faced with a really challenging Christian mystery like the Incarnation, we have two options:

- We can accept that there are certain aspects of Christianity that we'll never fully understand.

- We can take away the mystery by proposing a heresy that denies one or more of the underlying doctrines that have triggered the apparent "impossibility."

The easiest way to resolve the mystery of the Incarnation is to attack one of the two essential tenets it contains. The mystery vanishes if you assert either that Jesus is not fully divine, or that Jesus is not fully human.

Arianism: The Humongous Heresy

As you might expect, Christianity's greatest mystery (and the greatest miracle) also spawned Christianity's greatest Christological battle, the so-called Arian heresy, or Arianism. Arianism challenged the teaching that Jesus was truly God. Its proponent, a highly respected Christian cleric named Arius, saw himself as a committed Christian fighting an essential battle.

Arius (this is the Latinized version of the Greek name Areios) lived from 256 to 336. He was a Greek-speaking African churchman, possibly born in Libya, who served as a priest and deacon in Alexandria, Egypt, and was widely respected as an expert theologian.

Arius argued his case from his reading of Scripture. He maintained that only God the Father is wholly transcendent and eternal. He pointed out that God the Son was begotten, which meant to Arius that the Son hadn't existed eternally and was a creature of God—an "agent" that the Father had begotten to create the Universe.

Get Wisdom _____

While not exactly a heresy, nonbelievers—and skeptics in general—often allege that Christianity "borrowed" the concept of the Incarnation from Greek mythology. The Greek myths are populated with gods who walked the earth looking like men and heroes (or demi-gods) whose mothers were human and whose fathers were members of the Greek Pantheon (collection of pagan gods). Although there are superficial similarities, Jesus is not a mythological god in disguise or a demi-god. Christians assert a significantly different kind and quality of event when they claim that Jesus is the Incarnate God of the Universe—and is still alive today.

Arius acknowledged that Jesus contained as much of the "divine essence" as the Son of God provided, but refused to take the next step and acknowledge that Jesus was truly God. Arius was ultimately willing to grant Jesus every honor, accolade, attribute of divinity except membership in the Godhead. Arius insisted:

◆ Jesus was a man created by God.

◆ Jesus was a creature endowed with special powers and many of the attributes of divinity.

◆ Jesus' death could bring salvation to mankind.

◆ Jesus was worthy of honor and praise although he was not and had never been the Infinite and Omnipotent God.

Arianism was widely accepted as truth in the early church and came close to becoming established church doctrine.

Other Challenges to Jesus' Divinity

Adoptionists argued that God the Father had "adopted" the man Jesus at the time of his baptism by John the Baptist (see Matthew 3:13–17), making him divine, although not as fully divine as God the Father. Ebionites claimed that Jesus wasn't divine, but was merely a mortal human, a prophet who was the Messiah.

Challenges to Jesus' Humanity

Docetists believed that Jesus' physical body merely seemed real, that is was actually an illusion, that Jesus was a pure spirit who could not die (hence his crucifixion and death were also illusions). Gnostics argued that because matter was evil and corrupted, God would never take on a material body; they denied the full humanity of Jesus.

Welcome to Nicaea

The various Christological battles plagued early church leaders for many decades. It finally took two church councils—the First Council of Nicaea, in the year 325, and the First Council of Constantinople, in 381—to define the relationship of Jesus to the other "Persons" of the Trinity. (See Chapter 3 on the mystery of the Trinity.)

The councils adopted and refined the "Nicene Creed" that is still spoken by Christians of many denominations today. The relevant verses are:

"We believe in one Lord, Jesus Christ, the only Son of God, eternally begotten of the Father, God from God, Light from Light, true God from true God, begotten, not made, of one Being with the Father; through him all things were made."

"For us and for our salvation he came down from heaven, was incarnate of the Holy Spirit and the Virgin Mary, and became truly human."

But as we'll see in Chapter 4, it took another church gathering—the Council of Chalcedon, in 451—to resolve the thorny issues related to Jesus' dual natures.

A Useful Analogy

Before I became a Christian, the Incarnation was the most "foolish" Christian doctrine I'd come across—a true barrier for me. It struck me as impossible, irreverent, unnecessary, and unexplainable. Happily, a useful analogy changed my thinking. It literally popped into my mind one afternoon (I leave it to you to decide who put it there).

To set up the analogy, let me explain that my wife and I write romantic mystery novels; we tell stories about characters who extricate themselves from murderous situations and fall in love during the process. One day, while I was getting ready to participate in a critique group with other writers we know, I wondered what would happened if I "wrote myself" into one of my stories.

Faster than I can write about it, I realized that the idea of a self-portrait inside a novel was a wonderful analogy for the Incarnation. I had always thought of the Incarnation from an earthbound perspective, but the self-portrait analogy flipped the viewpoint around and forced me to adopt a "Creator's eye" view. All at once, I was imagining things from the perspective of God the Father, the Creator of all things.

The Creator's-Eye View of Things

"Ron Benrey" was my self-portrait in my imagined novel. I would be *fully author* and *fully character*. Similarly, Jesus was God's self-portrait in his creation. He is *fully God* and *fully man*. As I considered the analogy, I felt the idea of the Incarnation develop with a clarity that imposed a feeling of certainty.

That's the power of a good analogy—comparing something unfamiliar to something familiar makes the "target concept" seem possible. My long-held notions that the Incarnation was absurd or impossible fluttered away.

Why had I thought the Incarnation so difficult to fathom? The answer was that I expended too much mental energy worrying about the physical details, such as how could an infinite God fit "inside" Jesus. (Yes! I'd posed the same silly question that many nonbelievers worry about.) My analogy transformed the Incarnation into a simple idea for me to chew on. I could focus on the central concept of the creator entering his creation. Among painters, the self-portrait is incredibly popular. And many authors write autobiographical novels. Human creators often put themselves into their creations—so why not God?

As I continued to develop my analogy, I realized that the fictional world created by a novelist has many parallels with the real world God created.

A Novelist Has God-Like Powers

Imagine you are writing a novel. As the author of your own creation, you have many of the powers attributed to God: you are omnipresent; you have the power to move across time and space. If you choose, you can write a novel that spans thousands of years and put it in "a galaxy far, far away." Because you are essentially "transcendent" in your imaginary world, you can jump to any time, leap to any place, and move instantly forward or backward, simply by starting to write on a different page.

God spoke our world into existence, out of nothing—"And God said, 'Let there be light ....'" (Genesis 1:3, NIV) You create your fictional world, also out of nothing, simply by putting words down on paper.

As the author, you are wholly omniscient in your fictional world. You "know" everything that might happen and everything that any character thinks. You are also omnipotent; you determine the "laws of nature" and you can make anything happen that you want to happen, simply by writing it down. You control every aspect of your characters' pasts, presents, and futures.

God the Artist

I've since come to understand that other fiction writers have made a similar observation. Many teachers of fiction encourage beginning novelists to "think like God." And I've also discovered several Christian theology texts that offer fiction writing as an analogy that illustrates the notion of "God the Artist" creating the "handiwork of God." One example is *Introduction to Christian Theology* by Alister McGrath (see Appendix B).

Of course, like every analogy, the writer-of-fiction analogy has its limits. You can't push it too far or it will rip a plot. But it has helped me to demonstrate to myself that the idea of Incarnation is not as impossible, or mysterious, as it first seems. I hope that you will find it useful, too.

The Least You Need to Know

◆ Several aspects of the Incarnation are mind-bending—none more so than the notion that God the Son condescended to come to Earth and bond with humanity to create Jesus of Nazareth.

◆ It is essential for our salvation that Jesus has dual natures (full divinity and full humanity).

◆ The Incarnation did not change God into a man; God has not stopped being God.

◆ Arianism, the greatest of the heresies that challenged mainstream Christian teaching, argued that Jesus was a "special man" with many attributes of divinity, but not truly divine.

◆ Christians did not "borrow" the Incarnation from Greek mythology, which includes several tales of heroes (or demi-gods) whose mothers were human and fathers were gods from the Greek Pantheon.

◆ A good way to penetrate some of mystery of the Incarnation is to take a "creator's-eye" view of the Incarnation.

The Mystery of the Trinity

In This Chapter

- ◆ Is the Trinity logically impossible?
- ◆ Three divine Persons: Father, Son, and Holy Spirit
- ◆ The Father is God, the Son is God, and the Holy Spirit is God … but there is only one God
- ◆ Why the Trinity fits the Biblical witness
- ◆ How to contemplate the Trinity
- ◆ The most popular heresy

The words of one of Christianity's most beloved hymns were written in 1826 for Trinity Sunday, by Reginald Heber, the Vicar of Hodnet, a village in Shropshire County, England:

> Holy, holy, holy! Lord God Almighty!
> Early in the morning our song shall rise to Thee;
> Holy, holy, holy, merciful and mighty!
> God in three Persons, blessèd Trinity!

This hymn has introduced countless Christians to the central concept—and the core mystery—of the *Trinity*. Christianity claims that somehow, the one

God consists of "three Persons"—God the Father, God the Son, and God the Holy Spirit.

We'll examine the Trinity in this chapter, and look at both sides of the doctrine: what the teaching actually says, and why it's a necessary part of Christianity.

Why the Trinity Is Hard to Understand

The majority of Christians are Trinitarian—they accept the doctrine of the Trinity as true. I assume that your exposure to the inner workings of this curious teaching followed the pattern experienced by many other Christians:

◆ Someone attempted to explain the basic idea to you. I'll restate it once again: The *Godhead* has three Persons: God the Father, God the Son (Incarnate as Jesus of Nazareth), and God the Holy Spirit.

def•i•ni•tion

In Christianity, **Godhead** means deity or divinity—the unity comprised of God the Father, God the Son (Jesus Christ), and God the Holy Spirit. Godhead is not a synonym for "Trinity," although many people use it as such.

◆ That same person may have dressed up the explanation with a few highfalutin theological words: God is one being who eternally exists as a *mutual indwelling* of the three Persons of the Trinity.

◆ Your well-meaning teacher may have shown you an illustration—perhaps a church painting done by a famous artist—that depicted the Father as an elderly man with beard … the Son as crucified, or carrying a cross … and the Holy Spirit as a dove.

In time, you probably asked yourself the inevitable question: How can 1 = 3?

If you were lucky, your teacher said, "No! No! No! The Trinity is not an exercise in arithmetic. Think about it for awhile and you'll realize that one God can have three 'somethings.'" If you were less lucky, he or she said, "No one can answer that question; the working of the Trinity is an unfathomable mystery."

There's no doubt that the Trinity is a mystery chock full of impenetrable aspects. Augustine of Hippo, the famed fifth-century theologian known as St. Augustine to many Christians, reportedly wrote, "If you deny the Trinity you will lose your soul, but if you try to understand the Trinity, you will lose your mind." Happily, Augustine was exaggerating a bit. Like most other Christian mysteries, there's much about the Trinity that you can understand.

Three *What?*

Frankly the whole idea that the Godhead is a Trinity would have been much more comprehensible to modern Christians like you and me if the fourth-century theologians who invented the language to describe the Trinity hadn't used the Greek word *hypostasis* in Greek, which eventually was translated into the English word "person." The problem was they couldn't find a better word, despite searching for years. We can be sure of one thing. They definitely didn't share our concept of personhood: an independent individual, separate from other persons, with a mind of his/her own who has a well-developed sense of identity and powerfully expressed wants, wishes, and personal interests.

Get Wisdom

Hypostasis is a great conversation starter at Bible study, but otherwise is not very useful a word outside a seminary. It's a technical term used by ancient Greek philosophers that found its way into Christianity because theologians needed a word to label the three "somethings" in the Godhead. Hypostasis has a complex history; its literal meaning in Greek is "that which stands beneath" (the reality of a thing as opposed to what it seems to be).Because hypostasis also meant "being," we ended up with the doctrine of three Persons in the Trinity.

To us, three persons make a trio. The three persons may have many things in common, but if asked we could produce a long list of differences that enable us to identify each of the three as significantly different human beings. Even more important, there's no way we'd ever imagine the trio as a truly single being. We might think of it as one group, but its essential "three-ness" would always be in our minds.

The critical idea conveyed by the word *person* in the Trinity is that the three Persons of the Godhead—each divine, each God—are somehow sufficiently distinct that we can talk about each of the three separately.

There may be better words to convey this idea, but we're stuck with *person*, so I'll use it throughout this chapter.

The Most Maligned Christian Mystery

The Trinity has been misunderstood—and maligned—for more than 1,600 years. When skeptics throw rocks at Christianity, they often take aim at the Trinity. It's an easy target, because so many people presume that *three in one* is a logical impossibility.

Thomas Jefferson, no mean thinker himself, questioned the practical value of the doctrine of the Trinity on arithmetical grounds. He asked, in a letter to James Madison, "When we shall have done away with the incomprehensible jargon of the Trinitarian arithmetic, that three are one, and one is three; when we shall have knocked down the artificial scaffolding, reared to mask from view the very simple structure of Jesus; when, in short, we shall have unlearned everything which has been taught since his day, and got back to the pure and simple doctrines he inculcated, we shall then be truly and worthily his disciples."

But seemingly faulty "Trinitarian arithmetic" is not the only criticism leveled against the Trinity. Countless Christians—including many theologians—have argued that:

◆ The Trinity adds unnecessary complexity to Christianity, which is already a complex faith to explain and to understand.

◆ The Trinity drives nonbelievers away from the faith by forcing them to cope with a seemingly illogical concept early in their Christian walk.

◆ Because the Trinity is mind-blowing, the concept of three Persons in one God has invited a torrent of heresies to explain it away.

The Trinity Is *Not* in the Bible

The Trinity was invented by theologians. Countless students in confirmation classes have won wagers based on the fact that the word "Trinity" doesn't appear in the Old or New Testaments.

It seems incredible to some people that a central doctrine of Christianity—a doctrine that some consider to be the defining tenet of Christianity—is not set forth in Scripture. Not only won't you see *Trinity* in the Bible, you also can't find a neat verse that summarizes the threefold nature of the Godhead. The few references to Father, Son, and Holy Spirit (for example, Matthew 28:19 and 2 Corinthians 13:14) don't talk about their relationship.

For the record, it doesn't carry much meaning that *Trinity* is not in the Bible. You won't find the word *monotheism* in Scripture either, but few people argue against the concept that Christians worship the one God who created the Universe.

Get Wisdom _____

The word *Trinity*—to express *tri-unity*, the concept of three in one—was coined somewhere around the year 200 by Tertullian, a Latin theologian. He is believed to be the first Christian theologian to observe that the Father, Son, and Holy Spirit were "one in essence, but not one in person.

The Trinity Does Make Sense

This heading is not trying to take away any of the Trinity's mystery. What I mean is that those long-ago theologians had excellent reasons for proposing that God is three Persons "of one substance or divine essence." Saying they were of *one substance* meant they were of the *same being*—the one God.

God Revealed Himself Progressively

One of the more unusual things about the God whom Christians worship is that he has done a remarkable job of revealing himself to mankind. The Holy Scriptures provide a *progressive revelation*, with new details about God piling atop old details as each new Book was written.

The Old and New Testaments also provide information on God's face-to-face encounters with man. The most extraordinary of these encounters is the Incarnation (see Chapter 2) when God put on flesh and Jesus took up residence among us for more than 30 years.

But also important are the times—described in the Old Testament—when the Tabernacle, and later the Temples in Jerusalem, became God's houses on Earth. And since the Resurrection, the Spirit of God has played a vital role in the salvation of believers.

The point I want to make is that the triune (threefold) nature of God was revealed step by step in the Bible:

1. *God the Father*; Creator of the Universe

2. Jesus Christ, the *Word of God*; the eternal *Son* of God the Father

3. *The Holy Spirit*, the Inspirer; the Comforter and Counselor

As you can see, during the past 4,000 years, humanity met God in three significantly different forms. We're confident that there is only one God, but the simple word "God" doesn't seem sufficient to encompass important things we've learned about these different forms.

Closely related to this idea, Robert Jenson, a respected Lutheran Theologian, argues that we should think of the phrase "Father, Son, and Holy Spirit" as the proper name for the God whom Christians know in and through Jesus Christ.

Seven Simple Statements About God

We can sum up our chief observations about the Father, the Son, and the Holy Spirit in seven simple statements:

1. There is only one God.

2. The Father is God.

3. The Son is God.

4. The Holy Spirit is God.

5. The Father is not the Son.

6. The Father is not the Holy Spirit.

7. The Son is not the Holy Spirit.

Each of these statements represents a widely held belief among mainstream Christians. Moreover, each makes complete sense taken one at a time. But when we consider them as a collection of doctrines, we run into an apparent logical problem. We seem to be claiming that three Gods are one God.

This is the predicament that the formulators of the Trinity sought to resolve. They did it by asserting that God is numerically one, yet somehow exists eternally as a unity of three distinct Persons: Father, Son, and Holy Spirit.

"Three *in* one"—unlike "three *are* one"—is not a logical impossibility, although no one can explain how such a thing actually functions in the Godhead. The doctrine of the Trinity, mysterious though it may be, honors the Scriptural witness that mankind encountered God in different ways.

Take Warning! _____

A common misconception often causes confusion: Just as the definition of the Trinity doesn't say that "three Gods are one God," neither does it say that "three Persons are one Person." God is *not* a Person. *Person* is simply a convenient word for one of the three "somethings" within the Godhead. God is God—that's the only word we need to describe him.

Detailing Distinctness

The doctrine of the Trinity teaches that each Person in the Godhead is somehow distinct from the others yet shares the same divine essence (or substance).

Expressing the distinctness of the different Persons can be tricky, because as you'll soon learn, you can't really use the different work of the divine Persons to accurately distinguish among them. The authors of the ancient *Athanasian Creed* (see Appendix B) resolved the problem by focusing on the origins of the three Persons that can be drawn from Scripture:

♦ The Father is from none—not created or begotten.

♦ The Son is from the Father—not created, but begotten.

♦ The Holy Spirit is from the Father and the Son—not created, but proceeding.

Although Athanasias—the fourth-century Archbishop of Alexandria who lead the charge against the Arian heresy (see Chapter 2)—was credited with creating the Athanasian Creed, most scholars believe it was written at the start of the fifth century in western Europe. Its likely purpose was to definitively reject Arianism and other Christological heresies.

The Trinity also helps us understand how a *transcendent* God (a spirit beyond time, space, and our conception) can make himself *immanent* and accessible to mankind. Specifically …

♦ God can indwell, empower, and encourage us via his Holy Spirit.

♦ God can invade time and space in the man Jesus, without abandoning his control of the universe.

♦ God can relate to us on our terms—through Jesus and the Holy Spirit—and yet remain an infinite being.

The bottom line: the Trinity is a mystery, but not an inconceivable description of God.

> ### Get Wisdom
>
> The Trinity has strongly impacted worship in mainstream denominations. The Apostle's and Nicene Creeds, regularly recited by many different denominations, sets forth the Trinitarian nature of God: "I believe in God, the Father Almighty, the Creator of heaven and earth, and in Jesus Christ, His only Son, our Lord: Who was conceived of the Holy Spirit .... I believe in the Holy Spirit ...." Baptisms are performed "in the name of the Father, and of the Son, and of the Holy Spirit," in response to Jesus' Great Commission (Matthew 28:16–20). And, many familiar prayers in the liturgy are Trinitarian. The well-known Doxology is a good example: "Praise God, from Whom all blessings flow; Praise Him, all creatures here below; Praise Him above, ye heavenly host; Praise Father, Son, and Holy Ghost."

You'll sometimes hear it said that some Christians "believe in" the Trinity. In fact, Christians believe in the God who has revealed himself in the Bible to be Father, Son, and Holy Spirit. The Trinity is ultimately a way of describing God that the majority of Christians accept as true.

Is Any *Person* in Charge?

During the 1,500+ years since the doctrine of the Trinity was formulated, theologians and Christian thinkers have considered, and resolved, many legitimate questions about the relationship among the Father, Son, and Holy Spirit. One that comes up every time I've taught the doctrine of the Trinity to adults is, how do the Father, Son, and Holy Spirit make decisions?

For starters, the triune God is *not* a committee, with three members who express their individual wishes by taking votes. That kind of arrangement would be perilously close to tritheism, the wrong idea that the three divine Persons in the Godhead are independent and self-contained to the point of being separate individuals. Clearly, if this were true, we couldn't insist that there is only one God.

A closely related wrong idea is that each Person of the Trinity is only partially divine and that the Godhead isn't fully God until all three persons work together. The Trinitarian claim that each Person is truly God refutes this notion.

Father, Son, and Holy Spirit think with a single mind—God's mind—although the single mind of God somehow has a threefold consciousness that enables each Person of the Trinity to know himself. God the Son was aware that he had taken on flesh and become a man, but Jesus' thoughts and feelings were experienced by God the Father and God the Holy Spirit.

As for which Person is "in charge"? (Or as one of my Sunday-school students put it, which Person holds the TV remote control?) Christians have insisted from the earliest days of the doctrine that each divine Person is eternal, almighty, with none greater or less than another. Unlike an earthly trio, Father, Son, and Holy Spirit are not arranged in a hierarchy. The three Persons of the Trinity are all equal within the Godhead.

And yet, despite a lack of organizational structure, God the Father could employ God the Son: "Through him all things were made." (John 1:3, NIV) And later, the Father could send the Son and the Holy Spirit to do their humanity-saving work.

Keep in mind, though, that God acts as a single being, not as some kind of divine team. Somehow, Father, Son, and Holy Spirit function together as one force and jointly participate in everything that God does. However, it's convenient—and perfectly acceptable—for us to envision God's different activities as the responsibility of the Father, the Son, or the Holy Spirit.

Consequently, Christians often view God the Father as the creator and the lawgiver, God the Son as the Messiah and the savior of fallen humanity, and God the Holy Spirit as the advisor, sanctifier, and giver of spiritual gifts. In fact, all the Persons in the Trinity deserve credit for these accomplishments.

Take Warning!

Every discussion of Trinity must always honor the fact that the concept of a triune God doesn't in any way supplant the doctrine of monotheism. Rather, the Trinity sheds new light on the nature of the one God. Monotheism was at the heart of the early Christians' understanding of God. Jesus and his followers never contradicted the well-known Old Testament statement of God's oneness: "Hear, O Israel: The Lord our God is one Lord" (see Deuteronomy 6:4). In fact, Jesus repeated these words in Mark 12:28, when he answered the teacher of the law's question about which is the most important commandment.

Modalism: The Most Popular Heresy

Most of the heresies I've written about in this book are museum pieces. They represented significant threats to orthodox ("right thinking") Christianity many hundreds of years ago, but today only cause consternation among seminary students at exam time. Modalism is a striking exception. It's alive and well and winning converts throughout Christendom.

As I've said before, a fast way to eliminate a Christian mystery is to deny one or more of the theological facts that seem inconsistent. Modalism simplifies the Trinity by denying that the Father, Son, and Holy Spirit are distinct, divine Persons.

The Trinity Simplified ... While You Wait

Modalism argues that the one God is a kind of quick-change artist, sometimes playing the role of the Father, sometimes playing the role of the Son (as when Jesus was alive), and sometimes playing the role of the Holy Spirit.

Imagine God putting on three different masks during different times in history—or for different purposes—to reveal a specific *mode* of the Godhead. (The label *Modalism* is an expansion of the word *mode*.)

- In the role of the Father—the dominant mode in Old Testament times—God created the universe.

- Later, he switched to the role of the Son, took on flesh, and became Jesus, who was fully God and fully man.

- Now, God has made another switch to the role of Holy Spirit, enabling him to interact closely with Christians.

Modalism is a seductively simple explanation of the mysterious inner workings of God because it's so easy to understand and picture. It seems to explain how the Trinity works without the need for a single "somehow."

What's Wrong with Modalism?

Mainstream Christians begin their attack on Modalism by pointing out that the Gospels describe circumstances when more than one Person of the Trinity is present at the same time. A powerful example is the appearance of the Father and the Holy

Spirit at Jesus' baptism by John the Baptist. (Matthew 3:16) A similar challenge is posed by the different occasions when Jesus prayed to the Father (for example, Luke 22:42, when Jesus prayed on the Mount of Olives, minutes before he was arrested). It's hard to accept that Jesus was actually praying to himself.

Another objection is that Modalism, if true, would mean that humanity never enjoys a true revelation of God—we see God wearing a mask, never his real face. Jesus' well-known statement "Anyone who has seen me has seen the Father" (John 14:9, NIV) would take on a much different meaning.

A more subtle reason to challenge the idea of Modalism is that mainstream Christian theologians believe that the threefold nature of God witnessed by Scripture actually reflects the inner workings of the Godhead. In other words, the fact that mankind has experienced Father, Son, and Holy Spirit means that the one God has a triune nature.

Danger! Modalist Analogies

Ironically, two of the most popular analogies used to explain the Trinity are Modalist at their cores. Both are favorites of Sunday school teachers and even some pastors:

◆ The Trinity is like the head of a household, a man who is simultaneously a husband, a father, and an employee. This seems to be a good analogy of three in one, but take a closer look. Note that the man is simply adopting three different roles.

◆ The Trinity is like water, because water can be a liquid (water), a solid (ice), or a vapor (steam). Do you see the difficulty? Water, ice, and steam are different modes of one substance.

It's no surprise these analogies are still in circulation, because it's hard to come up with a valid analogy of the Trinity in the face of all those "somehows."

Another popular teaching tool is the egg. An egg has three interrelated parts that work together: a shell, a yoke, and the white. Unhappily, the analogy breaks down quickly; shell, yoke, and egg white are obviously of different substances. Looked at individually, they are parts of a whole egg.

The danger of the egg analogy is that it suggests that neither Father, Son, nor Holy Spirit is wholly God—rather that they are only parts of God. But as I've said many times in this chapter, each Person of the Trinity is fully divine.

The Least You Need to Know

◆ Christianity's doctrine of the Trinity teaches that the Godhead consists of three divine *Persons:* Father, Son, and Holy Spirit.

◆ The doctrine was formulated in response to mankind's understanding of God based on the Scriptural witness.

◆ The Trinity doesn't say that "three Persons are one Person" (*Person* is simply a convenient word for one of the three "somethings" within the Godhead).

◆ Christians don't "believe in" the Trinity (which is a description of God's inner working); rather we believe in the God who has revealed himself in the Bible to be Father, Son, and Holy Spirit.

◆ The concept of a triune God doesn't in any way supplant monotheism—the doctrine that there is only one God.

◆ The anti-Trinitarian heresy of Modalism is alive and well today, because it seems to explain the Trinity in simple terms without any "somehow."

Chapter 4

The Mystery of Jesus' Dual Natures

In This Chapter

- ◆ Jesus' two natures are essential for our salvation
- ◆ Two natures somehow coexist in one being
- ◆ The latest, greatest debates about Jesus
- ◆ What the church Council of Chalcedon accomplished

Whoa! Haven't we been here before? Chapter 2 introduced the mystery of the Incarnation. Well, the Incarnation quickly launched another mystery. Not only is Jesus fully God and fully human, he needs to be both at the same time! Jesus' divine nature and his human nature operate simultaneously inside the one Person of Jesus.

We'll look at this second mystery in this chapter, but I'll take a somewhat different approach than I've followed with other tough teachings in this book. First, I'll describe the mainstream doctrine of Jesus' dual natures, and then I'll tell you about the various concerns that led to the doctrine's refinement and affirmation by the Council of Chalcedon.

Don't Accept Less Than Two Natures!

The doctrine of the Incarnation (see Chapter 2) teaches that Jesus must be fully divine and fully human, not some hazy hybrid—a man who incorporates a few aspects of divinity, or a divine Person who has a handful of humanity.

If he weren't true God and true man, Jesus of Nazareth wouldn't represent the intersection of Heaven and Earth. He couldn't serve as the mediator who reconciles God and man, nor would he have the divinity required to save fallen humanity.

Walking with the Wise

The Incarnation was a historical and unrepeatable event with permanent consequences. Reigning at God's right hand today is the man Christ Jesus, still human as well as divine, though now his humanity has been glorified. Having assumed our human nature, he has never discarded it, and he never will.

—John Stott, *Authentic Christianity*

Not all Christians agree with the teaching that Jesus is both fully God and fully man. The mainstream two-natures doctrine posed a special problem for many early Christians who couldn't imagine how Jesus' dual natures—his divinity and his humanity—could coexist simultaneously in a single human body. On the one hand, they thought the idea of one being with two natures was logically impossible. On the other hand, they argued that both couldn't possibly work at full power: Jesus' divine nature would be tainted by his human nature—or his human nature would be inhibited by his divinity.

While a few opponents simply rejected the dual-nature idea, many others fudged the concepts. They softened Jesus' divinity or his humanity, with an eye toward making the dual natures more compatible with each other.

Take Warning!

Don't confuse the dual-nature concerns addressed here with the assertions made by Docetists (I talked about them in Chapter 2). Because they doubted that the divine nature of the second Person of the Trinity could exist within the truly physical body that Jesus was supposed to have, they claimed that his physical body merely seemed real.

A Convention at Chalcedon

Chalcedon (pronounced *kal-SEE-dun*; today called Kadiköy, Turkey) is an ancient maritime town on the eastern shore of the Bosporus. In 461, a church council met in Chaldedon to put an end to several challenges to the teaching that Jesus was fully God and fully human.

The Council of Chalcedon emphasized that Jesus alone is fully God and fully man, with *neither* nature diminished by the other. The participants produced the document theologians call the Chalcedonian Definition; it makes the following essential points about Jesus:

- Jesus is perfect in divinity—truly God.

- Jesus is perfect in humanity—a man born with a human soul, human mind, and human body; like us in all things but sin.

- Jesus' divinity and humanity come together to form one person and being, and are not divided or separated into two persons.

- Jesus' two natures are united without confusion or change.

- The distinction between Jesus' two natures was not abolished by their union.

- The character proper to each of Jesus' two natures was preserved as they came together in one person.

I need to end this section with a caveat, to reinforce the second point made at Chalcedon. When you see "human nature," don't think about the way people behave. It may be human nature for people to be greedy and selfish, but the theologians at Chalcedon had a much broader meaning in mind.

Theologically speaking, "human nature" is shorthand description of mankind's attributes. Our human nature has a material aspect (our bodies) and a nonmaterial aspect (our spirits or souls). The doctrine of the Trinity insists that Jesus took on both during the Incarnation. That's how he became fully human.

The Council of Chalcedon focused on theological details when it set out to defend the claim of Jesus' dual divine and human natures. You and I might have made a practical argument. I noted in Chapter 2 that the Incarnation gave mankind the ability to enter a personal relationship, through Jesus, with the God who created the universe. For this to be possible, Jesus must be both fully human and fully divine. If Jesus is only a man, we lose the ability to relate to God; if Jesus is only divine, we lose our communications link to God.

Hey! Who Says Jesus Has Dual Natures?

One of the fascinating things about the Council of Chalcedon is that it met so many years after Jesus died. The reason, of course, is that it took *centuries* for many of the most intelligent thinkers—the equivalent of today' rocket scientists—to explain the Jesus set forth in the Gospels. And so, it was probably inevitable that the last, great debates about Jesus would involve issues that were more compelling to theologians than Christian laymen.

> **Walking with the Wise**
>
> For the "incarnation of God" to be possible in a Christian sense, God must be able to come over to our side without leaving his own "side."
>
> —Hans Urs von Balthasar, *Elucidations*

Because the Council of Chalcedon did its work in response to specific challenges to the teaching that Jesus is fully God, fully man, this list of responses will take on greater meaning when we look at the specific objections that were raised to the majority-view doctrine about Jesus' dual natures.

What If Jesus Has Only a Divine Nature?

All the perceived problems of combining Jesus' divinity with humanity go away if you assert that Jesus gave up the lion's share of his human nature during the Incarnation.

The skeptics who advocated this viewpoint argued that much of Jesus' human nature ceased to exist at the moment that God the Son took on human flesh. They were willing to believe that Jesus of Nazareth had a body equivalent in substance to ours. But they claimed that every other aspect of Jesus' humanity—his will, his mind, his human soul—had been absorbed by his divinity, much like a single grain of sugar dissolving in a tall glass of water.

Of course, denying Jesus' human nature completely unhinges the mainstream doctrine of the Incarnation and completely rejects the Biblical witness that "The Word became flesh." (John 1:14, NIV)

Moreover, if Jesus isn't fully human, the foundations of other important teachings also crumble. For example, a nonhuman Jesus wouldn't be tempted by Satan (see Matthew 4:1–11). And a Jesus without a human soul could not have suffered in the Garden of Gethsemane, where he said, "My soul is overwhelmed with sorrow, to the point of death ...." (Matthew 26:38, NIV)

Consequently, it's no surprise that the actual Chalcedonian Definition starts with these words: "… we all with one accord teach men to acknowledge one and the same Son, our Lord Jesus Christ, at once complete in Godhead and complete in manhood, truly God and truly man …." The participants understood that few of the skeptics challenged Jesus' divine nature; that doctrine had been affirmed more than a century earlier. The goal of the Council of Chalcedon was to establish "complete in manhood" as an orthodox teaching.

What If Jesus Has Only a Human Nature?

At first glance, this argument against Jesus having dual natures looks like the heresy of Arianism I talked about in Chapter 2. Although the effect is the same—to deny the Incarnation—the thinking behind it is somewhat different.

Arius argued—and lost—on Scriptural grounds that Jesus couldn't be fully divine. The dual-nature naysayers claimed that Jesus had to have only a single human nature because a divine nature would be limited alongside a human nature. In other words, it would lose many aspects of divinity.

The Chalcedonian Definition attacks this assertion head on by insisting that the *hypostatic union* united Jesus' divine and human natures without change or alteration. Specifically, the character proper to each of Jesus' two natures was preserved as they came together in one Person. The council made no attempt to explain how such a thing is possible; Jesus' unchanged dual natures remain an ongoing Christian mystery.

def•i•ni•tion

Hypostatic union is the technical theological term to describe the union of the divine nature of the second Person of the Trinity (God the Son) with human nature to create Jesus, who is fully God and fully man in a single "hypostasis" (Person, in the theological sense). Because the hypostatic union is held to be a mystery that exceeds human comprehension and explanation, some Christians call it the "mystical union."

What If Jesus Consists of Two Separate Persons?

Not all dual-nature doubters insisted on eradicating Jesus' divinity or humanity. Instead, they invented alternative theories that would leave Jesus' dual natures intact.

One of these ideas claimed that Jesus was not a unified person, but rather two separate individuals sharing a single human body:

◆ Jesus the man—a human being with a fully human nature

◆ The Son of God—the second Person of the Trinity—who has a fully divine nature and who dwelt inside Jesus' body

This idea is called Nestorianism, after Nestorius, the Bishop of Constantinople, who was accused of advocating it. (He always denied that he did.)

The "solution" to the mystery of Jesus' dual nature that Nestorianism purports to offer is that because Jesus' divinity and human nature are kept separate, with no interactions that might compromise them, each remains intact and functional.

But these supposed benefits come at a high cost:

◆ The Son of God indwells the person of the Nestorian Jesus, making Jesus a "God-bearing man" rather than the *God-man* the Incarnation insists he is.

◆ The Nestorian Jesus who died on the cross is no longer fully God—taking away his power to save mankind and restore humanity's broken relationship with God.

Although Nestorianism has been considered a heresy for upward of 1,600 years, it's often dragged out of the closet today by people searching for a simple explanation of the Incarnation. The idea that the Son of God merely indwells the man Jesus eliminates many of the "somehows."

What If Jesus Has One United Nature?

Okay, back to the erroneous-doctrine drawing board. We want Jesus to incorporate both divinity and humanity, but having truly dual natures seems illogical. One way to resolve this dilemma is to claim that Jesus has only *one* nature, created by uniting divine and human attributes to yield a third sort of nature that blends divinity and humanity. This would be a one-of-a-kind nature, unique to Jesus.

Alas, some sort of hybrid nature that combines a little of this with a little of that means that some aspects of divinity and some aspects of humanity never make it to the mixing bowl. Jesus ceases to be fully God or fully man—and we lose the chief benefits of the Incarnation that we've talked about (including Jesus' power to be Savior).

The Chalcedonian Definition refutes the blended-natures notion in three ways. First, it states that Jesus' dual natures are united without confusion. Second, it asserts that the union of Jesus' two natures didn't abolish their distinction. Third, it insists that the character of each of Jesus' two natures remained intact after the hypostatic union.

What If Jesus Doesn't Have a True Human Mind?

One of the more bewildering assaults on Jesus' dual natures starts by acknowledging that he has most aspects of human nature—all except a truly human *mind*. The doctrine of Apollinarism claimed that Jesus' mind was divine—the mind of the God the Son, the second Person of the Trinity.

The doctrine, invented by a cleric named Apollinaris, did grant Jesus' human body a "lower soul" (which ancients considered the seat of emotions), so that Jesus could have human feelings. Apollinaris strongly disagreed that divinity and humanity could coexist within one person. His solution was to diminish the human nature of Christ by shifting rational thought and decision-making to God the Son.

Scripture doesn't agree. The Gospels depict Jesus thinking like a man, asking questions of people, growing in knowledge and wisdom, and not displaying essential divine attributes such as omniscience.

In fact, Apollinarism was declared to be a heresy 80 years before the Council of Chalcedon, but the Chalcedonian Definition taps the last nail into the doctrine's coffin by asserting that Jesus has a "rational human soul"—a human mind, in ancient theological terminology.

What If Jesus Doesn't Have Human Will?

Here we have a compromise position designed to please both mainstream theologians who defend Jesus' dual natures, and those who claim that Jesus only has one divine nature. Perhaps Jesus could have two natures, but only one will: a divine will. This would ensure that there would never be a conflict of wills that might cause Jesus to act the wrong way.

Once again, the Scriptural witness disagrees with this position: consider Jesus' poignant prayer in the Garden of Gethsemane: "My Father, if it is possible, may this cup be taken from me. Yet not as I will, but as you will." (Matthew 26:39, NIV) Jesus is clearly submitting his human will to the divine will of God the Father.

Jesus' Dual Natures Remain a Thorny Mystery

It took many decades after Chalcedon for the teachings to sink in throughout Christendom. Even then, countless well-meaning Christians continued to misinterpret the teaching that Jesus is fully God and fully man. Jesus must be a union of two distinct, changeless natures—divine and human—but Jesus can't have a split personality. Somehow his two natures operate without confusion, so he can be fully God and fully man. Not only does the Bible attest to Jesus' divinity and humanity, it also presents him as a fully integrated human being.

Get Wisdom

Here's an interesting analogy to use when you explain the mystery of Jesus' dual natures to a scientifically minded person. Point out that modern physicists understand that light sometimes acts like waves and other times like particles—a mysterious combination of significantly different dual natures. This "wave–particle duality" was first described by Albert Einstein in the early 1900s. Various experiments can be done on light to demonstrate its sometimes-particle nature and its sometimes-wave nature.

His dual natures, though distinct, don't operate independently. It's incorrect to say, "Ah, Jesus did this because of his divine nature, and that because of his human nature." Instead, we recognize that Jesus acted and spoke the way he did by virtue of his dual natures: deity *and* humanity.

The Least You Need to Know

◆ Jesus *must* have dual natures—be both fully God and fully man—to be a savior or to reconcile mankind with God.

◆ Hypostatic union is the theological term that describes the union of the divine nature of the second Person of the Trinity (God the Son) with human nature.

◆ Jesus doesn't have a split personality; his two natures operate without confusion.

◆ Most of the arguments against Jesus' dual natures begin with the wrong assumption that his divine nature and his human nature can't coexist inside a human being.

◆ Most of the alternative doctrines proposed by the naysayers ignore the Gospel teachings about Jesus.

◆ The church Council of Chalcedon wrestled with the major objections and produced a document—The Chalcedonian Definition—that reaffirms Jesus' dual natures.

The Mystery of Jesus' Resurrection

In This Chapter

- The crucified Jesus rose from the dead
- Christianity's most incredible teaching
- Belief in Jesus' Resurrection launched Christianity
- Arguments that the Resurrection happened
- What Jesus' Resurrection means to believers

Christians insist that Jesus was resurrected—that somehow He returned to life in a glorified body—on the third day after His execution.

For most nonbelievers, the Resurrection is the most incredible assertion that Christianity makes. They see the teaching as patently absurd, utterly impossible, and completely contrary to human experience. This skepticism has rubbed off on many believers; over the years, public opinion surveys have found that as many as one-third of all Christians doubt that Jesus' Resurrection was a historical fact.

We'll examine the mystery of the Resurrection in this chapter and seek to understand why the teaching has remained at the hub of Christianity for nearly 2,000 years.

That's Quite a Claim!

Christians claim that Jesus of Nazareth rose from the dead roughly 40 hours after His execution by the Romans and met with hundreds of people during the following 40 days. And therein lies a Christian mystery that's unexpectedly easy to talk about.

Take Warning!

Don't be confused when you come to he end of the Apostle's Creed, a statement of faith used by many Christian denominations, which asserts: "I believe in … the resurrection of the body, and life everlasting." A similar statement appears in the Nicene Creed: "We look for the resurrection of the dead, and the life of the world to come." These attestations refer to the "general resurrection" of dead humankind that Christian's believe will occur when Jesus returns to Earth. They do not affirm your belief in Jesus' resurrection.

Unlike the Trinity (see Chapter 3), we can easily picture in our minds what the Resurrection supposedly entails: Jesus came back to life in a uniquely different body. He met with his Apostles and other people in Jerusalem, near Emmaus (a village west of Jerusalem), and on the coast of the Sea of Galilee, and at other unnamed locations.

And unlike the Incarnation (see Chapter 2), we don't have to spend much time pondering how such an incredible thing might be accomplished. Even skeptics acknowledge that a God who created the universe would have the power to resurrect Jesus and glorify His body.

Biblical Resuscitations

The Bible has several examples of people "raised from the dead" (Lazarus, for example, in John 11:38–43). We can be confident that all their mortal bodies eventually died. But something different happened to Jesus on that Sunday morning in Jerusalem. He was *resurrected*, not resuscitated. His ordinary human body was somehow transformed, giving Jesus a glorified body that will never die again.

Christians assert that Jesus' physical resurrection is the preview of every believer's own resurrection in the future, that we, too, will have imperishable bodies on the New

Earth that God will make. As Paul wrote, "… Christ has been raised from the dead, the first fruits of those who have died." (1 Corinthians 15:20, NRSV)

But … People Don't Rise from the Dead!

But then we reach the mind-blowing aspect of the Resurrection: the idea that it took place at all.

Everyone—including the first-century followers of Jesus—knows that a man executed on Friday afternoon doesn't come back to life on Sunday morning. It would be hard to conceive of a more improbable event—even though Jesus' disciples all but disregarded Jesus' prediction of His resurrection. Matthew 16:21–22, NIV, reports the following conversation between Jesus and the Apostles: "From that time on Jesus began to explain to his disciples that he must go to Jerusalem and suffer many things at the hands of the elders, chief priests and teachers of the law, and that he must be killed and on the third day be raised to life."

Peter took him aside and began to rebuke him. "Never, Lord!" he said. "This shall never happen to you!" It's clear that Peter (speaking for the disciples) focused on Jesus' death and ignored His return to life.

Because Christianity is so rich in miracles, we can debate which miracle is most important. I've told you that I give the Incarnation top billing, but I won't argue if you save that honor for the Resurrection. It's certainly true that many of Christianity's recorded miracles seem significantly less miraculous than Jesus' Resurrection. Once a Christian accepts the Resurrection as a historical event, Jesus' other miracles are easy to believe.

Get Wisdom

One of the more curious findings of a recent public opinion study is that an astonishing 26 percent of *non-Christians* in America believe that Jesus was physically resurrected. What's startling about this statistic is that someone who believes in the Resurrection of Jesus is well down the road to becoming a Christian.

Christianity Is Pointless Without the Resurrection

From the earliest days of Christianity, Christians understood that the claim that Jesus of Nazareth had been raised from the dead was absolutely essential. Paul famously wrote, "And if Christ has not been raised, our preaching is useless and so is your faith. …. And if Christ has not been raised, your faith is futile; you are still in your sins." (1 Corinthians 15:14, 17, NIV)

Why is this so?

The Resurrection Confirmed What Jesus Said

The most important reason is that the Resurrection *vindicated* Jesus. His Resurrection proved to everyone who doubted Jesus that everything he taught, claimed, and said was true ….

◆ Jesus was Israel's long-awaited Messiah.

◆ Jesus was both Lord and Savior—and did have the divine power to save humanity.

◆ Jesus did have divine authority to modify the Law, as when He announced that, "… the Son of Man is Lord of the Sabbath." (Matthew 12:8, NIV)

◆ Jesus was right when he said, "Anyone who has seen me has seen the Father." (John 14:9, NIV)

This is the point that Paul hammered home when he spoke to the Athenians on Mars Hill (the Areopagus in Greek): "… he [God] has fixed a day on which he will judge the world in righteousness by a man whom he has appointed, and of this he has given assurance to all men by raising him from the dead." (Acts 17:31 NIV)

> ### Walking with the Wise
>
> If resurrections happened regularly, there would be nothing different about Jesus being raised from the dead. He would be one among many, just another statistic. … If [Jesus' Resurrection] is unique, then, by definition, there will be no analogous events. That makes it a lot harder to believe. It also makes it worth believing.
>
> —Alister E. McGrath, *What Was God Doing on the Cross?*

Some theologians argue that without the confirmation provided by the Resurrection, a sensible person would be foolish to call him/herself a Christian. Simply put, it makes no sense to follow a dead itinerant preacher—no matter how wise the things he said and how miraculous the deeds he performed during his short ministry.

However, because the Resurrection provided persuasive "proof" that Jesus had told the truth about himself and was the promised Messiah, the early Christians—most of whom were Jewish—came to believe that Jesus was the fulfillment of Old-Testament prophecies that the God of Israel was going to free Israel from exile and oppression.

In fact, Jesus' Resurrection changed their perspective. The cross that had seemed like an unqualified defeat came to be viewed as an extraordinary victory. These early Christians concluded that in Jesus, God had started a process that would, in time, lead to the elimination of evil, sin, and even death.

In many different ways, Jesus' Resurrection started the Good News flowing. It was an extraordinary demonstration of the power of God—a true miracle for the ages. It's not surprising then that Paul was the first of many Christians to recognize that Christianity ultimately rises or falls on the question of whether Jesus *actually* rose from the dead. As N. T. Wright, the theologian, author, and Anglican bishop, put it: "If Easter isn't good news, then there is no good news."

The word *actually* is what differentiates the Resurrection in Christianity from the "hero's return from death" stories found in many mythologies. Jesus wasn't a make-believe pagan "corn god" who symbolically died and came to life each year.

More than one skeptic has argued that Jesus' death and Resurrection represent a mythology that was widely accepted by first-century believers. To the contrary, the earliest Christians apparently believed in a literal Resurrection that happened recently, a few miles from their homes, not a mythological event in a faraway time and place. The Gospel accounts claim to communicate history. They're written in the style of historical accounts, not legends. Moreover, myths take decades to develop and spread slowly (if at all); reports of Jesus' Resurrection traveled widely across the Roman Empire within a few years of his death. Finally, it's hard to imagine a group of people less likely to emulate pagan myths than the Jews who became the first Christians.

Christians assert that the Resurrection of Jesus was an event in history—an event that had a date (the third decade of the first century) and a place (Jerusalem). If the Resurrection happened as Christians claim, it was as real as the Passover celebrations that year in Israel, or springtime maneuvers by Roman soldiers.

Walking with the Wise

If the first Christians had not believed that Christ rose from the dead there would have been no church and no New Testament .... If Christianity had been founded merely on the moral teaching of Jesus, it would no doubt have flourished for a short time as a well-meaning deviation from orthodox Judaism. It would quickly have lost its identity amid the innumerable varieties of religion and philosophy which occupied the minds of the ancient world.

—William Neil, *The Life and Teaching of Jesus*

Must Christians Believe in the Resurrection?

When I taught adult Christian education courses at our church several years ago, I often asked: "Which of the Christian mysteries do you have the most difficulty believing?" The answer I heard most often was, "The Virgin Birth" (see Chapter 9), but in nearly every class, one or two students acknowledged that they doubted that Jesus had been physically resurrected.

This response was likely to start a lively discussion about whether it's possible to be a Christian if you don't believe that Jesus was resurrected.

Naturally, I pointed to Romans 10:9, NIV, where Paul wrote, "that if you confess with your mouth, 'Jesus is Lord,' and believe in your heart that God raised him from the dead, you will be saved."

This is one of the earliest Christian professions of faith—a combination of confession (public statement) and sincerely held belief:

◆ It took great commitment in first-century Rome to say aloud that "Jesus is Lord" (this was a time when all non-Christians knew that Caesar was lord, and any other viewpoint could be dangerous).

◆ Only a true Christian believes in his/her heart that God raised Jesus from the dead—most others will think the teaching unbelievable.

The bottom line: it does seem that belief in the Resurrection is a hallmark of one's Christian faith.

Get Wisdom

George Carey, the Archbishop of Canterbury in the United Kingdom from 1991 to 2002, made two well-reported statements that illustrate the difficulties that Christians—including highly-trained Christian leaders—can have with the teaching of the Resurrection: in 1992, he said that "the resurrection is not an appendage to the Christian faith—it is the Christian faith." In 1999, he said, "I can tell you frankly that while we can be absolutely sure that Jesus lived and that he was certainly crucified on the cross, we cannot with the same certainty say that we know he was raised by God from the dead." Carey went on to explain that while he firmly believes in the Resurrection, "It goes against human experience and our first instinct is incredulity."

Jesus Wasn't Resurrected Because ...

Skeptics who doubt that Jesus was resurrected often test Christianity's claim by asking for direct evidence that the event really happened.

These people also know that the chief direct evidence of the Resurrection (evidence that stands on its own) can be found in the New Testament, in the Gospels and in several of Paul's letters. Not surprisingly, these skeptics also reject the truth of the Bible are not impressed by Scriptural witness. For example, the eyewitness accounts presented in the Gospels don't move them, because the evidence comes from the Bible. The same is true of Paul's statement (see 1 Corinthians 15:6) that the Resurrected Jesus was seen by more than 500 eyewitnesses.

On the other hand, these same skeptics know that they can't disprove that the Resurrection happened. The mere fact that rising from the dead is not part of the human experience is not evidence that Jesus stayed buried in his tomb.

Most of the doubters also acknowledge that early Christians acted *as if* they believed the Resurrection was true. Although they may disagree with Paul's contention that 500 "brothers" saw the resurrected Jesus, they agree that the detail presented in Paul's letters confirms that the Resurrection had become an "official" Christian teaching within a decade or two of Jesus' death.

Consequently, the cleverest doubters don't challenge the Scriptural accounts of the Resurrection or the sincerity of eyewitnesses. Rather, they claim that the people who experienced the Resurrected Jesus were misled—that they misunderstood what they saw and erroneously concluded that Jesus had risen from the dead.

Get Wisdom

A highly disputed piece of direct evidence about the Resurrection can be found in *Jewish Antiquities,* a history written by Flavius Josephus, a first-century Jewish historian: "Now there was about this time Jesus ... a teacher of such men as receive the truth with pleasure. He drew over to him both many of the Jews and many of the Gentiles. He was [the] Christ. And when Pilate ... condemned him to the cross, those that loved him at the first did not forsake him; for he appeared to them alive again the third day, as the divine prophets had foretold ..." While some Christian scholars accept the paragraph, most believe it was added after Josephus' death by a Christian scribe.

Improbable Theory 1: A Shared Vision

The vision argument goes like this: Jesus' followers were so shocked and saddened by his execution that they refused to admit that he was really dead. And so, they hallucinated him back to life. After all, Jesus predicted that he would be killed and raised on the third day (Matthew 16:21); his followers merely imagined the second half of Jesus' prophecy. Consequently, when Mary Magdalene reported seeing Him (Matthew 28:1–10), she fulfilled the disciples' expectations, and their imaginations did the rest.

An identical vision shared by all of Jesus' followers—a vision that lasted 40 days and then stopped—seems even less probable than His Resurrection, especially when the hallucination in question speaks, eats, drinks, and travels around the countryside.

Moreover, the Gospel record suggests that the Apostles were shaken, demoralized, and wholly discouraged after Jesus' execution. They had all seen crucified people before and were apparently terrified of becoming the Romans' next targets. It's hard to picture any of this group expecting Jesus to appear in the flesh—or having enough faith to share improbable visions.

Improbable Theory 2: It Wasn't Jesus Who Walked Around

One especially bizarre notion is that Jesus had an identical twin brother among his disciples (Thomas or Didymus, both of which mean *twin*) who substituted for the dead Jesus in a bogus resurrection. A thorny challenge for those who support this theory is to explain the reports of Jesus' glorified body. Presumably, Jesus' "twin brother" wasn't born with the ability to enter a room without using the door (see John 20:19–20).

Improbable Theory 3: Jesus Survived the Crucifixion

A fairly popular argument among doubters is that Jesus somehow survived his execution. There are several variations:

◆ Jesus swooned after several hours on the cross—perhaps because he was drugged by his followers—and was mistakenly assumed to be dead by the Roman soldiers.

◆ The great physical abuse Jesus endured caused a deep coma that caused the Roman executioners to believe he had died.

◆ Jesus appeared to be dead because he had epilepsy or another illness that caused a profound unconsciousness that mimicked death.

In all of these survival scenarios, Jesus was taken down from the cross by the Roman soldiers, who believed they had successfully completed their assignment. Jesus subsequently recovered later—probably with the help of his followers, possibly while lying inside the tomb.

The fundamental flaw in these survival theories is the idea that experienced Roman executioners were fooled by the mere appearance of death. If Jesus was crucified (which few skeptics doubt), His survival means that Roman soldiers who conducted countless crucifixions made an amateurish mistake—which is highly unlikely.

Christians Point to the Indirect Evidence

There may be little non-Biblical direct evidence of the Resurrection, but Christians can offer a flood of *indirect* (or *circumstantial*) *evidence* that the Resurrection actually occurred.

Many people—I'm one of them—find the indirect evidence highly compelling. Even before I became a Christian I agreed that "something momentous happened" about year 30 in first-century Jerusalem—something that altered the course of world history.

def•i•ni•tion

Indirect (or circumstantial) evidence provides a basis for inferring the truth or falsity of the fact in dispute. For example, wet pavement is indirect evidence of recent rain.

The Mightily Changed Apostles

The leadership of the early Christian church in Jerusalem during the days following Jesus' death consisted of a rag-tag band of followers who, as I noted, were dejected, demoralized, and fearful of arrest. It's difficult to imagine this bunch, cowering in a Jerusalem hiding place, as thinking of themselves as leaders of anything. Yet, this literally hopeless group was transformed into a team of zealous evangelists willing to die for their Christian beliefs—and all but one of them did! (See Chapter 20.)

What could have caused a transformation that substantial? Certainly not a decision to invent a sham resurrection; few people are willing to die for a lie. No; the most credible explanation (mysterious as it is) is that the Apostles were changed by seeing the risen Jesus.

Clearly, accepting this piece of indirect evidence requires *some* acknowledgment that the New Testament is truthful; I find that many nonbelievers are willing to go this far, because:

◆ They recognize that much the same argument can be made for the earliest Christians in and around Jerusalem, many of whom took significant risks to proclaim their new faith.

◆ They can't deny the spectacular spread of Christianity in the first century, from a small Jewish sect in Jerusalem, to a faith with adherents across the Roman Empire—including a significant group in Rome itself.

Both of these facts testify to a simple truth: the details of Jesus' Resurrection were accepted as true by many of His contemporaries, who would have heard if the story had been discredited.

Widespread Belief in a "Failed Messiah"

Some scholars believe there were upward of 100 people who claimed to be the Jewish messiah in the first century. All except Jesus were promptly forgotten or replaced after being killed by the Romans. (Many of them were crucified.) By definition, a dead messiah is a failed messiah—a messiah who has lost all his credibility.

Jesus of Nazareth was different. For some reason, this particular "dead messiah" wasn't abandoned by his followers. What's more, they journeyed far and wide throughout the Roman Empire to tell other people about him. The only explanation that makes sense is that Jesus' followers *knew* that He was special because they had seen Him alive after His crucifixion.

Widespread Belief in Jesus' Divinity

Within 20 years of his death, the early Christians proclaimed Jesus' divinity (see Chapter 2). Their numbers included many Jewish Christians whose faith insisted there was only one God. What prompted this shift in their understanding and their seemingly blasphemous assertions? Only a happening as persuasive as the Resurrection—an event that validated their belief that Jesus was fully God, fully man.

> **Walking with the Wise** _____
>
> The Resurrection is the keystone of the arch on which our faith is supported. If Christ has not risen, we must impeach all those witnesses for lying. If Christ has not risen, we have no proof that the crucifixion of Jesus differed from that of the two thieves who suffered with him. If Christ has not risen, it is impossible to believe his atoning death was accepted.
>
> —D. L. Moody, "Jesus Arose: So Shall We" (sermon)

The Early Christians Would Have Invented a Better Lie

If first-century Christians had made up the story of Jesus' Resurrection to somehow give credence to their efforts to launch a new religion (assuming that this is plausible, which it isn't!), they would have invented a more convincing lie. The Resurrection stories told in the Gospels are cluttered with details of the Apostles' doubts and concerns that get in the way of Jesus' triumphant return from death. He is forced to spend much of his 40 days on Earth holding their hands, instead of doing heroic deeds.

Another observation made by many historians is that the Gospels report the first eyewitnesses of the risen Christ were women. But women were not considered trustworthy witnesses in first-century Israel. A sham account would have featured eyewitnesses who had greater credibility.

Something Happened in the Holy Land

The first Christians clearly believed that Jesus had been resurrected and that he spent 40 days proving the point to his followers. This is such an odd belief for thousands of people to use as the foundation of their faith that the most plausible reason is that it was widely known—and accepted—that Jesus had actually risen from the dead.

To finish with another quote from N. T. Wright, "… the historian may and must say that all other explanations for why Christianity arose, and why it took the shape it did, are far less convincing as historical explanations than the one the early Christians themselves offer: that Jesus really did rise from the dead on Easter morning, leaving an empty tomb behind him."

The Least You Need to Know

◆ Christianity teaches that Jesus was physically resurrected after his crucifixion—
   that He rose from the dead and spent 40 days in the Holy Land.

◆ Most nonbelievers see the Resurrection as the most incredible assertion that
   Christianity makes because it seems completely contrary to human experience.

◆ Most direct evidence that establishes the truth of Jesus' Resurrection is found
   in the Gospels and Paul's letters—believers accept the evidence as true; skeptics
   reject most of the Scriptural witness.

◆ There is a wealth of compelling indirect evidence that corroborates Christianity's
   claim that the Resurrection was a historical fact.

◆ Skeptics have advanced arguments that the eyewitnesses to the Resurrection
   did not see the risen Jesus—but were fooled by impostors or a Jesus who hadn't
   actually died.

◆ Although opinion surveys find that some Christians doubt that Jesus was physically resurrected, most Christians feel that belief in the Resurrection is an essential of Christian faith.

Chapter 6

The Mystery of the Atonement

In This Chapter

- ◆ No Christianity without the Cross
- ◆ Jesus' atoning death somehow reconciled God and man
- ◆ How Jesus' work on the Cross "worked"
- ◆ Different denominations favor different theories of Atonement
- ◆ The related mystery of God's grace
- ◆ God's gracious (unmerited) gift to humankind

Christians say that the largest rescue mission ever launched achieved success 2,000 years ago on a bleak hillside outside of Jerusalem. Somehow, when Jesus of Nazareth was crucified, His death atoned for the sins of humankind.

How did Jesus' death accomplish this extraordinary result? This chapter will present many different answers to the question that Christian scholars have proposed during the past two millennia.

The *At-One*-Ment of God and Humankind

The principal message of Christianity is that through Jesus Christ, God reconciled sinful man with himself:

◆ The second Person of the Trinity took on flesh to become Jesus—fully God, fully man (see Chapters 2 and 3 on the Incarnation and the Trinity, respectively).

◆ Jesus led a sinless life, fully obedient to God in every way.

◆ Somehow, Jesus' willing death on the Cross crushed the powers of sin and death and made possible humanity's reconciliation with God.

◆ When Jesus' Atonement was complete, he spoke "It is finished" (John 19:30, NIV) and died.

The word "atonement" is of fairly recent vintage. It was invented by William Tyndale, the sixteenth-century scholar who created the first significant English Bible translation (it later served as the foundation of the famed King James Version). Tyndale searched for a single word that would communicate the two benefits of Jesus' sacrifice: the taking away of sin, and the reconciliation of humankind to God.

Get Wisdom

Matthew 27:50, NIV, reports that Jesus "cried out … in a loud voice," and Mark 15:37, NIV, states he made "a loud cry." Only the Gospel of John reports what Jesus shouted at his death: an idiomatic Greek word, *tetelestai* (which, when used in commerce, means "paid in full!"). Most Bible versions translate this as "It is finished," although the interpretation from commerce is even closer to the concept of atonement.

Tyndale finally invented his own word by creating a new word from the Middle English phrase *at oon*, which means *at one*. Thus, atonement—*at-one-ment*—is that which reconciles, or makes "at one."

Another theological word you are likely to see or hear when Christian scholars write or talk about the Atonement is soteriology—a word is based on the Greek word *soteria*, which means "salvation." Soteriology is the study of how salvation through Jesus Christ is possible, and how Christians should understand salvation.

It All Begins with Sin

Christians claim that sin created a massive gulf between God and humankind. As Paul said, "For all have sinned and fall short of the glory of God …." (Romans 3:23, NIV) And as John echoed, "If we claim to be without sin, we deceive ourselves and the truth is not in us." (1 John 1:8, NIV)

Most Christian denominations in North America teach that our sinful nature is inherited and is an inherent part of humankind's makeup.

Christians go on to say that by itself, humankind could do nothing to restore the shattered relationship. God Himself had to intervene. Thus, "All this is from God, who reconciled us to himself through Christ and gave us the ministry of reconciliation: that God was reconciling the world to himself in Christ, not counting men's sins against them." (2 Corinthians 5:18–19, NIV)

And, "For God was pleased to have all his fullness dwell in him [Jesus], and through him to reconcile to himself all things, whether things on earth or things in heaven, by making peace through his blood, shed on the cross." (Colossians 1:20, NIV)

Atonement Isn't Automatic

Let me start this section with a warning. The Atonement is an example of a Christian teaching that created an "in-house debate." This fracas has lasted almost 2,000 years. Not only do Christians argue among themselves about how Jesus' Atonement "works," we also disagree about what sinners need to do to take advantage of the salvation Jesus' death provided.

Some denominations teach that the only requirement is to accept Jesus as one's Lord and Savior—possibly (but not always) by reciting a sinner's prayer—a short prayer that acknowledges past sin and invites Jesus into the person's life as his or her Lord and Savior.

Other denominations insist that repenting of past sins is an essential first step. Still others claim that baptism is required for salvation. The advocates of these different positions can point to Scripture to support their beliefs.

> **Scripture Says**
>
> Acts 16:30–31, NIV, reports that the jailor in Philippi asked Paul and Silas, "Sirs, what must I do to be saved?" They replied, "Believe in the Lord Jesus, and you will be saved—you and your household." Acts 2:38, NIV, describes Peter's answer to a similar question: "Repent and be baptized, every one of you, in the name of Jesus Christ for the forgiveness of your sins."

I'll highlight in-house controversies where appropriate in this chapter (and this book), but I won't describe the pros and cons in great detail. Every sincere Christian must ultimately reach a personal conclusion about the "rightness" or "wrongness" of each alternative. A good way to begin is to search the Scripture for yourself, followed by a talk with a pastor or teacher at your church.

How Did the Atonement Work?

The central mystery of the Atonement is this: how could the death, 2,000 years ago, of an itinerant preacher in an obscure Roman province impact our relationship with God?

The Gospels provide lots of detail on Jesus' crucifixion and Resurrection but don't explain how Jesus' death "worked" to achieve atonement. Consequently, Christian scholars—beginning with the earliest Church Fathers in the second and third centuries—have come up with many "theories of atonement" to explain how Jesus accomplished his saving mission. Each so-called theory is a specific explanation of how the death of Jesus Christ reconciled humanity with God. (Don't be mislead by the word "theory." Scholars use the word differently than most of us do. To them, a theory isn't a guess or a gut feeling. Rather, it's a well-thought-out model or framework that explains how a complex phenomenon—like the atonement—works.)

Some denominations prefer—and teach—a single theory of atonement, but in fact the language of the New Testament suggests many possible explanations of the atonement. When set side-by-side, however, the various theories seem fundamentally dissimilar and in conflict with each other. This has caused considerable contention over the years, even though many Christian scholars point out that the various theories illuminate different aspects of Jesus' atoning work. If Christians focus on one, they warn, we ignore important Scriptural insights into what Jesus actually accomplished. Nonetheless, some theories have become more widely taught than others.

An interesting point worth noting is that the various theories of atonement you'll learn about in this chapter were *not* developed as responses to erroneous (heretical) beliefs. Many other leading Christian

> **Walking with the Wise**
>
> The central Christian belief is that Christ's death has somehow put us right with God and given us a fresh start. Theories as to how it did this are another matter. A good many different theories have been held as to how it works; what all Christians are agreed on is that it does work.
>
> —C. S. Lewis, *Mere Christianity*

teachings were created to defend against wrong ideas; the theories of atonement were proposed chiefly because Christians wanted to understand Jesus' "work" on the Cross.

The Earliest Theory: Keep Your Eye on the Incarnation

The first theory of atonement simply noted that the Incarnation of the Son of God unified God and man, and consequently lifted man up. To quote Gregory of Nazianzus, a highly respected fourth-century cleric, "… that which is united to God is saved."

This simple model leaves out much of the Scriptural witness (for example, it ignores Jesus' sacrifice and the familiar idea that he bore our sins) and at best provides a sketchy answer to "how does the Atonement work?"

Jesus Was a Sacrifice

Paul notes that "God presented him [Jesus] as a sacrifice of atonement." (Romans 3:25, NIV) The Gospel of John depicts John the Baptist describing Jesus as "… the Lamb of God, who takes away the sin of the world." (John 1:29, NIV) John may have analogized Jesus with the Passover Lamb.

In any case, Jesus was both the sacrifice and the priest who offered the sacrifice. Christians claim that Jesus was a perfect sacrifice who accomplished what the Old-Testament sacrifices could never achieve: a sacrifice covering humankind for all time.

The theory that Jesus died a sacrificial death is an example of an explanation that holds that something specific happened on the Cross that made salvation possible. In other words, Jesus' death somehow enabled humankind's sins to be forgiven, making the Cross an essential aspect of the process that reconciled God and man.

> **Get Wisdom**
>
> In the Old Testament, a sacrifice was an offering to God by one seeking atonement. The Passover Lamb was the lamb slain when the Israelites were seeking to leave Egypt. They smeared their doorframes with its blood and were spared the tenth plague: the death of firstborn males. (See Exodus 12:21.)

Jesus Was Our Ransom Paid

Jesus said of himself, "For even the Son of Man did not come to be served, but to serve, and to give his life as a ransom for many." (Mark 10:45, NIV) Moreover, Paul described Jesus' death as a ransom paid to free humankind: "You are not your own; you were bought at a price." (1 Corinthian 6:19–20, NIV) And, "... the man Christ Jesus, who gave himself as a ransom for all men." (1 Timothy 2:5–6, NIV)

A ransom is price paid for a person held against his/her will, most typically following a kidnapping. In the Atonement, the ransom paid for the lives of sinful humanity was the sinless life of Jesus. Although the ransom theory has obvious Scriptural support, it also has an equally obvious problem: if we push the figure of speech too far, sooner or later we're likely to ask: "Who collected the ransom?" The only credible answer is Satan, which introduces a host of theological issues:

 ◆ The theory gives Satan more power that he is granted in Scripture.

 ◆ Christianity teaches that sinners will ultimately be punished by a wrathful God; they may be led astray by Satan and be described metaphorically as "slaves of sin" (see Romans 6:16), but they remain in God's control.

 ◆ Where and how did Satan acquire binding rights to humankind that would force God to pay a ransom?

 ◆ Nothing in the Bible indicates that Satan had such rights or that he demanded a payment.

 ◆ The very idea of God paying a ransom to Satan is repugnant to most people.

Some early theologians modified the ransom theory to resolve the latter problem by adding the notion that God somehow deceived Satan during the transaction, because Satan didn't understand Jesus' divine nature, which made it impossible for him to maintain his hold on Jesus. This "solution" fails because it seems to change the character of God.

In the end, the idea of a literal ransom has been largely abandoned. The term *ransom* in Scripture is taken to be one of many useful metaphors to describe the effect of the Atonement.

Get Wisdom

The Bible also describes Jesus as our redeemer, a metaphor much like the payer of a ransom. "... Jesus Christ, who gave himself for us to redeem us from all wickedness." (Titus 2:13–14, NIV) And, "For you know that it was not with perishable things such as silver or gold that you were redeemed from the empty way of life ... but with the precious blood of Christ, a lamb without blemish or defect." (1 Peter 1:18–19, NIV) This figure of speech equates sin with a state of bondage that has entrapped humankind. Humanity must be redeemed by suitable price.

Jesus' Death Paid Our "Sin Debt"

This theory of atonement is often called the "satisfaction" theory. The six assumptions here are that:

1. Sin insults God and is an affront to God's honor.

2. Consequently humanity owes a debt to God Himself, because of the insult we've delivered.

3. God wants to forgive humanity, but, because he is a righteous Sovereign, he can't merely ignore the accumulated "sin debt."

4. The insult humankind has heaped upon God is so great that we have no way to satisfy (discharge) the debt.

5. A perfect sacrifice can satisfy the debt.

6. Jesus, fully God and fully man—and sinless—was able to offer the perfect sacrifice and satisfy the offended honor of God.

Jesus Suffered Our "Punishment"

A widely taught variation on the satisfaction theory is "substitutionary atonement," which views sin as a serious breach of God's law rather than as an insult to God's honor. As the term implies, the key idea is that Jesus died as a substitute for sinners—that he died vicariously for humankind. "Vicariously" used in this context means that humanity enjoyed the benefits of Jesus' atoning death; that God accepted Jesus' suffering in lieu of punishing sinful humanity.

The six-fold idea behind the substitutionary theory of atonement (sometimes called "penal substitution") is:

1. Humankind broke God's law by sinning.

2. Humanity incurred God's wrath and wholly deserved the punishment God has ordained for sin. "For the wages of sin is death." (Romans 6:23, NIV)

3. God wants to forgive humankind but—because he is a righteous Sovereign— can't merely waive the "curse of the Law" that hovers over humanity.

4. Jesus willingly and obediently died on the cross, took God's wrath upon himself, bore the curse of the law, and suffered and died for our sins.

5. When Jesus endured the punishment we deserved he simultaneously expiated (made amends for) our sins and propitiated (placated) God's wrath against us.

6. Thanks to Jesus' vicarious death, humanity has been reconciled with God and is saved eternally.

Advocates of the substitutionary theory often point to Isaiah 53:4–5, NIV, as the most convincing Old-Testament prophesy that a savior would be punished for humanity's sins:

> Surely he took up our infirmities and carried our sorrows, yet we considered him stricken by God, smitten by him, and afflicted.

> But he was pierced for our transgressions, he was crushed for our iniquities; the punishment that brought us peace was upon him, and by his wounds we are healed.

> We all, like sheep, have gone astray, each of us has turned to his own way and the LORD has laid on him the iniquity of us all.

> He was oppressed and afflicted, yet he did not open his mouth; he was led like a lamb to the slaughter, and as a sheep before her shearers is silent, so he did not open his mouth.

A simple analogy commonly used to describe the substitutionary theory of atonement is a courtroom overseen by an honorable judge. One day, the judge's child is prosecuted for violating the law. The judge faces a dilemma: on the one hand, he would like to forgive his child. On the other hand, justice (and the evidence) requires that the child be found guilty and punished. The judge's solution demonstrates both his love and his righteousness: He finds the child guilty, but pays the fine himself, then later "expunges" the record of guilt.

Walking with the Wise

You can say that Christ died for our sins. You may say that the Father has forgiven us because Christ has done for us what we ought to have done. You may say that we are washed in the blood of the Lamb. You may say that Christ has defeated death. They are all true. If any of them do not appeal to you, leave it alone and get on with the formula that does. And, whatever you do, do not start quarrelling with other people because they use a different formula from yours.

—C. S. Lewis, *Mere Christianity*

Jesus' Death Illustrates God's Love

Not all theories of atonement argue that Jesus' death paid a specific penalty or achieved vicarious punishment of sinful humanity. The "illustrative" theories argue that the Cross demonstrated a powerful affirmation of God's love … an example of sacrificial love too powerful to ignore. God assumed human nature and willingly endured all the sufferings of humanity. Consequently, Jesus' death should inspire in us a powerful response of love, which ultimately removes our sin.

Though the idea goes back nearly a thousand years, illustrative theories have won limited denominational support. Many Christian scholars point out that they ignore the Biblical witness that Jesus' death dealt with humankind's sins and propitiated God's wrath.

What's the Scope of Jesus' Atonement?

Another "in-house disagreement" within Christianity—and the topic of many lively debates among scholars—is the scope of Jesus' atonement. There are two leading schools of thought:

◆ The majority view is that Jesus died to save all of sinful humanity and that everyone has access to salvation by becoming a Christian.

◆ The significant minority view is that God foreordained a specific group of individuals to be saved—called the *elect* in Scripture—and Jesus died to save them, not all humankind.

The dispute—which on occasion has become noisy—will probably never be resolved to anyone's satisfaction because both sides can make strong arguments for their positions, each based on many passages in the Bible.

The Related Mystery of Grace

Once we've thought about the mystery of Jesus' atonement, we run smack into another mystery: *why* did the second Person of the Trinity became human to be the world's Savior and make possible sinful humanity's reconciliation with God?

This is the mystery of Grace.

Christians teach that Jesus' atoning death was the result of God's unmerited favor of humankind—the supreme example of God's Grace. Because we're all sinners, the gap between God and humankind is unbridgeable. Not only are we incapable of "earning our own" salvation, our behavior has earned God's wrath.

Get Wisdom

The New Testament Greek word that is usually translated "grace" is *charis* (pronounced *khar-ece*) a word that has several usages related to the root concept of being happy, joyful, delighted. Thus, grace can be something that brings joy (being favored by someone or receiving special treatment, for example) or it can be an expression of joy or thankfulness (as in saying grace before a meal). The Christian concept of divine Grace holds that because of God's unmerited favor, humanity received salvation through Jesus' atoning death.

Christians insist that humanity would have remained unsaved—and locked in a truly hopeless situation—if God hadn't taken the initiative and provided a path toward salvation.

As Paul wrote in Ephesians 2:8, NIV, "For it is by grace you have been saved, through faith—and this not from yourselves, it is the gift of God—not by works, so that no one can boast."

Stories of Unmerited Favor

The Gospels don't report Jesus talking about God's Grace directly, but two of his best-known parables teach lessons about unmerited favor.

The Parable of the Workers in the Vineyard (Matthew 20:1–16) tells of a vineyard owner who pays late-arriving workers the same wages as those workers who toiled all day—much to the chagrin of the all-day workers.

Jesus began the parable by saying "For the kingdom of heaven is like …" (Matthew 20:1, NIV), which indicates that we're supposed to see the vineyard owner as analogous to Sovereign God, and the "unearned wages" as equivalent to the unmerited gift of salvation.

Although Christian scholars have long debated "what Jesus really meant" by the parable, a simple interpretation is that God doesn't use measures of merit to decide who will be saved. All those who "show up for work" qualify for salvation.

The Parable of the Prodigal Son (Luke 15:11–31) tells of a "lost son" who demanded his share of the family fortune, squandered it on sinful living, then returned home expecting to become one his father's servants. Instead, the father welcomed him delightedly and lavishly: "… this son of mine was dead and is alive again; he was lost and is found." (Luke 15:24, NIV) Everyone in the household seemed happy, except the older brother who couldn't understand his father's graciousness.

Besides the father's obvious example of unmerited favor, the location of the parable in the Bible—just after The Parable of the Lost Sheep and The Parable of the Lost Coin—indicate that readers should also …

- Take away a message about God's love (it continues despite sinful behavior).

- Understand that God is joyful when a lost sinner is metaphorically "found."

Did You Spot a Common Denominator?

The "Vineyard" and the "Prodigal Son" illustrate another often-seen phenomena. The all-day workers in the vineyard and the loyal older brother didn't like the idea of unmerited favor—even though it didn't diminish them. The very idea of the Grace of God is contrary to human notions of "fair treatment" and "getting what we deserve."

That turns out to be a good thing!

The Least You Need to Know

- Christianity teaches that when Jesus of Nazareth was crucified, his death some-how atoned for the sins of humankind.

- The word *atonement*—at-one-ment—encompasses two concepts, the taking away of sin and the reconciliation of humankind to God.

- Christian scholars have invented several "theories of atonement" to explain how Jesus' atoning death "worked."

- The theories of atonement are not core Christian doctrines—they are attempts to explain one thorny Christian mystery.

- Some Christian denominations disagree and assert the truth of a specific theory of atonement; this is an example of an "in-house debate" (a disagreement among Christians that can become contentious).

- Christianity teaches that the salvation provided by Jesus' atoning death is the supreme example of God's Grace—God's unmerited favor of humankind.

The Mystery of the Last Things

In This Chapter

- ◆ The "last things" written about in Scripture
- ◆ The future of the world and humankind
- ◆ Different views about the Millennium
- ◆ The time of Great Tribulation
- ◆ The last judgment and the Resurrection
- ◆ Understanding the Book of Revelation and apocalyptic writing

Caution! This chapter may annoy you. Although I'll do my best to walk a middle line, the doctrine of the last things—eschatology to theologians—is one of the most controversial topics in Christendom. It often seems there are as many opinions about the last things as there are Christians.

I'll give you a broad-based introduction to the different aspects of the mysterious last things. I apologize in advance if I've left out a key point in your denomination's (or your pastor's) teachings. I can only provide a brief overview of eschatology in a single chapter.

And, because The Book of Revelation—and other Scripture written in apocalyptic language—play key roles in teaching about the last things, I'll end this chapter with an overview of Revelation and the unique style of apocalyptic writings.

Do the End Times Mean the End of the World?

Let's jump in with one of the many arguments that keep students of *eschatology* stewing. Some Christians believe that one of the last things is the end—the literal destruction—of our world. Others say the *eschaton* marks the start of a new age when resurrected humanity will live on a restored New Earth.

def•i•ni•tion

Eschatology (pronounced ess-cat-ology) comes from a Greek word that means "the study of the last things" (the Greek for "last things" is *ta eschata*). A closely related—and useful—word is **eschaton**, (pronounced ess-cat-ton), which is the end of the age. (For example, most Christians believe the Great Judgment will occur at the eschaton.)

Blame This Battle on *Aion*

One of the factors that drive this disagreement is the challenge of translating the Greek word *aion* (pronounced ahee-ohn), found in several eschatological passages in the New Testament. Here are two translations of Matthew 13:39 (I've bolded the words that were aion in the original Greek):

> He [Jesus] answered "… the harvest is the end of the **world;** and the reapers are the angels. As therefore the tares are gathered and burned in the fire; so shall it be in the end of this **world.**" (Matthew 13:39–40, NIV)

> He [Jesus] replied: "… the harvest is the end of the **age,** and the harvesters are angels. Therefore just as the weeds are gathered and burned in the fire, so it will be at the end of the **age.**" (Matthew 13:39–40, HCSB)

As any good Greek-to-English dictionary will tell you, *aion* can mean "an unbroken age," "a vast period of time," "the total time the world exists," and by implication "the world." These various English meanings paint distinctly different mental images when we read them.

I'll go with "age" in this chapter, because it's more consistent with the idea that Christianity is an eternity-centered faith and that believers will be resurrected and someday live on a New Earth.

Get Wisdom

An oft-seen expression in prayers and many Bible translations is "world without end," which is equivalent to "forever and ever" and "to the end of time." For example, "Unto him be glory in the church by Christ Jesus throughout all ages, world without end." (Ephesians 3:21, KJV) In this verse, "world without end" translates a Greek phrase that means "from the age to the ages." Interpreting the language used in scripture is a fundamental challenge in eschatology, because many of the key writings are written in an apocalyptic style that is especially difficult to understand two thousand years after it was written. Consequently, many eschatological battles are actually fights over what Biblical passages mean.

The Expanding Joys of Eschatology

Before the twentieth century, theologians who focused on the last things tended to deal with four fairly narrow subjects:

◆ The general resurrection of the dead ("general" because this is the resurrection of humankind, not the special Resurrection of Jesus)

◆ The "last judgment" of humanity by Jesus

◆ Heaven (one of the so-called "eternal states")

◆ Hell (the other eternal state)

Although these are still the leading eschatological topics, most modern scholars now appreciate that it's impossible to isolate the end times from other Christian teachings. A perfect example is the collection of doctrines about Jesus Christ. The Incarnation, Jesus' dual nature, his miracles, his role as Messiah, and his death and resurrection can't be fully understood without looking at how these teachings (and events) impact the ultimate future of humankind, nature, and history. Pay attention as you read the rest of this chapter; you'll find all of them intertwined with the last things.

The Second Coming

Christianity teaches that at the eschaton—the end of the age—Jesus Christ will return to Earth in a personal, bodily form (for example, see Acts 1:11 and Matthew 24:30). Virtually all Christians believe this will happen.

You've probably seen the bumper sticker: "Jesus is Coming Back and He's Annoyed." Well, theologically speaking, that idea isn't far off from mainstream teachings. Most

Christians believe that Jesus will come back to destroy evil throughout the world and establish his reign of justice and peace.

Jesus' return will also inaugurate key Messianic prophecies, including the resurrection of the dead, the last judgment of the living and the dead, and the establishment of the Kingdom of God.

Because no one, not even Jesus himself, knows exactly when the Second Coming will occur (see Matthew 24:36), the event will likely catch most Christians by surprise, even those who watch diligently for the signs. Jesus emphasized the uncertainty by analogizing his return to the coming of a thief in the night (see Luke 12:39–40).

It's interesting to note that the exact phrase *Second Coming* is not found in Scripture. Rather, the New Testament uses the Greek word *Parousia*, which means "to be present" (in the active sense of the term).

Take Warning!

Over the years, many students of eschatology—some well-meaning scholars, others charlatans—have "prophesied" the precise time of the Second Coming. Clearly, the past predictions have been wrong. Unfortunately, countless ordinary Christians have wasted time, money, and faith on end-times claims that proved incorrect. It's best to listen to Jesus: "No one knows about that day or hour [when I will return], not even the angels in heaven, nor the Son, but only the Father." (Matthew 24:36, NIV)

The Mysterious Millennium

We've arrived at one of the biggest and noisiest eschatological warzones. There are three divergent views—premillennialism, postmillennialism, and amillennialism—each based on different readings of Scripture. The cause of the brouhaha is the millennium mentioned in the first half of Revelation, chapter 20:

> Then I saw an angel coming down from heaven …. He seized the dragon, that ancient serpent who is the Devil and Satan, and bound him for 1,000 years. He threw him into the abyss, closed it, and put a seal on it so that he would no longer deceive the nations until the 1,000 years were completed. After that, he must be released for a short time. Then I saw thrones, and people seated on them who were given authority to judge. I also saw the souls of those who had been beheaded because of their testimony about Jesus and because of God's word, who had not worshiped the beast or his image, and who had not accepted the

mark on their foreheads or their hands. They came to life and reigned with the Messiah for 1,000 years. The rest of the dead did not come to life until the 1,000 years were completed. …. When the 1,000 years are completed, Satan will be released from his prison …. (Revelation 20:1–7, HCSB)

Several issues are up for grabs. What will inaugurate the millennium? Will Jesus Christ come to Earth before the start of the 1,000-year period? Or will He do His reigning in heaven at the right hand of the Father?

The Premillennialist Teaching

Premillennialists believe that Jesus will return to Earth to inaugurate this 1,000-year period. "Pre" signals the idea that the Parousia will happen *before* the millennium.

Most premillennialists also believe that a dramatic (almost cataclysmic) series of event will occur before Jesus returns, including:

- Major wars and conflicts

- Vast natural disasters

- The appearance of an antichrist who will deceive much of the world and win the allegiance of many people who professed to be Christians but were not faithful believers

- The widespread growth of evil as a controlling force

- A Great Tribulation (see "A Time of Great Tribulation," later in the chapter)

It's difficult to be more specific about the antichrist, because surprisingly, the word is not found in the Book of Revelation. The antichrist mentioned in two of John's letters (for example, see 1 John 2:18) are Gnostic preachers, not the evil leader that many premillennialists anticipate before Jesus' Second Coming. The "end-times Antichrist" is often associated with the "beast" coming out of the sea (see Revelation 13:1) or the "false prophet" (see Revelation 19:20).

When Jesus arrives after these tumultuous events, He will restrain evil and usher in a 1,000-year period of peace, justice, and morality. God's curse (see Genesis 3:17) will be removed from the world and humankind will no longer toil to produce food. Some premillennialist scholars claim that martyred Christians will be resurrected in glorified bodies and reside on Earth.

Get Wisdom

Most people know that the "Mark of the Beast" in the Book of Revelation is the infamous number 666. John describes it as the "number of a man" (see Revelation 13:17–18). The obvious question is which man? Although many Christians believe the beast has yet to appear, some scholars note that Hebrew numerology applied to the Hebrew transliteration of the name "Nero Caesar" yields the number 666. Nero, of course, was an especially cruel persecutor of Christians. Moreover, many of John's first-century contemporaries believed the emperor Nero to be alive (mostly because few people had witnessed his death) and likely to return and avenge himself on those who deposed him.

The millennium will end with a final attack by Satan's forces against Jesus and the Earth's believing Christians. God's heavenly fire will destroy the vast armies of evil (see Revelation 20:9), leaving Jesus free to resurrect all the dead, conduct the last judgment, and consign those not "written in the book of life" (see Revelation 20:15) to hell.

The premillennialist position has become widely known among Christians (and nonbelievers) who are fans of the hugely popular *Left Behind* series of novels written by Tim LaHaye and Jerry Jenkins.

The Postmillennial Teaching

Postmillennialists believe that Jesus Christ will return to Earth after the millennial period specified in the Book of Revelation (although some say that the actual length of the period may exceed 1,000 years, because the number is figurative rather than literal).

In any case, the millennium will be a time of Christian revival and growing influence of church, brought about by successful preaching and teaching that transforms the world into a more righteous, more peaceful, place characterized by broad belief in Jesus Christ.

This new age will resemble the present age in many respects—although the most pressing social and economic problems will be resolved as Christianity's teachings are widely applied. Evil will still rear its ugly head from time to time, though much less than today.

At the end of the millennium, Jesus Christ will return to inaugurate the resurrection of the dead and perform the last judgment.

The Amillennial Teaching

Amillennialists (the *A* means "not" or "no") view the 1,000-year period mentioned in Revelation 20 as a figurative label for Christ's reign during the present church age (that's already spanned almost 2,000 years, and may last considerably longer). They reject the idea that Christ will reign on earth. Rather, they believe that He will continue reigning at the right hand of God (see Mark 16:19) until his eventual Parousia.

Two significant events described in Revelation 20 will occur during this period. First, Satan will be bound, thus enabling the spread of Christianity throughout the world. Second, the Christian martyrs will live and reign with Jesus Christ in Heaven.

Amillennialists further claim that the Kingdom of God arrived when Jesus was alive (see Matthew 12:28) and is currently present in the world—although the forces of evil will remain active until Jesus returns. Consequently, we experience both good and evil during the present age.

When Jesus returns at the end of the figurative millennium, he will oversee the resurrection of the dead and the last judgment.

A Time of Great Tribulation

Jesus spoke of a time of Great Tribulation (see Matthew 24:21–22) that would take place in advance of his Parousia. Although Jesus wasn't specific about what would happen, some Christians believe that the word *tribulation* encompasses the horrific "seal judgments," "trumpet judgments," and "bowl judgments" described in chapters 6, 8, 9, and 16 of the Book of Revelation.

Some Christians associate the time of the Great Tribulation with the last "week of years" (in other words, seven years) described in the Book of Daniel, Chapter 9:24–27. Part of this group believe that the time of tribulation will span 7 years, the rest believe that it will have two 3½ year periods: the "beginning of sorrows" and the "Great Tribulation," the worst of the events occurring during the second half, the Great Tribulation proper.

> **Scripture Says**
>
> For at that time there will be great tribulation, the kind that hasn't taken place from the beginning of the world until now and never will again! Unless those days were limited, no one would survive. But those days will be limited because of the elect. (Matthew 24:21–22, HCSB)

The Posttribulationist View

We've reached another topic of theological disagreement. Some Christians believe that Jesus will not return until the tribulation is over, and that the church—including Christians alive at the time—will experience the worst of what happens to the world. This teaching is called posttribulationism.

The Pretribulationist View

By contrast, pretribulationists interpret 1 Thessalonians 4:16–18 as teaching that Jesus will remove—or "rapture"—faithful Christians from the world before the start of the tribulation, so that they don't have to experience any of the terrible events. Because Jesus meets the faithful in the air, not on the ground, this preliminary return does not count as his Second Coming.

Get Wisdom

The word *rapture* doesn't appear in the New Testament, but has an interesting history. Paul wrote that Christians will be "caught up" with the risen dead (see 1 Thessalonians 4:17). This is the English translation of the Greek word *harpazo*. However, Greek Scripture was first translated into Latin; thus *harpazo* was transformed into *raptus*, a word that has two meanings: "carried off by force" and "carried away with exhilaration." It is this second meaning that becomes *rapture* when translated into English.

The Midtribulationist View

Midtribulationists believe that Jesus will return to rapture faithful Christians at the end of the 3½-year long "beginning of sorrows." This is halfway through the time of tribulation, but before the worst events of the Great Tribulation occur.

Has All of This Already Happened?

Not all Christians read Revelation as unfulfilled prophecy. The "full preterist" view is that all of the prophetic verses in Revelation were fulfilled during the first century, including the Second Coming—and that all can be seen to have occurred in the destruction of Jerusalem by the Romans in the year 70. Partial preterism asserts that most of Revelation's prophecies have come to pass, with the exception of the Parousia and the last judgment.

Preterists base their arguments on the various end-time prophecies Jesus made that indicated the end of the age would occur within the lifetimes of many early Christians. After Jesus described the end of the age and his Second Coming (see Matthew 24: 1–23), he said, "I tell you the truth, this generation will certainly not pass away until all these things have happened." (Matthew 24:34, NIV) (See also Matthew 16:28.)

The Last Judgment

Virtually all Christians believe that Jesus will return at the end of the age to judge humankind—all that have lived and those still alive. The last judgment is described in the final third of the Book of Revelation:

> Then I saw a great white throne and One seated on it. Earth and heaven fled from His presence, and no place was found for them. I also saw the dead, the great and the small, standing before the throne, and books were opened. Another book was opened, which is the book of life, and the dead were judged according to their works by what was written in the books. Then the sea gave up its dead, and Death and Hades gave up their dead; all were judged according to their works. Death and Hades were thrown into the lake of fire. This is the second death, the lake of fire. And anyone not found written in the book of life was thrown into the lake of fire. Then I saw a new heaven and a new earth, for the first heaven and the first earth had passed away, and the sea existed no longer. (Revelation 20:11–15, HCSB)

An alternate description of the last judgment appears in Matthew 25:31–43, HCSB: "He will sit on the throne of His glory. … and He will separate them one from another, just as a shepherd separates the sheep from the goats. He will put the sheep on His right and the goats on the left. Then the King will say to those on His right, 'Come, you who are blessed by My Father, inherit the kingdom prepared for you from the foundation of the world.' … Then He will also say to those on the left, 'Depart from Me, you who are cursed, into the eternal fire prepared for the Devil and his angels!'"

Christianity teaches that the last judgment is an either/or situation: those who are saved in Christ will be separated and receive an eternal reward; the unforgiven will receive eternal punishment.

The Book of Hebrews provides an interesting link between the last judgment and Jesus' atoning death (see Chapter 6): "… so also the Messiah, having been offered once to bear the sins of many, will appear a second time, not to bear sin, but to bring salvation to those who are waiting for Him. (Hebrews 9:28, HCSB)

Get Wisdom _____

Some Christians, especially those who advocate premillennialism, believe that the "Sheep and Goats Judgment" and the "Great White Throne" judgments are two separate events—the first, the judgment of people alive after the Great Tribulation, and the second, the judgment after the general resurrection.

The Resurrection (Ours!)

This is a teaching that can surprise any Christian who pictures the afterlife as limited to angels flying around heaven, possibly strumming a harp. This greeting card image of life after death ignores the key doctrine taught in the New Testament that Christians hope for a bodily resurrection in a new "incorruptible body" (see 1 Corinthians 15:51–54). The lost will also be resurrected—into eternal death and punishment (see John 5:28–29).

Jesus affirmed that faithful Christians will be resurrected when he spoke to Martha before he raised Lazarus from the dead: "Jesus said to her, 'I am the resurrection and the life. The one who believes in Me, even if he dies, will live. Everyone who lives and believes in Me will never die—ever. Do you believe this?'" (John 11:25–26, HCSB)

Scholars recognize that Christianity's hope of resurrection had its roots in Jewish teachings. For example, consider Daniel 12:2, HCSB: "Many of those who sleep in the dust of the earth will awake, some to eternal life, and some to shame and eternal contempt." But first-century Christians could also point to the resurrection of Jesus as a preview of what would happen to them.

There were apparently many different first-century Jewish views of resurrection, but historians who study Jewish writings of the time have concluded that the majority of Jews believed in the resurrection of the dead. Here, for example is a passage from the apocryphal Book of Enoch that was probably written between 150–80 B.C.: "The righteous and elect ones shall rise from the earth and shall cease being of downcast face. They shall wear garments of glory."

Early Christians accepted the teaching of resurrection, as can be seen in Romans 8:11, HCSB: "And if the Spirit of Him who raised Jesus from the dead lives in you, then He who raised Christ from the dead will also bring your mortal bodies to life through His Spirit who lives in you."

When I wrote about the mystery of Jesus' Resurrection, I noted that the Bible offers several examples of dead people being resuscitated, but provides only one instance of a true resurrection that leads to eternal life. The difference is that resuscitated people—brought back to life in their original corruptible bodies—eventually died again, whereas Jesus is still alive today.

Christians consider physical death to be the separation of the soul from the body. Scripture teaches (see Hebrews 9:27)—as do the obituary pages in any newspaper—that all people die. Death is inevitable, except for those who are alive when Jesus returns. Most Christians believe in an "afterlife," the continued existence of the soul after death.

But true resurrection is much more than an afterlife; it is the complete *reversal* of death: the restoration of a physical body (a glorified body not subject to death and decay) living in a restored world.

Walking with the Wise

In the New Testament ... the fact of Jesus' resurrection is closely linked to our own ultimate resurrection, which isn't life after death—it's life *after* life after death. Whatever life after death is, being with Christ which is far better, being in Paradise like the thief, etc, the many rooms where we go immediately ... that is the temporary place. The ultimate life after life after death is the resurrection in God's new world.

—From a 2007 interview with theologian N. T. Wright at Asbury Seminary

The Intermediate State (Heaven?)

This definition raises an obvious question: what happens to the dead before they are resurrected. Scholars use the term *intermediate state* to label the soul's circumstances between death and eventual resurrection of the body. Although there are many different ideas of the intermediate state, the mainstream Christian notion has two aspects:

- Dead believers enjoy conscious bliss in "heaven" (or paradise) because they are with Jesus.

- Dead unbelievers experience anguish (in "hell") because they are separated from the presence of God.

Many contemporary Christian scholars define *heaven* as the place (possibly another dimension) where God lives and reigns. (This idea is not in conflict with the Christian teaching that "God is everywhere.")

It's important to emphasize the word *intermediate* when speaking about "heaven" or "paradise." Christian scholars note that these places are not eternal and represent a waypoint on the complete journey to "life after life after death."

The Final State (Also Heaven?)

Let me give you a challenge: try to imagine the "final state" that comes after the intermediate state I just described. Most Christians find it difficult because few of us have grabbed on to the notion of being resurrected in glorified bodies. We can picture (sort of!) souls existing in a heavenly spirit realm. But where will resurrected bodies live?

On a "New Earth," of course! When God restores the creation after Jesus Christ's Second Coming, the "New Earth" (see Revelation 21:1–3) will be the eternal home for humankind. It will also be the "New Heaven," because God will live with humanity.

The Book of Revelation goes on to describe a part of New Earth, the New Jerusalem (see Revelation 21:9–27). Even acknowledging that Revelation is written in an image-filled apocalyptic style, the leading city of New Earth seems a place worth visiting.

> ### Walking with the Wise
>
> We've heard it said, "This world is not our home." It's true, but it's a half-truth. We should qualify it to say "This world—as it now is, under the curse—is not our home." But we should also say, "This world—as it once was, before sin and curse—was our home." And we should add, "This world—as it one day will be, delivered from the curse—will be our home."
>
> —Randy Alcorn, "Looking Forward to a New Earth" (sermon)

Revelation: The Source of the Prophecies

The New Testament is chiefly a collection of biographies (the Gospels), letters to different churches and groups of Christians (the various epistles), and a history (the Book of Acts). And then there's Revelation—the New Testament's only book of prophecy.

Theologians believe that Revelation was written early during a time of intense Roman persecution against Christians. Two periods are likely: the years 54–68 (when Nero ruled the Roman Empire) and the years 81–96 (when Emperor Domitian reigned). Scholars who hold the preterist view that Revelation's prophecies have been fulfilled argue that Revelation was written before Jerusalem was destroyed (in the year 70).

Christians have long held that the author of Revelation is the Apostle John, the son of Zebedee (see Matthew 10:2). John meets the key requirements: a Jewish-born church leader well versed in Hebrew Scripture (Revelation includes many Jewish themes) who would be a credible critic of the seven "Churches of Asia" (see Revelation 1:4).

Over the years, the *Book of Revelation* has had several alternative titles, including *Revelation to John*, *Apocalypse of John*, and *Revelation of Jesus Christ*.

Some scholars argue that the primary messages in Revelation were aimed at the seven Churches of Asia, and that the book should be understood in that context. Specifically, John exhorted the churches withstand pressures to worship the Roman Emperor—even in the face of death—and offered assurances that God would eventually triumph over the forces of evil.

Other Bible experts see Revelation in broader terms—as a collection of fundamental truths and end-times prophecy we can interpret today.

Apocalyptic Writing Is Highly Symbolic

The Book of Revelation is written in a distinct literary style: *apocalyptic*. This highly symbolic style writing was popular from roughly 165 B.C. through the first century and was often used to express thoughts that if communicated directly would bring punishment from local authorities. The best-known apocalyptic passages in the Old Testament are the four visions and dreams in the Book Of Daniel (chapters 7 to 12).

Apocalyptic writing overflows with coded language filled with symbolic imagery that was completely familiar to the pious readers of the day. For example, Daniel saw a beast with iron teeth and ten horns (see Daniel 7:7) that most scholars interpret as a symbol for Rome. Alas, interpreting the majority of apocalyptic symbols has become guesswork today, making it difficult to interpret Revelation and other apocalyptic documents accurately.

def•i•ni•tion

Although the word **apocalypse** is commonly used in English to label a great disaster, possibly the end of the world, that is not its real meaning. Apocalypse comes from a Greek word that means "to reveal" or to "disclose something hidden." Thus the Greek title of the Revelation of St. John is "The Apocalypse of St. John."

Here are four other aspects of apocalyptic writings:

◆ They are written in the first-person ("I saw") as personal experiences.

◆ Future events are typically seen within a dream or vision.

◆ Eschatology is a key element—especially predictions about the end of the age.

◆ The seer often foresees a worldwide catastrophe during which God will overcome the forces of evil.

Because apocalyptic writings are so tricky to unravel, our knowledge of the last things is filled with uncertainty. We really won't know which of the viewpoints is the most correct until this age is over.

The Least You Need to Know

◆ Christianity has a collection of teachings about the eschatology—the "last things"—that predict what will happen to the world and to humankind.

◆ Eschatology is an unsettled area of theology because many Christian denominations and theologians hold significantly different views.

◆ A chief driver of the debate is that eschatological prophesy is written in image-filled apocalyptic language that's subject to many interpretations.

◆ Virtually all Christians believe that Jesus Christ will return to Earth in a personal, bodily form at the end of the age.

◆ Two key events will follow Jesus' Second Coming: the general resurrection of the dead the last judgment of humankind.

◆ The resurrected faithful will spend eternity with God in the restored New Earth—and the resurrected unbelievers will spend eternity separated from God in a state of anguish.

Part 2

Other Mysteries About Jesus

Now that you've examined the really tough mysteries that surround Jesus of Nazareth—fully God, fully man, the Messiah promised in the Old Testament—it's time to move on to even more mysteries about Jesus, including his birth, life, and death.

As Christian mysteries go, these are among the easiest to talk about and envision. So sit back and enjoy yourself! We're going on a journey that will take us from Ancient Israel, to India, to Japan, and England. And possibly a short visit to Hades.

The Mystery of Jesus as the Revelation of God

In This Chapter

- ◆ Jesus decisively reveals God to humankind
- ◆ Jesus shows us what God is like and how He thinks
- ◆ Everything we know about God was revealed by God Himself
- ◆ What we learn from "general revelation"
- ◆ What we learn from "special revelation"

Christianity teaches that God—the creator of the Universe—somehow revealed Himself to humankind in the person of Jesus of Nazareth. This is more than the idea that Jesus is fully divine, as discussed in Chapter 2. The other side of this teaching is the notion that God is Christ-like. Consequently, when you know Jesus, you know God.

In this chapter, you'll learn about the different ways that God reveals himself to humanity and, in particular, what Jesus makes known about God.

When Philip Asked Jesus for More ...

The Gospels provide a lot of information about the Apostle Philip. He lived in Bethsaida on Lake Genesareth (John 1:44) and was apparently linked to Peter and Andrew, who also hailed from the same town. It was Philip who recruited Nathanial, telling him, "We have found the one Moses wrote about in the Law, and about whom the prophets also wrote ...." (John 1:45, NIV) And, Philip's name always appears fifth on the various lists of apostles presented in the Gospels (Matthew 10:2–4, Mark 3:14–19, and Luke 6:14–16).

But what Christians remember most about Philip is how he responded when Jesus said, "No one comes to the Father except through me. If you really knew me, you would know my Father as well. From now on, you do know him and have seen him." (John 14:6–7, NIV)

Philip, clearly confused, said, "Lord, show us the Father and that will be enough for us." (John 14:8, NIV)

Jesus answered: "Don't you know me, Philip, even after I have been among you such a long time? Anyone who has seen me has seen the Father. ... The words I say to you are not just my own. Rather, it is the Father, living in me, who is doing his work." (John 14:9–10, NIV)

The Bible doesn't explain how Jesus' disciples responded to Jesus' amazing declaration that to see him was the same thing as seeing God. As good Jews, they all knew that the God revealed in the Hebrew Scriptures was a spirit completely beyond their comprehension—a being of such majesty and holiness that anyone looking at God's face would die (see Exodus 33:20). More than one of the Apostles must have been bewildered to the point of giddiness.

Scripture Says

No one has ever seen God. (John 1:18, HCSB)

Can you find out the deep things of God? Can you find out the limit of the Almighty? It is higher than heaven—what can you do? Deeper than Sheol—what can you know? (Job 11:7–8, NRSV)

For my thoughts are not your thoughts, nor are your ways my ways, says the LORD. For as the heavens are higher than the earth, so are my ways higher than your ways and my thoughts than your thoughts. (Isaiah 55:8–9, NRSV)

Even today, many Christians—including the vast majority who believe in the Incarnation—aren't always sure how to deal with the mysterious notion that Jesus reveals God to humankind. After all, we're taught that Jesus' revelation is designed to do more than convey mere information. It's also what sets the stage for a personal relationship with God (see Chapter 1).

Okay ... But How Does This Revelation Thing Work?

Theologians teach that there's only one way for people to learn specific details about God: God must *reveal* them to us. He must take the initiative, because there's nothing we can do to "examine God" through our own efforts.

Simply put, humankind can't "reach up to find God." Instead, God must reach down to our level and "condescend" to reveal himself. It's been said, "By God alone can God be known."

Christians believe that God has engaged in two kinds of revelation to make himself known to humankind: *general revelation* and *special revelation*. Both concepts are important and—I promise—are easy to understand.

Look Around—at General Revelation

The Bible doesn't provide formal proofs that God exists. One of the few verses on the subject notes, "The fool says in his heart, 'God does not exist.'" (Psalms 14:1, HCSB) Rather, Scriptures assert that "The heavens declare the glory of God and the firmament showeth his handiwork." (Psalm 19:1, KJV) Because creation—from tiny bacteria to vast clusters of galaxies—is so spectacular, Christianity teaches that one way to know that God exists is to look around. When someone really does look around it's hard for him or her not to reach the indisputable conclusion that there must be a creator. This is an example of God's general revelation to humanity.

Learning from Morality and History

Scholars point to two other aspects of general revelation. Most people have a conscience that reflects an innate knowledge of fairness and morality. Christians assert that our personal moral compasses came from a creator who "defined" right and wrong.

Another indicator of God's presence is history. Many historical events are difficult to explain without assuming that the providential hand of God somehow played a role. Contemplate the remarkable survival of the Jewish people despite concerted efforts over three millennia to destroy them. Every nation—every leader—who has tried to eliminate the Jewish people has itself been destroyed. (See God's promise to Abraham in Genesis 12:3.) And consider the implausible growth of Christianity from a small sect in ancient Jerusalem to the largest faith in the modern world (see Chapter 22).

The Trouble with General Revelation ...

General revelation—confirming the existence of God through his creation—is available to everyone, but it does have a major limitation. Although we may come away confident that there is a creator we can call God, His handiworks and actions give us little specific information about Him. All we can deduce is a handful of basic attributes, such as:

- He exists and is somewhere "out there."

- He's exceedingly powerful.

- He established a universal moral compass.

- He plays a providential role in humankind's history.

- He's timeless.

- He acts without making Himself visible.

- He appreciates beauty and variety.

This is the stuff of many primitive and pagan religions, but it's not enough to give us a useful understanding of God's nature and will, or the appropriate ways to worship him. If God had stopped at general revelation, Judaism and Christianity could never have arisen.

Even more important to us as individuals, we would never have learned that God had made provisions to save sinful humanity—nor would we have been taught how to take advantage of God's plan for salvation.

Scriptures + Jesus = Special Revelation

Special revelation is in-depth information about God Himself that God has provided, including specific facts and details that mankind can't deduce simply by looking around at the natural world. God's special revelation involves communication that is comprehensible to humanity—using ways or languages that we can understand.

During Old-Testament times God communicated his power and his commitment to the people of Israel by getting them out of Egypt. Years later, God reminded them, via prophets, that "I am the LORD your God, who brought you out of Egypt, out of the land of slavery." (For example, see 1 Samuel 10:18.)

For Christians, the two most important "media" of special revelation are …

◆ Holy Scripture (the Bible) *inspired* by God.

◆ The person of Jesus of Nazareth, who manifested (revealed) God.

Christianity teaches that the Bible is the primary source of specific information about God—and about Jesus Christ—for believers. Martin Luther said Scripture is the "the manger in which Christ is laid." And, as the well-known hymn declares:

> Jesus loves me! He will stay
> Close beside me all the way;
> Thou hast bled and died for me,
> I will henceforth live for Thee.
>
> Yes, Jesus loves me!
> Yes, Jesus loves me!
> Yes, Jesus loves me!
> The Bible tells me so.

Get Wisdom

The ubiquitous hymn "Jesus Loves Me"—a children's favorite for nearly 150 years—has an interesting history. The lyrics first appeared as a poem inside an 1860 novel entitled "Say and Seal" written by Susan Warner (the poem was co-written by Anna Warner, Susan's sister). The words were spoken in the story to comfort a dying child. The familiar tune was added in 1862 by William Batchelder Bradbury.

An important aspect of special revelation is that it is progressive. Christians teach that the earliest readers of Hebrew Scriptures had the five *Books of Moses*, commonly called the *Pentateuch* ("five-volumed book"). These books reveal much about the nature of God by describing how God interacted with "his people," the Israelites.

Christians believe that the human authors and editors of the Holy Scriptures—including the Old and New Testaments—were somehow inspired by God. There are different views on how this inspiration worked, but virtually all mainstream Christians agree that because of God's leading or influencing, the Bible can be considered the word of God, and trusted as humankind's paramount authority in matters of faith and life practice.

The story of God dealing with his people expanded with each addition to create a vast tapestry spanning some 2,000 years from Abraham to Jesus. Each new Book brings fresh insights into God's purposes, will, and character.

Some people wrongly think of progressive revelation as a journey through faulty teachings that eventually leads to truth. Not so. Christians argue that the earliest revelations are true, but only tell part of the whole story.

Jesus Is the Revelation of God

The idea that Jesus is the special revelation of God is less well-known among Christians, and much more mysterious. Because believers tend to emphasize that Jesus is Lord and Savior, we may overlook that God demonstrated himself to humanity in the fully divine, fully human person of Jesus Christ.

Back in Chapter 2, I described Jesus as "God's self-portrait." This is a simpler way of conveying the theological concept that in Jesus, humankind can see the glory of God manifested in human flesh.

> **Walking with the Wise**
>
> When Holy Scripture speaks of God, it concentrates our attention and thoughts upon one single point and what is to be known at that point … from first to last the Bible directs us to the name of Jesus Christ.
>
> —Karl Barth, *Church Dogmatics*

John 1:18, HCSB, begins by noting that "No one has ever seen God." The verse then goes on to say, "The One and Only Son—the One who is at the Father's side—He has revealed Him."

Colossians 2:9, NRSV, builds on this theme: "For in him the whole fullness of deity dwells bodily …." And Hebrews 1:1–2 adds, "Long ago God spoke to our ancestors in many and various ways by the prophets, but in these last days he has spoken to us by a Son …." Christians infer from these verses that one of the principle purposes of the Incarnation was to reveal God's nature to humanity.

Jesus Didn't Reveal All of God's Attributes

Christianity teaches that Jesus is fully divine, but that he is also fully human and was perceived as an ordinary man by almost all of the people he met during his ministry in the Roman Province of Judaea. Consequently, God must have somehow reduced or limited the aspects of divinity that people could see, touch, and sense when they interacted with Jesus.

This is probably one of the reasons that many of the people Jesus knew—including his family and his disciples—remained skeptical about the bold claims he made. At first glance, Jesus the man simply didn't meet their expectations of God.

Practically speaking, Jesus revealed God in a manner that was consistent with both his divinity and his humanity. For example, Christians affirm that when Jesus spoke it was God speaking, and that when Jesus healed people, it was God doing the healing. But believers are also confident that God *did not* die when Jesus died.

The point is, when his disciples saw Jesus, they saw God—but not "all" of God. Jesus emphasized the distinction when he called himself "The Way" (see John 14:6). Christianity teaches that we *go through* Jesus to reach the totality of God.

Scripture Says

Philippians 2:5–7, NRSV, teaches, "Let the same mind be in you that was in Christ Jesus, who, though he was in the form of God, did not regard equality with God as something to be exploited, but emptied himself, taking the form of a slave, being born in human likeness." Bible scholars have long argued about the exact meaning of "emptied himself," but all seem to agree that Jesus didn't reveal all of God's attributes to the people around him.

This is a good point to remind you that although Jesus claimed that seeing him was like seeing the God the Father, this does not imply that Jesus was merely the Father in some sort of disguise—or that Jesus and the Father are the same Person. Jesus was also careful to affirm that he and God the Father could, and should, be distinguished (see Chapter 3):

- ◆ The purpose of the Son's ministry as God Incarnate was to bring glory to the Father (see John 14:13).

- ◆ The Son had been sent by the Father (see John 14:24).

- ◆ Jesus would return to the Father after he completed the work his Father commanded him to do (see John 14:28).

We can be sure of one thing: those who knew Jesus two millennia ago did not learn everything there is to learn about God. Nonetheless, although we, too, will never know God completely this side of Heaven, we can take advantage of special revelation to learn much about him. We do that when we study the Gospels.

The idea of reading about the revelation of God through Jesus in the Bible can be a tad confusing if you don't think it through. Jesus remains a distinctive revelation of God—separate from other Scriptural revelations—because the details of Jesus' life, death, and Resurrection described in the Bible give us specific insights into God's nature.

What Did Jesus Teach Us About God?

Let me anticipate your next question: when I read about Jesus I imagine a bearded man in sandals walking down a dusty road. What part of that picture do I interpret as the revelation of God?

The Gospel reports of Jesus' words and deeds—including the retelling of his parables—reveal much about what we might label God's "personality," including his feelings about humankind. Through Jesus we learn …

- The Father's tenderness and forgiveness.

- The chief characteristics of the Kingdom of God, including justice and peace.

- Which of humanity's shortcomings most disappointed the Father, starting with a chronic indifference to others.

- Which of humankind's character flaws the Father considers the major stumbling blocks to our salvation—a litany of faults ranging from an unreasonable love of money to rank hypocrisy.

- The depth of the Father's desire to save mankind.

- The nature and extent of God's love—and what Christians mean when they say "God is Love."

- How the Father would respond to different people and circumstances.

What would Jesus do? The answer to that popular question is, "The same thing that God the Father would do."

> **Get Wisdom** _____
>
> When the Gospel authors wrote about Jesus, they followed "the rules" of ancient biography, which did not require relating events in chronological order. Ancient biographers reported events that revealed a person's nature and character, but were less concerned with getting time precisely right. As Plutarch, the first-century Greek biographer, said, "I am not writing histories, but rather lives." A good example of this in the Gospels is the story of Jesus overturning the moneychangers' tables in the Temple. It appears early in John's ordering of Jesus' deeds (see John 2:23), but only a few days before Jesus' crucifixion in the other Gospels (see Luke 19:45). Some Bible scholars believe that John's early placement emphasizes that Jesus had replaced the Temple—a key Jewish institution—with himself.

A Different Side of God

One of the more surprising aspects of Jesus' revelation of God is the notion of a supremely loving and forgiving God who invites close personal relationships. I say that because the God of Hebrew Scriptures kept his distance from all but a handful of people, once nearly destroyed all life on Earth, hurled fire and brimstone when appropriate, and killed rather than loved many of Israel's enemies.

He also delivered destructive object lessons to the Egyptians after repeatedly hardening Pharaoh's heart, punished his people with numerous military defeats and a long exile, and could be a super-strict disciplinarian at times—remember what happened to Uzzah when he foolishly decided to hold the Ark of the Covenant steady after an oxen pulling the cart stumbled. (See 2 Samuel 6:6.) *Zap!* God had previously made known the Ark was not to be touched.

This apparent difference between the God Jesus revealed in his person and the God described in the Old Testament prompted the *Marcionite heresy*. Marcion—a second-century bishop—claimed that God of the Old Testament was actually an "Evil Creator" (not Jesus' Father) and that Jesus had been sent by an unknown "Redeemer God" to save humankind. Marcion argued that creation itself was malignant because it had been created by an "inferior God" who focused most of his attention on judgment. According to Marcion, Jesus' mission on Earth was to reveal the "God God" and deliver humanity from the "Bad God."

Marcion discarded the Old Testament because he considered the Hebrew Scriptures the result of "evil inspiration." He also rejected the Gospels of Mark, Matthew, and Luke; the Book of Hebrews; and several of Paul's letters—because they include many verses and ideas found in the Hebrew Scriptures.

Marcion's notions were condemned as heresy in 144. The first verse of the Apostle's Creed, which many scholars believe written around 150, is widely held to be a response to Marcionism. It confesses unambiguously that God the Father talked about by Jesus is the Creator of heaven and earth revealed in the Old Testament: "I believe in God, the Father Almighty, the Creator of heaven and earth, and in Jesus Christ, His only Son, our Lord …"

Take Warning!

It's a common mistake to picture Jesus as exclusively "meek and mild." In fact, he often became angry (as when he cleansed the Temple (see Matthew 21:12–13), rebuked religious leaders in Jerusalem (see Matthew 15:3–7), and chewed out his disciples (see Matthew 8:26 and Mark 8:23). And of course the Book of Revelation 1:14–16 describes a Jesus of awesome power who made John collapse at his feet. No surprise; we can expect that kind of reaction when someone sees a man with eyes blazing like fire, glowing feet, a voice like rushing waters, and a face shining like the sun.

God Is Love

If you asked a roomful of believers what was the single most important attribute of God that Jesus demonstrated, there's no doubt what answer you'd hear. Love! The best-known verse in the New Testament proclaims, "For God so loved the world that he gave his one and only Son, that whoever believes in him shall not perish but have eternal life." (John 3:16, NIV)

Christians teach that God so loved humanity—the saints and the sinners—that for all our sakes (and at incalculable cost to Himself) He devised the rescue mission that culminated in Jesus' crucifixion and resurrection. You don't need to be a theologian to recognize that Jesus Christ crucified is a unique and unmatchable proof that God is love.

A Different Kind of Love

We've reached another occasion when our language fails to capture an important concept that Scripture communicates. Three different Greek words are translated as "love" in English Bibles:

- *Eros*—love of what is lovable, or desirable; a longing for what is prized (we get our the word *erotic* from eros)

- *Philia*—love based on compatibility and similar interests; "friendship" or "tender affection"

- *Agape*—uncalculating, self-giving love; often expressed through a decision to act in someone's best interest, regardless of the personal cost

The Septuagint, the translation of the Hebrew Scriptures into Greek, uses the word eros twice; the New Testament (the oldest copies we have are in Greek) doesn't use it at all.

Scripture Says
Whoever does not love does not know God, because God is love. (1 John 4:8, NIV)

God's Love Is Agape

By far, the most common New Testament word expressing the concept of love is *agape*—a word that paints a dramatically different image than "love" in the way we use the word:

- Agape is embodied in actions, not in talk or emotions.

- Agape is not self-seeking (you don't expect to receive anything in return) nor is it a reflection of your "feelings"—you may loathe the person being "loved."

- Agape may be based on sense of duty; you do it because you've been told to do it or it's the right thing to do.

God's love for humankind as revealed by Jesus is agape. It is love that forgives, sacrificial love given graciously, without being earned. Jesus is willing to die to find and redeem sinful humanity, his "lost sheep," without any guarantee that his love will be reciprocated.

The King James Version of the Bible often translates agape as "charity." Notice how different 1 Corinthians 13:4–5 sounds when we use charity rather than love: "Charity suffereth long, *and* is kind; charity envieth not; charity vaunteth not itself, is not puffed up, Doth not behave itself unseemly, seeketh not her own, is not easily provoked, thinketh no evil ...."

We have lots of "institutionalized agape" in our culture; for example, when military doctors provide medical care to enemy soldiers wounded on the battlefield, this illustrates "agape your enemies." And a firefighter running into a burning building to save a stranger demonstrates "agape your neighbor."

Is the Holy Spirit a Source of Revelation?

Many Christians see the Holy Spirit sent by Jesus (see John 15:26) as an ongoing force of revelation as he teaches, comforts, and conveys knowledge of God. Countless believers (including me) have experienced God's presence via the Spirit; these mysterious encounters continue today.

Although Christians assert that the Holy Spirit inspired the authors of the Bible—and that the Holy Spirit helps believers to interpret and understand Scripture—most theologians do not consider the Spirit a component of special revelation. One reason is that special revelation via Scripture is available to everyone who chooses to pick up the Bible. By contrast, any revelation provided by the Holy Spirit is personal and individual. (I'll describe the mystery of the Holy Spirit in Chapter 19.)

The Least You Need to Know

- Christianity teaches that we can learn the basics about God—such as the truth that God exists—by looking around at God's creation.

- But this "general revelation" doesn't teach us how to take advantage of Jesus' atoning death.

- Information about salvation is found in God's "special revelation"—the Bible and the "express image" of God that Jesus provided during his earthly ministry.

- Many see this notion of God as different from the picture painted in the Old Testament; nonetheless, they are the same God.

- Most Christians consider *love* to be the single most important attribute of God that Jesus demonstrated.

- A significant point to keep in mind that the kind of love Scripture attributes to God is agape love—sacrificial, and not expecting anything in return.

9

The Mystery of the Virgin Birth

In This Chapter

◆ Jesus was conceived by the Holy Spirit and born of a virgin

◆ The Mystery is described the Gospels of Matthew and Luke

◆ Not all Christians accept the Biblical accounts as historical

◆ Some skeptics claim the doctrine is based on mythology

◆ The Virgin Birth is often "explained away" by secular media

◆ Why the Virgin Birth matters

It happens every Christmas—a new round of debates about whether the Biblical story of Jesus' Virgin Birth is true or merely a "metaphor" or a "convenient myth." Ironically, the leading skeptics tend to be Christians who you might guess would be the strongest supporters of the teaching: theologians and pastors.

I'll tell you why that's so in this chapter—as we review the doctrine of the Virgin Birth and its significance to Christianity.

Here's Your Chance to Disagree with a Scholar

For most of the past 2,000 years, Christians have asserted without much disagreement that Jesus of Nazareth was born of a virgin after being conceived by the Holy Spirit. Believers accepted the Virgin Birth as a historical event that helped to explain how Jesus could be both fully God and fully man. (Over the years, many scholars have pointed out that the event described in the Gospels of Matthew and Luke was really a "virgin conception." However, I'll continue to use the term that almost all Christians recognize: the Virgin Birth.)

The Virgin Birth is another example of a miracle that we can picture in our minds. Like the Resurrection (see Chapter 5), the central mystery of the Virgin Birth is, how did God pull it off?

But, since the eighteenth century—and the so-called Age of Enlightenment—the teaching of the Virgin Birth has prompted another question: *did it really happen?*

Curiously, Christian laypeople like you and me overwhelmingly come down on the "yes it did!" side when queried by pollsters. A Harris Interactive poll conducted a few years ago found that more than 90 percent of Americans who identify themselves as Christians believe in the Virgin Birth—and close to 30 percent of non-Christians do, too. An older and often-cited poll of Protestant clergy reportedly conducted by the late Jeffrey Hadden, a sociologist who did much of his work while at the University of Virginia, found that between 20 and 60 percent of clergy in different mainstream denominations doubted the Virgin Birth. More recent polls of Anglican clergy in the United Kingdom found that upward of 30 percent rejected the teaching.

Get Wisdom

The Age of Enlightenment, a term that contemporary philosophers gave to much of the eighteenth century prior to the French Revolution, was a time of scientific progress and increasing civil rights coupled with declining power of royalty and the Church. Many leading thinkers of the day believed that reason and science provided truth, as opposed to "outmoded" religious doctrines— such as the Virgin Birth.

If you compare similar opinion studies conducted in years past, you'll find that the percentage of Americans (and Christians) who believe the Virgin Birth is a historical fact actually *increased* during the twentieth century.

And yet, many theologians and pastors continue to be troubled by the teaching. They dispute that the Virgin Birth occurred and question whether the doctrine is necessary. And they appear on a seemingly endless stream of TV shows that seek to "prove" that the story of the Virgin Birth is based on mythology, represents an attempt to demonstrate that Jesus is the promised Messiah, or was even aimed at defending Jesus' reputation.

Richard Longenecker summarized the situation in "Whose Child Is This?" an article published by *Christianity Today* in 1990:

"Today, scholars are sharply divided regarding the Virgin Birth:

1. Is it a fact of history—that is, that Jesus was conceived in the womb of a virgin without the aid of a human father? Or …

2. Should the Virgin Birth be considered an attempt of the early church to translate the mystery of God becoming a human being into terms intelligible to unsophisticated people, and so to be taken as a symbol of the truth that Jesus' birth was God's gift to humanity given entirely by grace …."

Walking with the Wise

Here's an example of a well-known skeptical theologian's comments on the Virgin Birth. "[The Biblical stories recounting Christ's birth] are a collection of largely uncertain, mutually contradictory, strongly legendary and ultimately theologically motivated narratives, with a character of their own. Unlike the rest of Jesus' life, there are dream happenings here and angels constantly enter on the scene and leave it—as heavenly messengers of God announcing important events.

—Hans Küng, *On Being a Christian*

The second possibility that Longenecker raises deserves a brief explanation. The idea in a nutshell is this: when faced with the mind-bending mystery of the Incarnation (see Chapter 2), the earliest Christians invented an alternative history to convey a theological truth—a kind of little white lie to a emphasize that Jesus was the Son of God. (Scholars call this kind of well-intentioned invention a *theologoumenon*—a story invented to make a theological point. Believers are free to consider the historical details a fiction, and reject them.) In time, this theory goes on, the invented story became part of the oral tradition about Jesus and found its way into Matthew's and Luke's Gospels.

As you can imagine, this idea doesn't play well with Christians who believe that the Bible is the inspired word of God. They argue that the presence of the Virgin Birth in two Gospels is conclusive evidence that the story is true and should be accepted as a valid Christian teaching.

In recent years, there have been several crises in mainstream Christian denominations caused by pastors and occasionally senior leaders speaking out against the doctrine of the Virgin Birth. In one recent case, a group of denomination members wanted the leader tried for heresy.

While some of the loudest disagreements are between "liberal Christians" and "conservative Christians," these labels don't do much to resolve the differences of opinion. Scholars who support the Virgin Birth acknowledge that Christians on the other side of the debate raise legitimate questions that need to be answered.

Get Wisdom _____

Some scholars point out that another piece of evidence that argues against the Virgin Birth being a hastily added theologoumenon is that Luke's account has a noticeably Jewish style in its language, theology, and storytelling flavor—which suggests that Luke (a Greek by birth) retold a story that had wide circulation in the Holy Land.

Why Are Scholars Divided?

The theologians and pastors who question the Virgin Birth typically point to a list of four "objections" that have been debated for hundreds of years. I'll tell you about each of them, in turn.

There's Not Enough Biblical Witness

Given the significance of the Virgin Birth in Matthew and Luke, why aren't there more mentions of the miracle in the New Testament?

- The Virgin Birth is described in "only" two Gospels: Matthew and Luke.

- Mark—the author of what scholars believe is the Gospel written first—chose not to write anything about Jesus' unique birth.

- John—the author of the Gospel that presents the highest Christology (see Chapter 2)—also ignored the Virgin Birth.

- The oldest of Christianity's documents—Paul's letters—are equally silent about the Virgin Birth, which seems surprising to many.

The implication is that the earliest Gospel—and the earliest letters—written 20 to 30 years after Jesus' death and resurrection don't talk about the Virgin Birth because it was not part of the early Christian beliefs about Jesus.

Consider Philippians 2:6–11, NIV, for example. Paul writes: "Christ Jesus … being in very nature God, did not consider equality with God something to be grasped, but made himself nothing, taking the very nature of a servant, being made in human likeness. And being found in appearance as a man, he humbled himself and became obedient to death—even death on a cross! Therefore God exalted him to the highest place and gave him the name that is above every name …."

Scholars believe this hymn or confession reflects the earliest Christian understanding of Jesus Christ. Why didn't Paul include a few words about Jesus' unique birth?

Get Wisdom

Matthew's and Luke's telling of the Virgin Birth are so different that Biblical scholars doubt that they based their accounts on common written source material. And, neither author seems have seen the other's words. Rather, they seem to have started with oral traditions that Jesus was conceived by the Holy Spirit. This indicates that Christians had begun to talk about the Virgin Birth before Matthew or Luke wrote their accounts.

Advocates of the Virgin Birth point out that Mark's Gospel begins 30 years after Jesus' birth—with the start of his public ministry. Mark wrote a fast-paced narrative that intentionally leaves out the details of Jesus' earlier life.

John clearly sees the Word becoming Flesh as miraculous (see John 1:14) but his largely poetic introduction doesn't try to explain the specific details of the Incarnation. Because most scholars believe that John wrote late in the first century, they assume that John had Mark's, Matthew's, and Luke's Gospels as resource materials. John seems to have chosen not to repeat what he thought was well covered in the other accounts.

As for no mention of the Virgin Birth in Paul's letters, a few scholars have tried to find indirect references, but the explanation I like best is that Paul hadn't heard the story. Why should he have heard about the Virgin Birth? The details were known to a few people, at most, and were not likely part of the oral tradition that circulated throughout the Holy Land when Paul lived there.

In fact, the Virgin Birth is the sort of thing that would have been closely guarded secret until long after Jesus' death to protect the surviving members of Jesus' family. The Romans were keenly aware of the messianic prophecies and would have seen the account of the Virgin Birth story as a threat.

And as for Paul reading the Gospels—Paul seems to have died before Luke was written and before Matthew was widely distributed (although historians continue to debate the dates of these three key events).

Get Wisdom _____

Some scholars insist that the Virgin Birth story was added to Matthew and Luke to counteract persistent rumors that Jesus was illegitimate. This notion lasted late into the second century, when Celsus, a Platonic philosopher and avowed opponent of Christianity claimed that Jesus was actually the illegitimate son of a Roman centurion named Panthera.

The Earliest Christian Preachers Ignored It

The Book of Acts presents various sermons presented by the apostles. None of them mention the Virgin Birth. A well-known example is Peter's Pentecost speech (see Acts 2:14–36). He talks about Jesus as Lord and Messiah, and states that Jesus "was a man accredited by God to you by miracles, wonders and signs," (Acts 2:22, NIV) yet says nothing about Jesus' unique birth—a highly relevant miracle.

Defenders of the Virgin Birth offer two explanations:

◆ When evangelizing, the apostles focused on Jesus as Lord and Savior—and so they stressed the events of his ministry and his death, resurrection, and ascension.

◆ The lion's share of their audiences were Jewish Christians who might have been put off by the "Pagan associations" of Virgin Birth.

It's Based on Pagan Mythology

The ancient world was chock full of myths about miraculous births. So some skeptical scholars assert that Matthew and Luke borrowed the concept of the Virgin Birth from Pagan religions, maybe to interest Pagans in Christianity, or perhaps to make Jesus seem as special as the many Pagan heroes who were sons (and daughters) of gods.

For example, Perseus, the first of the mythic heroes of Greek mythology, was supposedly the son of Danaë (a mortal woman) and Zeus, the king of the gods, the ruler of Mount Olympus.

Another illustration is a fable—well known throughout the Roman Empire during the first century—that Romulus and Remus, the mythical founders of Rome, were the twin sons of Mars, the Roman God of war and Silvia, a mortal Vestal Virgin.

There are four credible counterarguments:

◆ The idea that early Christianity wanted to "out-Pagan" Paganism doesn't make much sense; Christianity grew because it offered (and delivered) what Pagan religions lacked.

◆ The large group of Jewish Christians would have strongly opposed any attempt to import Pagan mythology into developing Christian teachings about the Messiah.

◆ At the very least, Jesus' family would have rejected the Virgin Birth if it had been merely a Pagan add-on.

◆ The Pagan myths involving miraculous births are fundamentally different than the story of the Virgin Birth.

> **Walking with the Wise**
>
> The virgin birth has never been a major stumbling block in my struggle with Christianity; it's far less mind-boggling than the Power of all Creation stooping so low as to become one of us.
> —Madeleine L'Engle, *A Stone for a Pillow*

It's Only a Sign of Jesus' Messiahship

Finally, some naysayers claim that the doctrine of the Virgin Birth appears in Matthew's and Luke's Gospels largely as a sign of Jesus' messiahship. This argument flows from a reading of Isaiah 7:14, KJV: "Therefore the Lord himself will give you a sign: The virgin will be with child and will give birth to a son, and will call him Immanuel."

Simply put, says this group of doubters, the Virgin Birth was added to Matthew's and Luke's Gospels merely to further identify Jesus as the fulfillment of Old Testament prophecy: the promised Messiah, and the Son of God. Other than that, they go on, it is "theologically unimportant."

Those who oppose this view point out that holding up Isaiah 7:14 as simply a sign would have been irrelevant, because Jewish believers did not expect the Messiah to be born of a virgin; most historians agree that Isaiah 7:14 was *not* considered a Messianic prediction by the Jews of the day.

As I noted earlier, Jewish Christians would have opposed the Virgin Birth as Pagan concept. And, many gentile converts were sophisticated thinkers whose first reaction would be to view the Virgin Birth as some kind of fairy tale. Consequently, the early Christians had every reason *not* to assert Jesus' miraculous birth, unless it was true.

Why the Virgin Birth Matters

Christians who, like me, affirm the Virgin Birth claim that it is one of Christianity's central teachings. While that's true, keep in mind that the Virgin Birth is chiefly the mechanism that God used to achieve the Incarnation. The familiar statement in the Nicene Creed, "I believe … in one Lord Jesus Christ … who for our salvation came down from heaven and was incarnate by the Holy Spirit of the virgin Mary and was made man …," makes an important theological point.

> **Take Warning!**
>
> Some Christians wrongly assume that "Immaculate Conception" is a synonym for "Virgin Birth." In fact, the Immaculate Conception is a Roman Catholic doctrine, adopted as dogma in 1854, which holds that Mary, the mother of Jesus, was conceived without sin. This explains how Jesus could be sinless when he was born. Protestant denominations do not accept the teaching and consider Jesus' lack of sin as another aspect of the mystery of Jesus' dual natures (see Chapter 4).

The phrase "incarnate by the Holy Spirit of the virgin Mary and was made man" teaches that the Virgin Birth was God's way of entering creation and achieving the unity of deity and humanity in one person.

Clearly, God could have used a different approach to accomplish his purpose, but none would have conveyed the same impact:

◆ God might have chosen not to use Mary, but rather to create Jesus from materials on Earth (echoing the story of Adam) or send a complete Jesus down from heaven—but either of these alternatives might have made Jesus seem less than fully human.

◆ Or, God might have started with a perfectly ordinary Jesus born of Mary and Joseph, and then somehow "inserted" some divinity—but this approach runs the risk of making Jesus seem less than fully God.

To a great extent, the theologians, scholars, and pastors who remain committed to the truth of the Virgin Birth are those who perceive the strongest link between the teaching and the Incarnation. They point out that the essence of Christianity is that God took on human flesh—a mystery made possible by the Virgin Birth.

The Least You Need to Know

- The doctrine of the Virgin Birth teaches that Jesus was born of a virgin after being conceived by the Holy Spirit.

- The account of the Virgin Birth appears in the Gospels of Matthew and Luke, but is directly mentioned nowhere else in the New Testament.

- The great majority of Christian laypeople (and many nonbelievers) accept the teaching as true, but some theologians and pastors doubt the Virgin Birth was a historical event.

- Some naysayers claim that the Virgin Birth was imported from Pagan mythology or placed in the Bible as evidence of a sign—foretold in Isaiah 7:14—that Jesus is the Messiah.

- Immaculate Conception is not a synonym for the Virgin Birth, but rather the Roman Catholic teaching that Mary, the mother of Jesus, was conceived without sin.

- Scholars note that the Virgin Birth was prophesied and explained in Scripture so that Christians can better understand the Incarnation and how Jesus can be both fully man and fully God.

The Mystery of Jesus' Missing Years

In This Chapter

◆ Where was Jesus from age 12 to 30?

◆ The Gospels are silent about the "missing years"

◆ Several contradictory legends

◆ Could Jesus have lived in England, India, or Japan?

◆ The best answer: he lived quietly in Nazareth

Fasten your seatbelts! We're entering the speculation zone—an area of blatant conjecture, counterfeit artifacts, and bizarre guesswork. I'll cover Jesus' so-called missing years in this chapter—a rather straightforward mystery, because Scripture is silent on where Jesus was (or what he was doing) between age 12 and the start of his earthly ministry.

The solutions range from modest proposals that Jesus studied with leading philosophers in Egypt and Greece (many of them Jewish), to outlandish notions that Jesus traveled to India and Japan to learn the ins-and-outs of eastern religions.

Jesus—Where Were You?

The Gospels of Mark and John begin Jesus' biography with the start of his earthly ministry. This is quite typical of ancient biographies, which traditionally left out "irrelevant" childhood details and began with the subject's first public act. By contrast, Matthew and Luke both describe Jesus' unique birth.

Matthew ends this "preface" of Jesus' ministry story with Joseph bringing Mary and Jesus back from Egypt after Herod's death (see Matthew 2:21–23).

Matthew provides a minimalist explanation regarding where Jesus lived after his return from Egypt and before the start of his ministry: "… and he went and lived in a town called Nazareth. So was fulfilled what was said through the prophets: He will be called a Nazarene." (Matthew 2:23, NIV)

> **Walking with the Wise**
>
> For the first thirty years of his life Jesus lived a human life that was so ordinary that the people of Nazareth who knew him best were amazed that he could teach with authority and work miracles.
>
> —Wayne Grudem, *Systematic Theology: An Introduction to Biblical Doctrine*

Luke says nothing about Jesus, Mary, and Joseph fleeing to Egypt but adds another detail about Jesus' late boyhood: he describes Jesus at age 12 going off on his own during a family visit to Jerusalem. His frantic (and upset) parents found him in the Temple three days later, talking theology with the learned teachers. (see Luke 2:41–49)

Luke summarizes the missing years (after Mary and Joseph found Jesus talking to the elders in the Temple) in a couple of sentences: "Then he went down with them and came to Nazareth, and was obedient to them. His mother treasured all these things in her heart. And Jesus increased in wisdom and in years, and in divine and human favor." (Luke 2:51–52, NRSV)

Was Jesus Really a Carpenter?

Although most Christians assume that Jesus was a carpenter, this familiar belief is based on two guesses. The first guess is that Jesus followed Joseph's occupation; however, Scripture says nothing about this. The second guess is that Joseph was a carpenter. Although many Bible translations use the word *carpenter* in Matthew 13:55, the actual Greek word that describes Joseph is *tekton*. This can mean a craftsman of wood products, a builder of houses (made of wood or stone), a designer, or even a scholar.

Did Jesus Began Preaching at Age 30?

This is largely an educated guess. On the one hand, the minimum age for priestly service was 30 (see Numbers 4:1–4) and the Book of Hebrews describes Jesus as our High Priest (see Hebrews 2:17). On the other hand, specific historic events mentioned in the Synoptic Gospels suggest that Jesus began preaching in the year 27 and that he was born a few years before 1 B.C. Put these facts together, and "age 30 or a bit older" seems right.

... That Leaves Roughly 17 Unexplained Years

Specifically, we are talking about the period mentioned in Luke during which Jesus "increased in wisdom and in years, and in divine and human favor." (Luke 2:52, NRSV) Seventeen years is a long time and Luke provided a downright vague description that doesn't satisfy modern readers who believe that childhood events influence adult behavior.

History—like nature—seems to abhor a vacuum, and so a number of odd theories have emerged to fill in the details of the 17 missing years.

Could Jesus Have Left the Holy Land?

Two details presented in the Gospels encourage some scholars to believe that Jesus did not spend the 17 missing years in Nazareth:

◆ John the Baptist, talking about Jesus, makes the comment: "I myself did not know him ...." (John 1:31, NRSV) This strikes many scholars as odd, because John and Jesus were cousins. At the very least, they should have seen each other during routine family visits to Jerusalem.

◆ Many historians believe that the two drachma temple tax Jesus was asked to pay in the incident recorded in Matthew 17:24–26 was a tax paid by Jews living outside the Holy Land. The implication is that Jesus was presumed to be a foreigner by the tax collectors.

These interpretations of the Scriptural witness, while not definitive, at least make it possible to speculate that Jesus traveled overseas during those 17 years. Most proponents of the away-from-home idea claim that Jesus used his time abroad to master different religions, from Druidism, to Hinduism, to Buddhism, and even Shinto, in Japan.

Jesus in Nazareth Is More Probable

Most Christians—including me and I'll guess you—assume that Jesus spent those 17 years in Israel, working, studying, praying, and preparing himself for his ministry. There are several reasons to doubt that Jesus took a long trip abroad:

◆ A multiyear journey to England, India, or Japan would have been such a significant part of Jesus' life that one of the Gospel authors would certainly have included the details.

◆ The townsfolk of Nazareth seemed familiar with Jesus at the start of his ministry—familiar enough to be astonished when the Jesus they'd known for years began to speak like the Messiah and demonstrate miraculous powers (see Matthew 13:54–56).

◆ A well-traveled Jesus would have included foreign-language idioms in his speech, foreign values in his teaching, and foreign details in his parables.

◆ The cost of a long overseas journey would have exceeded Jesus' meager financial resources (unless you assume that some of the gold given to him as a baby was available, or that someone else footed the bill).

For me, the most conclusive argument is that Jesus' teachings were based on the Hebrew Scriptures (which he could quote effortlessly), not eastern religious ideas. The temple leaders who opposed Jesus would certainly have spotted any foreign influences in his teachings—and would have spotlighted the theological inconsistencies to discredit Jesus. The fact that Jesus spoke, taught, thought, and behaved like a Jewish rabbi undermines the notion that he studied abroad and proves to my satisfaction that Jesus mastered Judaism close to home.

Get Wisdom

Some Christians believe that because the divine nature in Jesus of Nazareth was omniscient, Jesus was born knowing everything and did require any kind of formal education. This idea fights with the teaching that Jesus was fully human—and recognized as such by the people around him. Moreover, Luke tells us that "Jesus increased in wisdom and in years and in divine and human favor" after his twelfth year. (Luke 2:52, NRSV) An increase in wisdom implies a learning process and suggests that Jesus received training in Hebrew Scriptures and Jewish thought.

Does It Matter Where He Was?

Probably not—especially if we reflect on the other things we don't know about Jesus. We don't know what Jesus looked like, for example. Nor do we know his actual vocation, or the nature of his formal education in Jewish law. And, Scripture doesn't spell out the makeup of his immediate family (or what happened to Joseph).

The missing years represent just one more mystery about Jesus—one that's unlikely to be resolved. Nonetheless, the different theories to account for the missing years are as entertaining as they are improbable. So let's join Jesus on an improbable journey to the far corners of the world.

Theory: Jesus Lived Safely in Egypt or Greece

During the first century, the leading cities of Egypt and Greece were centers of learning—many with large Jewish communities. There would have been individuals and schools who could have taught and nurtured Jesus. Jesus would have been relatively close to Israel, but also far enough away to be safe from Herod's family.

Some scholars believe that Jesus' life was in danger even after Herod was dead. They assert that Matthew proves that Joseph worried about Herod's heirs after the return from Egypt: "But when he [Joseph] heard that Archelaus was ruling over Judea in place of his father Herod, he was afraid to go there. And after being warned in a dream, he went away to the district of Galilee." (Matthew 2:22, NRSV)

Most scholars presume that Jesus spoke Aramaic and Koine, the widely spoken "everyday" Greek dialect. But since he spent several years as a child in Egypt, he may have learned some of the Egyptian language and would have naturally chosen Egypt for sanctuary again.

This theory is one of the most plausible explanations of the missing years. It fits all of the Scriptural witness and leaves all of Jesus' future ministry intact. Nonetheless, it's all speculation.

Theory: Jesus Lived in India

This idea was popularized by the writings of a late-nineteenth-century Russian journalist named Nicolas Notovich. He claimed to have seen an ancient document in a Tibetan monastery that recorded the journey of "Saint Issa"—a 13-year-old prophet who, to avoid being forced into marriage, joined a merchant caravan and traveled from Israel to India.

Once in India, Issa studies Hinduism, preaches to the masses, is befriended by some Indian castes, opposed by others, and is forced to flee to the Buddhists, where he studies some more. The pattern repeats itself, and Issa is forced to flee to Tibet and Persia. He eventually returns to his homeland, begins his ministry in Israel, and is executed by the Romans at the behest of Pontius Pilate.

Alas, the ancient scrolls that inspired Notovich have never been produced, nor has any hard evidence that they actually exist. However, the legend that Jesus lived and preached in India is widespread today.

The India explanation of the missing years breaks down for the reasons I listed earlier: a long caravan trip to India seems implausible, but even more implausible is the notion that Jesus would study (and become expert in) polytheistic Indian religions. By age 12, Jesus would have totally committed to the central Jewish teaching that there is only one God.

Theory: Jesus Lived in England

This fascinating fable revolves around Joseph of Arimathea—the very same Joseph of Arimathea who gave his tomb for Jesus' burial (see Matthew 22:57) and boldly asked Pontius Pilate for Jesus' body (see Mark 15:43). Some Christians believe that Joseph was the Virgin Mary's uncle, thus Jesus' granduncle.

According to legend, Joseph amassed his great wealth importing tin from mines in the region of England that is now called Cornwall (many of the tin miners may have been Jewish immigrants from Israel). Joseph supposedly made many long trips to England, sometimes accompanied by Jesus. Consequently, some Christians insist that Jesus spent most of the missing years in what is now Cornwall and Somerset—safe from Herod's heirs and able to study the teachings of the Druids.

The legend goes on to claim that after the crucifixion, Joseph moved to Somerset—with several other followers of Jesus—bringing the religion of Christianity to the British Isles.

The inspirational power of this legend can be seen in its effect on the famed British poet William Blake (1757–1827). He wrote a poem called "Jerusalem" that has become one of Britain's most popular hymns:

> And did those feet in ancient time
> Walk upon England's mountains green?
> And was the holy Lamb of God

On England's pleasant pastures seen?
And did the Countenance Divine
Shine forth upon our clouded hills?
And was Jerusalem builded here
Among these dark Satanic Mills?

While it's within the realm of possibility that Jesus might have traveled to England, it seems totally unlikely that a thoroughly Jewish Jesus would have studied with pagan Druids.

Another fundamental problem with this legend is that Joseph of Arimathea's links to tin—and to Cornwall—are pure speculations. Scholars point out that beginning in the second century, *many* other legends grew around Joseph, including that he was one of the 70 disciples sent out by Jesus (see Luke 10:1–12) and the eventual keeper of the Holy Grail.

Theory: Jesus Lived in Japan

Yes, I'm serious. Japan!

The legends I've seen tell a rather curious tale that begins with Jesus—at age 21—making a four-year long voyage from Nazareth to a region of Japan near Mount Fuji, near the middle of the Island of Honshu. He then spent a decade or so studying Shinto, other aspects of Japanese theology, and the Japanese language.

Jesus journeyed back to Judea to preach, was rejected, and sentenced to be crucified. But, in a significant plot twist, his younger brother was executed in his place.

Consequently, Jesus was able to return to Japan and settle in the village of Herai, in the Aomori Prefecture of Japan, at the top of the Island of Honshu. There, Jesus married, fathered three daughters, and lived to a ripe old age (one version of the story says 108). Herai exists today; visitors can see tombs dedicated to Jesus and his younger brother.

A major problem with the Japanese legend is that it ignores Jesus' divinity (see Chapter 2) and the salvation brought by his atoning death (see Chapter 6). The story seeks to account for the missing years by completely destroying the purpose of his ministry.

The Least You Need to Know

◆ Scripture is silent on where Jesus lived—and what he did—between age 12 and the start of his earthly ministry (somewhere around age 30).

◆ The mystery of the "missing years" has become a subject of great speculation.

◆ Many theories have emerged to fill the years—including guesses that Jesus traveled to Egypt, Greece, England, India, and even Japan.

◆ A few of these theories are especially improbable because they assert that Jesus studied pagan or polytheistic religions while abroad.

◆ The simplest explanation is probably true: Jesus led an uneventful life in Israel during the missing years preparing for his earthly ministry.

Chapter 11

The Mystery of Jesus' Descent into Hell

In This Chapter

- ◆ Where was Jesus before he rose from the dead?
- ◆ Did he descend into hell?
- ◆ This view is taught by Christianity's leading creed
- ◆ Many scholars say the Apostle's Creed is wrong
- ◆ A look at the "hell" Jesus may have visited

I could have also titled this chapter, "The Mystery of Where Jesus Was Between His Death and Resurrection." Over the years, that has become one of Christianity's enduring uncertainties—with enthusiastic proponents on both side of the divide.

Many (perhaps the majority of) Christians say that Jesus descended into hell, while others insist the doctrine is not Scripturally based and was created in the fourth century to counter the heresy that Jesus was not fully human.

It's in the Creeds

If you belong to a Christian denomination that accepts the Apostle's Creed or the Athanasian Creed (see Appendix B) as a summary statement of Christian faith, you've probably confessed aloud that Jesus descended into hell.

◆ *Apostle's Creed:* "Jesus Christ, His only Son, our Lord ... who suffered under Pontius Pilate, was crucified, died, and was buried. He descended into hell. The third day He arose again from the dead."

◆ *Athanasian Creed:* "[Jesus Christ] suffered for our salvation, descended into Hell, rose again the third day from the dead."

The popular *Nicene Creed*, however, doesn't express the doctrine: "For our sake he [Jesus Christ] was crucified under Pontius Pilate; he suffered death and was buried. On the third day he rose again in accordance with the Scriptures ...."

Because the creeds are widely used and influential—and because they make clear, unambiguous statements about Jesus—many Christians take for granted that he spent at least part of the time between his death and resurrection in hell. However, as you'll see in this chapter, the Scriptural witness is much fuzzier. Consequently, some scholars insist that the idea of Jesus going to hell is either a misinterpretation or a convenient fabrication.

A Brief Tour of Hell

Virtually all of the theologians on both sides of the issue agree on one thing: The "hell" that Jesus may have descended into is *not* the place of eternal punishment that John describes in the Book of Revelation. Three words in the Bible are commonly translated into the English word hell:

◆ *Sheol*—the final abode of the dead (sometimes translated as "grave" or "the pit"). When Job described sheol, he said, "There the wicked cease to make trouble, and there the weary find rest. The captives are completely at ease; they do not hear the voice of their oppressor. Both the small and the great are there, and the slave is set free from his master." (Job 3:17–19, HCSB)

◆ *Hades*—the Greek equivalent to sheol that is used throughout the *Septuagint*, the Greek translation of the Hebrew Scriptures. Hades has a long tradition in Greek mythology—it means "the underworld" where the dead reside and is also the name of the Greek god of the dead.

◆ *Gehenna* (or geenna)—a fiery site of eternal punishment. Jesus spoke about gehenna when he advised his disciples to remove offending body parts rather than stumble into sin, go to hell, and end up in "the unquenchable fire." (See Mark 9:43–47 and Chapter 17.)

Most theologians agree that gehenna—also known as the lake of fire (see Revelation 20:14)—is the final destination of the unsaved; it will not become a place of eternal punishment until *after* Jesus' Second Coming and the Final Judgment (see Chapter 7).

Get Wisdom

Scholars believe that "gehenna" is based on a real place, "Ge Hinnom" (the Valley of Hinnom), a garbage dump not far from the south wall of ancient Jerusalem. Fires burned continuously in Ge Hinnom to destroy garbage, animal carcasses, and unburied bodies, making the valley a place of unquenchable fire, a literal hell on Earth. According to some reports, the stench of Ge Hinnom could be smelled several miles away.

The Two "Sides" of Sheol

Devout Jews in the Holy Land who looked forward to a general resurrection of humankind apparently believed that sheol had two "sides"—a place where the righteous dead waited for judgment in comfort and a place where the ungodly dead waited in torment. This division is clearly seen in the story of the rich man and the beggar Lazarus:

> In Hades [sheol], where he [the rich man] was being tormented, he looked up and saw Abraham far away with Lazarus by his side. He called out, "Father Abraham, have mercy on me, and send Lazarus to dip the tip of his finger in water and cool my tongue; for I am in agony in these flames." But Abraham said, "Child, remember that during your lifetime you received your good things, and Lazarus in like manner evil things; but now he is comforted here, and you are in agony. Besides all this, between you and us a great chasm has been fixed, so that those who might want to pass from here to you cannot do so, and no one can cross from there to us." (Luke 16:23–26, NRSV)

The good side of sheol is called paradise or "Abraham's Bosom," and the bad side simply "sheol" or "Hades" (suggesting that it had no special name). Christians believe that paradise is now in Heaven, or part of Heaven, or was somehow absorbed in

Heaven and is no longer connected to the place where the unrighteous dead wait for the Final Judgment.

Jesus May Have Descended into Sheol

If Jesus descended into "hell" after the crucifixion, he traveled to sheol or Hades, the abode of the dead, not to gehenna, which may not have existed then (and may not yet exist today).

A journey to the comforting side of sheol would be consistent with Jesus' well-known statement to the thief on the adjacent cross: "And He [Jesus] said to him, I assure you: Today you will be with Me in paradise." (Luke 23:43, HCSB)

It might also comfort many Christians to know that while Jesus' body was in the grave, his human soul (see Chapter 4) was in "Abraham's Bosom," a place of repose and happiness.

Alas, this solution doesn't resolve the conflict or solve the Mystery, because …

- Many proponents of Jesus descending to Hell claim that he also traveled to the hellish part of sheol—the abode of the unrighteous dead, a place of torment.

- Many opponents of Jesus descending to hell argue that the Scriptural evidence for a visit to paradise is as weak as the evidence for a visit to the hellish part of sheol.

For convenience, I'll use "Hades" to label the unpleasant half of sheol throughout the rest of this chapter.

The Arguments for Jesus' Descent into Hell

The Scripture used to support the notion that Jesus traveled to Hell—either paradise or Hades—is murky, in the sense you won't find a simple, straightforward, direct statement about his descent anywhere in the New Testament. There is one *sort-of* direct passage—1 Peter 3:18–20—but it's anything but simple or straightforward.

Probably the most commonly cited Bible verse in support of Jesus' descent into Hades is Ephesians 4:7–10. I've provided two translations—one old and one modern.

Here's a modern translation of Ephesians 4:7–10: But to each one of us grace has been given as Christ apportioned it. This is why it says: "When he ascended on high, he led captives in his train and gave gifts to men." (What does "he ascended" mean except that he also descended to the lower, earthly regions? He who descended is the very one who ascended higher than all the heavens, in order to fill the whole universe.) (Ephesians 4:7–10, NIV)

If you read Ephesians 4:7–10 with the idea that sheol is located somewhere below the Earth—as did Jews in the first century—you can extract the notion that Jesus met with the righteous dead in paradise and was seen from afar by the tormented dead in Hades.

Here's a much older translation of Ephesians 4:7–10: But unto every one of us is given grace according to the measure of the gift of Christ. Wherefore he saith, When he ascended up on high, he led captivity captive, and gave gifts unto men. (Now that he ascended, what is it but that he also descended first into the lower parts of the Earth? He that descended is the same also that ascended up far above all heavens, that he might fill all things.) (Ephesians 4:7–10, KJV)

The two versions of Ephesians 4:7–10 demonstrate that the "lower parts of the Earth" in older translations (a phrase often interpreted to mean Hades) is now translated as "lower, earthly regions" (a phrase that seems to mean the surface of the Earth). This has led many scholars to suggest Paul was writing about Jesus' Incarnation (see Chapter 2) rather than a possible descent into Hell.

The Most Difficult Verse in the New Testament

I'm sorry to do this to you, but the time has come to show you 1 Peter 3:18–20, which is widely considered to be the single most difficult verse to interpret in the entire New Testament:

> For Christ also suffered for sins once for all, the righteous for the unrighteous, in order to bring you to God. He was put to death in the flesh, but made alive in the spirit, in which also he went and made a proclamation to the spirits in prison, who in former times did not obey, when God waited patiently in the days of Noah, during the building of the ark, in which a few, that is, eight persons, were saved through water. (1 Peter 3:18–20, NRSV)

See what I mean about hard to interpret? Well, the phrase "he went and made a proclamation to the spirits in prison" is used to support the idea that Jesus descended into Hades.

There are numerous ideas about what the passage says, but assuming that Jesus did descend into the "prison" (a metaphor for Hades), one of the simpler interpretations holds that Jesus preached to dead in Hades who ignored God in years past (possibly people who lived in Noah's era).

Happily we don't need to understand the passage, other than to recognize that many have used it as evidence that Jesus descended into Hell.

What Jesus Accomplished in Hell

Various theologians who support Jesus' descent to hell have used these verses as evidence of three things he accomplished during his journey to sheol:

◆ He retrieved the souls of the righteous dead in paradise and brought them to Heaven (or else he proclaimed the Good News of their coming deliverance).

◆ He released the righteous souls captive in Hades and brought them to Heaven (this is called the "Harrowing of Hell").

◆ He preached in Hades, possibly proclaiming his victory won on the Cross over sin and death.

Get Wisdom

Some scholars—perhaps with tongue in cheek—suggest that Jesus might have descended to Hell to get the "keys of Hell and death" talked about in Revelation 1:18. In fact, John used "keys" as a metaphor to affirm that Jesus has complete control over Hell and death.

Other scholars combined the teachings about Jesus' atoning death (see Chapter 6) with the idea of a visit to Hades and proposed that he used the opportunity to destroy the power of Hell.

A few theologians claim that Jesus continued to suffer in Hades, as a continuing component of his atonement for humankind's sin. This view, however, conflicts with the mainstream Christian teaching that Jesus' atoning work was complete when he said, "It is finished." (John 19:30, HCSB, although most Bible translations use the same three words.)

The Arguments Against Jesus' Descent into Hell

The arguments you are most likely to hear zero-in on the limited Scriptural evidence in support of Jesus visiting Hades. The truth is that the New Testament tells us almost nothing about Jesus' location or actions during the period between his crucifixion and the Resurrection. The claim that Jesus descended into Hell is based on a few passages that don't provide clear-cut evidence.

Why the Apostle's Creed Was Changed

Opponents of the teaching also point out that the statement about Jesus descending into hell is not found in the earliest versions of the Apostle's Creed. Scholars believe that the Creed developed out of an early Christian baptismal confession. A version of the Creed dating back to the year 140 didn't assert that Jesus descended into Hades.

The first known appearance of the phrase in any Christian creed dates to the early fourth century, when the Latin words meaning "descended into Hades" crept into one of the many versions of the Apostle's Creed.

Some scholars speculate that the phrase was added to counter the heresy of Apollinarism, which taught that Jesus did not have a rational human soul. Clearly, if Jesus was truly human and had a truly human soul, that soul would have to spend the three days after Jesus' death in Abraham's Bosom, as I noted earlier.

In Conclusion ...

The opponents of the phrase recognize that "descended into Hades" was added to the Apostle's Creed to ensure that mainstream Christianity recognized that Jesus' death was as fully human as he was. Thus, his human soul was separated from his dead body while his body lay in the tomb.

In time, however, the phrase took on the unintended (and more ominous) meaning that Jesus descended into the place of eternal punishment. Consequently, the opponents argue that the phrase has become misleading and confusing and should be eliminated.

Every Christian has to decide for him- or herself. I've sided with the naysayers. Our church recites the Apostle's Creed every Sunday. I usually remain silent during "He descended into Hell."

The Middle Ground: "Hell" Is Metaphorical

There is a middle ground, one that I considered and you should, too. Some interpretations of the creedal phrase say that "he descended into Hell" encompasses the extraordinary pain and spiritual torment that Jesus experienced when he was crucified, separated from God, and took on the sins of humankind.

In particular, the feeling of aloneness expressed in Mark 15:34—"*Eloi, Eloi, lama sabachthani?* (My God, my God, why have you forsaken me?)"—is an indication that Jesus experienced the complete torment of hell while on the Cross.

The opponents of the phrase argue: Maybe so, but to acknowledge that Jesus "suffered hellishly" is a long way from asserting that he "descended into Hell."

The Least You Need to Know

- The "hell" in the Creedal statements is not a place of eternal torment, but refers to "sheol" (or "Hades"), the abode of the dead mentioned in the Old Testament.

- The Apostle's Creed and the Athanasian Creed teach that Jesus descended into Hell between his death and resurrection to perform works related to salvation.

- Some Christians reject this notion and say that Jesus finished his redemptive work on the Cross and his human soul went directly to paradise.

- Other Christians argue Jesus traveled to Hades to preach to the dead who had ignored God in years past.

- Still others say that the Scriptural witness is too limited to say anything about Jesus' pre-resurrection location.

Chapter 12

The Mystery of Jesus' Ascension

In This Chapter

- The resurrected Jesus Christ spent forty days on Earth
- Jesus' ascent to Heaven
- Jesus is still alive, sitting at the right hand of God
- The Book of Acts, rather than the Gospels, tells the story
- The claim that the Ascension was metaphorical

There are many mysteries connected with Jesus' ministry on Earth. The last of them, in chronological order, was his ascension back to heaven some 40 days after the Resurrection. I'll tell you about it in this chapter.

Let me make a little bet with you: I'll wager this is a Christian mystery you've all but ignored. Oh, you've heard about Jesus ascending to Heaven, but the event doesn't seem all that special. After all, Heaven is where God lives and Jesus is God.

Did I win my bet? In that case, you owe me the time it will take you to read this chapter carefully.

The Miracle of the Ascension

Jesus often had to work hard to help his disciples understand the purpose and price of his ministry on Earth. One example can be found in John 6:48–60. Jesus watched the Apostles struggle with the challenge of "getting" his teaching about eating his flesh and drinking his blood.

When Jesus saw his disciples complain among themselves about his "hard saying," he asked them, "Does this offend you? Then what if you were to observe the Son of Man ascending to where He was before?" (John 6:61–62, HCSB)

In other words, if you find it hard to understand my meaning when I say I'm the bread of life, how will you react when you see me, ascending to Heaven in a glorified body?

Many Christians view this question as Jesus' prophecy of his eventual ascension. It may be—but it also indicates that Jesus had a sense of humor and understood the limitations of his disciples. Moreover, Jesus expected his followers to freak out when they realized that a flesh-and-blood man—not a spirit—was on his way to Heaven.

The Ascension in Scripture

Because only a few Bible passages describe the Ascension, I can show you all of the key verses:

◆ *Mark 16:19.* Then after speaking to them, the Lord Jesus was taken up into heaven and sat down at the right hand of God. (Mark 16:19, HCSB)

◆ *Luke 24:50–51.* Then He led them out as far as Bethany, and lifting up His hands He blessed them. And while He was blessing them, He left them and was carried up into heaven. (Luke 24:50–51, HCSB)

◆ *Matthew and John.* Matthew wrote nothing about the ascension; neither did John, except for quoting Jesus's prophetic words, as I described above. (John 6:62)

◆ *Acts 1:9–11.* After He had said this, He was taken up as they were watching, and a cloud received Him out of their sight. While He was going, they were gazing into heaven, and suddenly two men in white clothes stood by them. They said, "Men of Galilee, why do you stand looking up into heaven? This Jesus, who has been taken from you into heaven, will come in the same way that you have seen Him going into heaven." (Acts 1:9–11, HCSB)

◆ *1 Timothy 3:16.* And most certainly, the mystery of godliness is great: He [Jesus] was manifested in the flesh, justified in the Spirit, seen by angels, preached among the Gentiles, believed on in the world, taken up in glory. (1 Timothy 3:16, HCSB)

Take Warning!

Don't be confused by the apparent time discrepancy between the Ascension accounts in Acts and Luke. Acts 1:3 states that the resurrected Jesus appeared for 40 days, while the Lukan story seems to cover a shorter period. Scholars remind us that ancient biographers often ignored precise chronology that wasn't essential to understanding the achievements of the subject. Luke's Gospel actually says nothing about timing, other than the Ascension happened after Jesus "led the observers out as far as Bethany."

The Importance of the Ascension

It's easy to overlook the significance of the Ascension. After all, if Matthew, Mark, and John gave the event so little ink in the Gospels, why should ordinary Christians consider it important?

To many believers, the chief benefit of the Ascension is that it enabled Jesus to leave. Consequently—as Jesus explained in John 16:7—humankind could enjoy the advantages of the Holy Spirit, the counselor and comforter Jesus would send after he departed.

Some scholars have argued that the Gospel writers downplayed the details of Ascension because they weren't essential to tell the "Good News." And yet, to echo part of the quotation from C. S. Lewis I shared with you in Chapter 6: "The central Christian belief is that Christ's death has somehow put us right with God and given us a fresh start."

Consequently, an essential aspect of the Good News is that Jesus can continuously repair and rebuild the new relationship. The Ascension of the human Jesus makes this possible.

Get Wisdom

Many Christians assert that the location of the Ascension is given indirectly in Acts 1:12: "Then they [the witnesses to the Ascension] returned to Jerusalem from the mount called Olive Grove [Olivet in many translations], which is near Jerusalem—a Sabbath day's journey away." (Acts 1:12, HCSB) Consequently, believers have long assumed that Jesus ascended from Mount Olivet.

Jesus' Humiliation and Exaltation

To understand what I mean by humiliation and exaltation, consider the summary of Jesus' mission that Paul provides in Philippians 2:5–11. Paul tells Jesus' story in a way that suggests there were two phases (or "states"). Theologians have named these two states the *Humiliation* and the *Exaltation:*

> Let the same mind be in you that was in Christ Jesus, who, though he was in the form of God, did not regard equality with God as something to be exploited, but emptied himself, taking the form of a slave, being born in human likeness. And being found in human form, he humbled himself and became obedient to the point of death—even death on a cross. Therefore God also highly exalted him and gave him the name that is above every name, so that at the name of Jesus every knee should bend, in heaven and on earth and under the earth, and every tongue should confess that Jesus Christ is Lord, to the glory of God the Father. (Philippians 2:5–11, NRSV)

Jesus' Humiliation consisted of four events:

1. Being born as a human (the Incarnation)

2. Suffering under Pontius Pilate and being crucified

3. Dying

4. Being buried

Jesus' Exaltation undid his Humiliation. It consisted of four subsequent events:

1. The Resurrection

2. The Ascension

3. Sitting at the right hand of God

4. Receiving all authority in Heaven and on Earth

Keep Your Eye on the Living Jesus

The Exaltation sequence reveals that the Ascension is an essential aspect of Jesus' success story. It's the mechanism that gets the *living* Jesus—a man restored to life by the Resurrection—back to Heaven.

Note that I've emphasized *living*. This is vital, because it means that the second Person of the Trinity (see Chapter 3) returned to Heaven—to the Godhead's home—but in a different form than before the Incarnation. He left Heaven as pure spirit, but came back as God-Man, divinity somehow joined to a human body and soul.

Unfortunately, too many Christians mistakenly believe that Jesus discarded his glorified human body—and human nature—during the Ascension. They picture Jesus in Heaven as a spiritual being rather than a glorified human being.

I admit that I often fall victim to this mistake. It seems much easier to think, talk, and write about Jesus in the past tense than in the present tense. Every Easter Sunday, countless Christians answer the statement, "Christ is risen" with the exclamation, "He is risen, indeed!" The Ascension didn't change Jesus' aliveness.

To the contrary, the central teaching of the Ascension is that the *fully human* Jesus was inexplicably taken up to Heaven. This is the core mystery of the Ascension, not the rather vanilla notion that Jesus returned home to Heaven after finishing his work on Earth.

The Benefit of the Ascension to Humankind

Because Jesus Christ is fully divine, fully human, fully alive, and at the right hand of God, he is uniquely equipped to serve as the *mediator* who understands both sides and can bridge the gap between humankind and God.

This concept was expanded in Hebrews 4: "Since, then, we have a great high priest who has passed through the heavens, Jesus, the Son of God, let us hold fast to our confession. For we do not have a high priest who is unable to sympathize with our weaknesses, but we have one who in every respect has been tested as we are, yet without sin. Let us therefore approach the throne of grace with boldness, so that we may receive mercy and find grace to help in time of need." (Hebrews 4:14–16, NRSV)

def•i•ni•tion

Mediator is the English translation of a Greek word that means "go-between" or "reconciler." Christianity teaches that only Jesus—both fully God and fully human—is able to reconcile the differences between God and man.

The point is that not only did Jesus provide a priestly sacrifice with his atoning death, he now has become the only human being who can enter the presence of God and intercede with God for each of us.

Is the Ascension Metaphorical?

Some modern theologians assert that that Luke meant the Ascension a metaphor to convey the truth that the exalted Jesus returned to the Father and is sitting at the Father's right hand. They argue that Luke never intended to convey the notion that Jesus literally ascended into a cloud. Rather, Luke described Jesus' sudden disappearance from the disciples' presence—something that must have happened often during Jesus post-resurrection period on Earth.

Ascension skeptics also argue that the idea of Jesus going upward into Heaven presupposes an old-fashioned three-level model of the universe that we know is wrong.

Other Christian scholars point out that nothing in the Scriptural accounts of the Ascension is hard to understand, imagine, or accept—if you are willing to believe the miracles described in the Bible. Some Christians assert that the cloud (singular!) described in Acts 1:9 was another appearance of God the Father in a "pillar of cloud" (see Exodus 13:21).

> ### Get Wisdom
>
> The "three level" model of the universe was accepted until relatively recent times. Heaven was above the Earth. For example, "He [Solomon] said: LORD God of Israel, there is no God like You in heaven above or on earth below …." (1 Kings 8:23, HCSB) And *sheol*, the abode of the dead (see Chapter 11) was below the Earth. For example: "Sheol below is eager to greet your coming." (Isaiah 14:9, HCSB)

Two Alternative Views

I found it worthwhile to consider two alternative views on the Ascension story from leading theologians in different camps. Despite their differing opinions about reading the Scriptural witness literally, both provide useful and interesting insights.

Don't Focus on the Literal Language

Marcus Borg, a liberal theologian, wrote in *The Ascension of Jesus*, an essay published in 2006, that, "The Luke-Acts narrative isn't a 'beam me up' story. Rather, it conveys Jesus' lordship and freedom from space-time limitations. … What we do know, of course, is that heaven is not literally 'up.' Therefore, we legitimately cannot imagine Jesus literally moving upward into the sky on his way to heaven. Something else must be meant."

This view holds that the most important aspects of Jesus' Ascension story are its metaphors and symbols, because they generate specific truths we take away when we read the Bible. Metaphorically speaking, the idea that Jesus has ascended to heaven and is at God's right hand is another way of saying that Jesus truly has the authority required to rule the world. In other words, the ascended Jesus is Lord.

Heaven Is a Real Place

The opposite view encourages us to interpret the Ascension story as a historical account of something that really happened. For example, Wayne Grudem, a well-known theologian, wrote in *Systematic Theology: An Introduction to Biblical Doctrine*:

> These [the Ascension] narratives describe an event that is clearly designed to show the disciples that Jesus went to a place. … Admittedly we cannot now see where Jesus is, but that is not because he passed into some ethereal 'state of being' that has no location at all in the space-time universe, but rather because our eyes are unable to see the unseen spiritual world that exists all around us.
>
> Of course we cannot now say exactly where heaven is. Scripture often pictures people as ascending up into heaven … so we are justified in thinking of heaven as somewhere 'above' the earth. Admittedly the earth is round and it rotates, so where heaven is we are simply unable to say more precisely—Scripture does not tell us. But the repeated emphasis on the fact that Jesus went somewhere … and the fact that the New Jerusalem will come down out of heaven from God (see Revelation 21:2), all indicate that there is clearly a localization of heaven in the space-time universe.

See Appendix B for details on this book.

Sitting at the Right Hand of God

Whether or not you believe the Father—a spirit—sits on a throne and that Jesus literally sits on his right side in a place of honor, (or stands at God's right hand, as Acts 7:55 states) keep in mind the concepts that the well-known phrase conveys. Sitting down at God's right hand …

◆ Asserts that the risen Jesus is an equal member of the Trinity.

◆ Affirms that Jesus had been exalted—and had received unique honors and glory (see Acts 2:33 and Philippians 2:9).

◆ Demonstrates the successful completion of the first stage of Jesus' ongoing mission to restore the relationship between God and humankind.

- Sets the stage for Jesus serving as a mediator that represents God to humankind and humankind to God (see 1 Timothy 2:5).

- Confirms that "all authority in heaven and on earth" (see Matthew 28:18) has been given to Jesus.

These are some of the key messages of the Ascension story; it's truly more important for you and me to grasp them than to resolve the mystery of how a living person can be taken up to Heaven.

The Least You Need to Know

- The story of Jesus Christ's ascension to Heaven is often downplayed by Christians who don't understand its importance.

- The significance of the Ascension lies in the fact that Jesus returned to Heaven as God-Man—divinity somehow joined to a human body and soul.

- Christianity teaches that Jesus returned to Heaven alive, and is alive today.

- Saying that the risen Jesus sits at the right hand of God affirms that he is an equal member of the Trinity.

- The Ascension demonstrates the successful completion of the first stage of Jesus ongoing mission to restore the relationship between God and humankind.

- Because Jesus is fully God, fully man, and fully alive, he is uniquely able to serve as the mediator between God and humanity.

The Mystery of the Dead Messiah

In This Chapter

◆ A dead messiah should have been a failed messiah

◆ Why Jesus was seen as the promised Messiah

◆ A triumphant king from the line of David

◆ A suffering servant who would bear humanity's iniquity

◆ Jesus of Nazareth: a wholly unexpected kind of Messiah

The earliest Christians claimed that Jesus was the Messiah promised by the Old Testament and expected by some (but not all) of the Jews in ancient Israel. This was not an obvious conclusion because the Old Testament prophets foretold different kinds of messiahs. Moreover, a dead Messiah seemed contrary to everyone's notion of a successful Messiah—everyone except Jesus himself.

This chapter will explain the various conflicting expectations that first-century Christians mysteriously brought together in the person of Jesus of Nazareth.

Jesus' Perplexing "Last Name"

Okay … I admit it. I used to be one of the countless crowd of people—a group that includes both Christians and nonbelievers—who think that "Christ" is Jesus' last name.

I also acknowledge feeling foolish when I learned that *Christ* is a *title* that means "one anointed by God"—in other words, the *Messiah*.

Paul Loved to Call Jesus the Messiah

The early Christians called Jesus the Messiah shortly after His death. One powerful piece of evidence is that Paul used *Christ* more than 350 times in his letters—the oldest surviving Christian writings. First Thessalonians, the earliest of Paul's letters, was written scarcely two decades after Jesus' death and resurrection.

This widespread recognition of Jesus' Messiahship happened even though He rarely identified himself directly as the Messiah. The most notable occasions recorded in the Gospels are:

◆ In the conversation between Jesus and the Samaritan woman, she said, "I know that Messiah … is coming," and Jesus replied "I who speak to you am he." (John 4:25–26, NIV)

◆ When Jesus was interrogated in Jerusalem, the high priest asked, "Are you the Christ …?" and Jesus answered, "I am." (Mark 14:61–62, NIV)

◆ When Jesus asked Peter "Who do you say I am?" Peter answered, "You are the Christ," and Jesus didn't disagree. (Mark 8:29, NIV)

Get Wisdom

The Hebrew term for "one anointed by God" is *moshiyach* (*messiah* in English). The term is used in the Old Testament to describe kings, priests, prophets—and even Cyrus the Great of Persia. When the Hebrew Scriptures were translated into Greek, *moshiyach* became *Christos* (based on a Greek term for rubbing with oil), which soon transliterated into the Latin word *Christ*.

The third example is especially interesting, because Mark goes on to report that "Jesus warned them not to tell anyone about him." (Mark 8:30, NIV)

Later of course, Jesus semi-directly proclaimed Himself the Messiah when he rode into Jerusalem on a colt as described in Luke 19:29–45. This fulfils the unmistakably messianic prediction in Zechariah 9:9, NIV: "Rejoice greatly, … O Daughter of Jerusalem!

See, your king comes to you, righteous and having salvation, gentle and riding on a donkey, on a colt, the foal of a donkey."

Jesus Preferred "Son of Man"

By contrast, Jesus referred to himself as the Son of Man more than 80 times in the Gospels. According to Bible scholars, most of these references are allusions to Daniel 7:13, a clearly messianic vision. One "like the son of man" is an exalted ruler who will receive—from God—the power to rule the world.

Scripture Says
Daniel 7:13, NIV, presents, via Daniel's dream, a preview of the coming Messiah: "In my vision at night I looked, and there before me was one like a son of man, coming with the clouds of heaven. He approached the Ancient of Days and was led into his presence. He was given authority, glory and sovereign power; all peoples, nations and men of every language worshiped him. His dominion is an everlasting dominion that will not pass away, and his kingdom is one that will never be destroyed."

Some theologians interpret Jesus' repeated use of Son of Man as communicating both his Messiahship and his divinity (see Chapter 4). The Son of Man will have everlasting dominion and receive worship; these are attributes of God.

The most likely explanation for Jesus' apparent reluctance to loudly proclaim himself as the promised Messiah is that Jesus understood that *messiah* was a word loaded with different meanings in first-century Israel. As you'll learn later in the chapter, not everyone in ancient Israel believed in the coming of a messiah, and those who did believe had widely varying views on what a "real" messiah should—and should not—do.

Jesus: An Unexpected Kind of Messiah

Modern Christian apologists often say that Jesus of Nazareth met most of the Old Testament prophecies about the promised Messiah. It's easy to make this claim from our twenty-first century perspective (a vantage point with "20-20 hindsight"), but few of Jesus' contemporaries would have recognized him as the messiah promised in Hebrew Scriptures.

The Gospels point out that his own family doubted his capabilities. (See Mark 3:21) This is so because Jesus was truly a bewildering sort of Messiah.

The Gospels also teach that John the Baptist announced the impending arrival of the Messiah by proclaiming, "… I baptize you with water for repentance, but one who is more powerful than I is coming after me; I am not worthy to carry his sandals. He will baptize you with the Holy Spirit and fire. His winnowing fork is in his hand, and he will clear his threshing floor and will gather his wheat into the granary; but the chaff he will burn with unquenchable fire." (Matthew 3:11–12, NRSV) (Ancient farmers used winnowing forks to fling recently harvested grain into the air. The heavier grain seeds fell to the ground, while the breeze blew lighter chaff and insects some distance away from the grain, where they could be collected and destroyed.)

This is an image that makes us picture Jesus as a kind of first-century "Terminator." In fact, John is expressing the commonly held hope for a Messiah who would expel the Roman occupiers from the Holy Land ("clear the threshing floor"), completely end the exile of faithful Jews ("gather his wheat into the granary"), and punish wrongdoers (winnow and burn the "chaff").

Jesus did none of this during his ministry; to the contrary, he preached the radical idea of "loving your enemies." It's not surprising, then, that John would become puzzled when his core messianic expectations weren't met.

And so, John sent word to Jesus from prison: "Are you the one who is to come, or are we to wait for another?" (Matthew 11:3, NRSV) Jesus replied to John's messengers, "Go and tell John what you hear and see: the blind receive their sight, the lame walk, the lepers are cleansed, the deaf hear, the dead are raised, and the poor have good news brought to them." (Matthew 11:4–5, NRSV)

Get Wisdom

John the Baptist was not only person who'd met Jesus who was confused about the nature of His Messiahship. Consider the story told in Mark 10:35–40, NRSV, about two of Jesus' disciples: "James and John, the sons of Zebedee, came forward to him and said to him, 'Teacher, we want you to do for us whatever we ask of you.' And he said to them, 'What is it you want me to do for you?' And they said to him, 'Grant us to sit, one at your right hand and one at your left, in your glory.; But Jesus said to them, 'You do not know what you are asking. Are you able to drink the cup that I drink, or be baptized with the baptism that I am baptized with?'" When they made their request, James and John obviously thought that Jesus had come to restore the Davidic kingship.

John the Baptist would have understood immediately that Jesus' curious answer was meant to recalibrate John's vision of the Messiah, based largely on prophecies found in the Book of Isaiah. Jesus the Messiah didn't plan to march through Israel punishing with "unquenchable fire." Rather, he intended to be a priestly and prophetic Messiah who is the Savior of humankind: "... my righteous servant will justify many, and he will bear their iniquities." (Isaiah 53:11, NIV)

Jesus clearly recognized that John the Baptist and other Jews might become angry at his failure to meet their well-entrenched messianic expectations. He added, "And blessed is anyone who takes no offense at me." (Matthew 11:6, NRSV) I also like to think that Jesus' polite reply was a gentle way of reminding John that, "The next day he [John] saw Jesus coming toward him and declared, 'Here is the Lamb of God who takes away the sin of the world!'" (John 1:29, NRSV)

Jewish Hope for the "Messiah" Is Hard to Pin Down

Many historians studying Ancient Israel believe that Jewish hope in the coming of a messiah grew more widespread as the Romans became more oppressive occupiers. That fact raises an obvious question: What kind of messiah did first-century Jews want?

This can be a tricky question to answer, because Judaism in the Holy Land had multiple mainstream threads plus many sects and splinter groups, much like Christianity has today in America. Consequently, *messiah* was a verbal moving target with meanings ranging from "righteous man," to "prophet," to "general of an army," to "king of the Jews," to "conqueror of the world," to the possibly divine "Son of Man" described in Daniel 7:13.

And, many residents of the Holy Land undoubtedly considered it safer to accept the "King of the Jews" put in place by the Romans (members of the Herodian family) and not believe in the coming of a messiah who would start a war with Rome.

Start with Jewish Prayer About the Messiah

One way to determine the mainstream expectations of first-century Jews is to look at the prayers they offered in regard to the messiah. A source of Jewish prayer that is routinely studied by historians and theologians is the book titled *Psalms of Solomon* (a collection of 18 prayers written about 50 years before Jesus was born).

Get Wisdom _____

The *Psalms of Solomon* were not the work of King Solomon, who lived 900 years before the prayers were written. Neither are they an accepted part of Hebrew Scripture. However, many historians believe that they reflect widespread Jewish hopes during the Roman occupation for a kingly messiah who would lead Israel, restore the Jewish nation's sovereignty, and establish a government focused on righteousness and justice.

Here's a passage from the seventeenth Psalm of Solomon that describes the messiah—the "Anointed of the Lord." I've added emphasis when appropriate:

> Behold, O Lord, and raise up unto them their *king*, the *son of David* … that he may *reign over Israel* Thy servant.
>
> And gird him with strength, that he may *shatter unrighteous rulers* …
>
> With a *rod of iron he shall break in pieces all their substance*,
>
> He shall *destroy the godless nations* with the word of his mouth; And he shall *reprove sinners* for the thoughts of their heart.
>
> And he shall *gather together a holy people*, whom he shall lead in righteousness …
>
> He shall have the heathen nations to *serve him under his yoke* …
>
> And he shall glorify the Lord in a place to be seen … And he shall purge Jerusalem, making it holy as of old
>
> And he shall be a *righteous king*, taught by God … And there shall be *no unrighteousness in his days* in their midst. …
>
> And he shall judge the tribes of the people that has been sanctified by the Lord his God. … For all shall be holy and their king *the Anointed of the Lord*.

As you can see, the "messiah" in this prayer will be …

◆ A descendent of King David.

◆ Crowned as the new king of Israel.

◆ A valiant military leader strong enough to rescue Israel from its oppressors by destroying the godless nations (the author certainly had the Roman Empire in mind as the principal godless nation).

◆ A king who ends Israel's exile and brings the Jewish people back to a restored Holy Land and a "purged" capital city (free of unrighteous leaders and priests).

◆ Worthy to rebuild the Temple in Jerusalem.

◆ A righteous judge who ushers in a time of justice and ends sinfulness in Israel.

◆ The author of peace throughout the world, because he will also rule over the heathen nations.

Actions Speak Louder Than Claims

The first-century Jews who believed in a kingly messiah presumed that he would make himself known by successful actions, not merely with claims to his messiahship. They expected a leader to arise, inspire the Jewish people, expel the Romans, triumphantly enter Jerusalem, reclaim David's throne, rebuild the Temple, and judge Israel.

At that point, people would see for themselves that the Messiah had in fact arrived and believers throughout the world would begin to enjoy the many promised benefits of the messianic age.

Suffering Servants Need Not Apply

The priestly messiah pictured in Isaiah who suffered and died an atoning death simply doesn't fit with mainstream expectations of a triumphant military leader and political ruler who would liberate Israel from the Roman occupation and restore the Jewish people to their promised land.

Some ancient rabbis apparently held a "Two-Messiah" theory. They believed that *two* Messiahs were necessary—one a triumphant conqueror, the other the redeemer—to harmonize the different notions of what the Messiah would do. This notion is just steps away from the Christian teaching that Jesus is both Lord and Savior.

People Expected a Live Messiah

A Messiah who was a Davidic king—a leader who some people believed would live and reign forever—would certainly not die a shameful death at the hands of the Roman occupiers. Even a priestly and prophetic messiah needed to be alive to do his work. Consequently, most first-century Jews, including many of Jesus' followers, perceived a dead messiah as *a failed* messiah. He might have been an exceedingly righteous man—a man whose spirit now lived in Heaven with God—but he could not have been the promised Messiah.

It's no wonder that the Apostles couldn't accept the notion that Jesus would die. "From that time on Jesus began to explain to his disciples that he must ... be killed and on the third day be raised to life. Peter took him aside and began to rebuke him. 'Never, Lord!' he said. 'This shall never happen to you!'" (Matthew 16:21–22, NIV)

And it's not by accident that Pontius Pilate chose the title King of the Jews to mock Jesus. As described in John 19:19–20, NRSV: "Pilate also had an inscription written and put on the cross. It read, 'Jesus of Nazareth, the King of the Jews.' ... and it was written in Hebrew, in Latin, and in Greek." Many paintings of the crucifixion and some crucifixes depict a titulus (plaque) bearing the letters INRI above Jesus' head. INRI is a Latin acronym that stands for IESVS NAZARENVS REX IVDÆORVM— Jesus the Nazarene, King of the Jews.

Finally, it shouldn't surprise you that—as I noted in Chapter 5—the Apostles were shaken, demoralized, and wholly discouraged after Jesus' execution. They must have assumed Jesus' ministry was over and that he would soon be forgotten like the failed or false messiahs who had walked the dusty roads of Ancient Israel.

Judas the Galilean

Let me tell you about one whose name you've probably seen. Judas the Galilean was the Jewish rebel leader mentioned in the Book of Acts (see Acts 5:37) and written about by Josephus, the first-century Jewish historian. Judas led a rebellion of Zealots in the year 6 when the Roman governor of the province of Judaea tried to establish new taxes. Acts 5:37, NIV, reports that Judas the Galilean "... was killed, and all his followers were scattered."

Get Wisdom _____

Josephus was a Jewish military leader who somehow managed to survive the First Jewish-Roman War of 66–73, when all of his compatriots committed suicide after their defeat by the Romans. He eventually became a Roman citizen—Titus Flavius Josephus—and became the leading Jewish apologist in the Roman world. He is best known for writing two histories (*History of the Jewish War* and *Antiquities of the Jews*) that managed to survive two millennia. These books provide vital looks into first-century Jewish history—and many of the details he provided (for example, the location of Herod's tomb) have proven to be true—even though modern historians believe that Josephus's writings are self-serving and include pro-Roman propaganda.

According to Josephus ...

- Judas founded Zealotism, a political movement that incited the people of Judaea to revolt against the Roman Empire.

- The Zealots believed that God was their only Ruler and Lord, and were willing to die rather than call the Roman Emperor lord.

- The Zealots became the driving force that led to the First Roman-Jewish War (66–70) and the eventual destruction of Jerusalem by the Romans in the year 70.

After his death, Judas's sons and grandsons took over the movement, and each, in turn, was called *the messiah*. This makes it likely that Judas had claimed the same title and that his national liberation movement was seen as messianic.

Why Not James the Messiah?

When a supposed "messiah" like Judas the Galilean was killed, leadership of the movement (if it survived) would pass to a close relative. Early Christianity could have followed the same pattern and declared James, the brother of Jesus, the new "messiah." After all, James was a highly respected elder of the church in Jerusalem (see, for example, Acts 21:18).

But the earliest Christians continued to claim that Jesus was the promised Messiah, even though he'd been executed by the Romans, and even though he hadn't met the mainstream expectations of what the Messiah should accomplish. Given the circumstances—including close Roman scrutiny of potentially rebellious sects—their assertion of Jesus as Messiah seem both foolish and foolhardy ... *unless* they were confident that Jesus was alive, because he had been resurrected (see Chapter 5).

Making Sense of the Messiah

History doesn't record who among the earliest Christians were most instrumental in making sense of the conflicting messianic expectations. Paul probably played an important role—although by the time he wrote his letters, Jesus the Christ was a well-established teaching.

The first-century Christians considered it important that Jesus of Nazareth was of King David's line, but they apparently didn't declare that the resurrected Jesus would reestablish King David's throne in Jerusalem.

These same early Christians didn't raise bands of rebels or do anything that the Romans would perceive as a direct military threat. And yet, they confessed that Jesus is Lord, a politically charged proclamation that refuted Roman claims that Caesar was lord.

Above all, the earliest Christians redefined the common notion of the warrior messiah. Rather, they saw in the resurrected Jesus the power to bring God's love, justice, and kingdom of peace. And soon after that they came to believe that Jesus' atoning death restored humankind's relationship with God.

The Least You Need to Know

◆ The term *messiah* conjured up many different images in Ancient Israel—although not all first-century Jews believed that a Messiah was coming.

◆ The most prevalent belief was that the Messiah promised in the Hebrew Scriptures would be a triumphant king from the line of David who would kick out the Roman occupiers and restore Israel's freedom.

◆ Some first-century Jews believed in a different kind of messiah—a priestly Messiah who would be the suffering servant who would take on humanity's iniquity.

◆ Jesus' followers were shaken, demoralized, and wholly discouraged by Jesus' execution, because a dead messiah was considered a failed messiah.

◆ Jesus' Resurrection gave followers the confidence to proclaim that Jesus was the promised Messiah, although in a wholly different way than most people in Ancient Israel had anticipated.

◆ Christians teach that Jesus' Messiahship was prophesied in the Old Testament—and is easy to identify once you recognize that Jesus is both Lord and Savior.

Part  3

The Mysteries of Jesus' Ministry

Before Jesus became a Savior, he was a healer, an exorcist, a teacher, and a prophet. Throughout his short ministry, he performed miracles that demonstrated his power over nature, demons, disease, and disability.

On the one hand, Jesus helped people in need. On the other hand, he provided "credentials"—indisputable evidence that proved he was the promised Messiah.

There's intriguing mystery in every aspect of Jesus' miracles, and also in the bewildering things that Jesus said during his ministry.

14

The Mystery of Jesus' Healings

In This Chapter

- ◆ Twenty of Jesus' thirty-six recorded miracles were healings
- ◆ Jesus healed to established his "credentials" as the Messiah
- ◆ Some healings taught lessons about grace and the Kingdom of God
- ◆ Did Jesus really perform miracles?
- ◆ Jesus: a miracle-worker with an unusual style
- ◆ Miracles 101

Jesus of Nazareth was a successful healer during his short ministry in Judea, Galilee, and Samaria. Before Jesus saved humankind with his atoning death, he saved (in a different sense) dozens, perhaps hundreds, of people by healing and occasionally raising them from the dead.

In this chapter, I'll tell you about the relevance of these miracles and the broader messages that Jesus may have wanted to send with his healings (in addition to his obvious desire to help people in need). And because this is the first chapter that examines Jesus' miracles, I'll also give you an overview of miracles—and the arguments for and against the possibility that miracles actually happen (see the section "A Short Course on Miracles" later in the chapter).

Jesus Heals and Saves

Christians view Jesus of Nazareth as a miracle worker in every sense of the term. For starters, there were the miracles that led to his being fully God, fully man: the Incarnation (see Chapter 2) and the Virgin Birth (see Chapter 9). After his death came the miracle of the Resurrection (see Chapter 5). And then there were the numerous miracles he performed during his ministry. These fall into four categories:

- ◆ Healings of many people with various diseases and birth defects (including several mass healings that make it impossible to total the number of individuals he helped)

- ◆ A handful of resuscitations that brought dead people back to life (these are considered resuscitations rather than resurrections, because we must take for granted that the people eventually died)

- ◆ Exorcisms to drive out demons (see Chapter 15)

- ◆ Miracles that displayed his power over nature—for example, by turning water into wine and calming a storm (see Chapter 16)

Jesus Focused on Healing

Most of all, Jesus the miracle worker was a *healer*. Twenty of the 36 reported miracles were healings and resuscitations (for convenience, I'll group them together). Of course, unlike many so-called "miracle workers" today, Jesus did not perform miraculous healings for personal gain.

Scripture Says
Although the best-known healing miracles have Jesus healing individuals, he also performed mass healings. For example: "Jesus left there and went along the Sea of Galilee. Then he went up on a mountainside and sat down. Great crowds came to him, bringing the lame, the blind, the crippled, the mute and many others, and laid them at his feet; and he healed them. The people were amazed when they saw the mute speaking, the crippled made well, the lame walking and the blind seeing. And they praised the God of Israel" (see Matthew 15:29–31).

We can be sure that stories about Jesus' miracles circulated throughout Judea, Samaria, and Galilee long before the Gospels were written—in fact, long before Jesus' ministry was over. The proof can be found in the large crowds that reportedly followed Jesus around. In an age of limited medical care, many of these people would have seen Jesus the miracle worker as their only source of help for otherwise incurable ailments. Others who followed Jesus probably had heard stories of his astonishing healings and wanted to witness Jesus at work.

Consider that healing the sick, blind, and lame demonstrated Jesus' truly supernatural powers in an easy to understand—and wholly nonthreatening—manner. Witnesses to Jesus' nature miracles were often frightened by the experience (see Mark 4:39–41). On the other hand, onlookers were amazed (ostensibly in a gentle way) by Jesus' healings (see Luke 5:24–26).

Surprisingly, even the resuscitations of dead people didn't seem to frighten the onlookers. (See Luke 8:41–53, the resuscitation of Jarius's daughter, and John 11:38–44, the resuscitation of Lazarus after three days in his tomb.)

Apparently, the only group of people who remained wholly unimpressed by Jesus' prowess as a healer were the residents of Nazareth, his home town. The story told in Mark 6:5–6 implies that the Nazarenes had such little faith in Jesus that few of them thought about asking Jesus to perform a significant miracle. And so, during his stays in Nazareth he only had the opportunity to perform a few traditional healings done with laying on of hands.

Why Jesus Healed People

The Gospels make clear that Jesus healed people for three primary reasons.

First, Jesus healed people because he had compassion for people living with birth defects (such as congenital blindness), individuals afflicted with chronic illnesses (such as leprosy), or those who'd lost loved ones (such as Mary, the sister of Lazarus). A good Scriptural example of this motivation can be found in Matthew 14:14, NIV: "When Jesus landed [in his boat] and saw a large crowd, he had compassion on them and healed their sick."

Second, Jesus healed people to establish his messianic credentials by providing signs and wonders to onlookers (I'll talk about these in the next section). Acts 2:22, NIV, offers a fine summary description of this idea: "Jesus of Nazareth was a man accredited by God to you by miracles, wonders and signs, which God did among you through him …." The healing miracles, performed by Jesus himself rather than in God's name, were evidence that Jesus was much more than a mere rabbi.

Third, Jesus used healings to fulfill the prophecies about the promised Messiah. Perhaps the best known example can be found in Matthew 8:16–17, NIV: "When evening came ... he healed all the sick. This was to fulfill what was spoken through the prophet Isaiah: 'He took up our infirmities and carried our diseases.'" (This refers to Isaiah 53:4—Matthew couldn't identify the specific verse, because the verse numbering system wasn't developed until the thirteenth century.)

Christians who read the Bible carefully find three more reasons for Jesus' healings.

> **Scripture Says**
>
> John 10:37–38, NIV, is another oft-cited New-Testament passage that demonstrates how Jesus used miracles to establish his credentials: "Do not believe me unless I do what my Father does. But if I do it, even though you do not believe me, believe the miracles, that you may know and understand that the Father is in me, and I in the Father."

Fourth, some of the people healed by Jesus went on to become his followers, possibly out of gratitude, but more likely because of even deeper belief in Jesus generated by the healings, coupled with a sense that each healing included a call to follow Jesus.

Fifth, Jesus used some of his healings in much the same way as he used his parables—to teach onlookers about salvation and the Kingdom of God. A good example of this is the long discussion toward the end of John 9:1–41, NIV. After curing the man born blind at birth, Jesus challenges the Pharisees who had launched a formal investigation into the healing. He uses "seeing" as a metaphor for understanding. Jesus said, "For judgment I have come into this world, so that the blind will see and those who see will become blind." Some Pharisees who were with him heard him say this and asked, "What? Are we blind too?" Jesus said, "If you were blind, you would not be guilty of sin; but now that you claim you can see, your guilt remains. (John 9:39–41, NIV)

Jesus' point seems to be that of all the people in ancient Israel, the Pharisees were the best equipped in terms of education and training to "see" the real Jesus. Yet they refused to recognize who Jesus was.

Sixth, Jesus took advantage of a few healings to communicate more about himself, his ministry, and the ultimate purpose of the Incarnation. The most obvious example is the story, told in Luke 5:18–25, of the paralytic lowered in front of Jesus through a hole in the roof: "When Jesus saw their faith, he said, 'Friend, your sins are forgiven.'" (Luke 5:20, NIV) This was tantamount to claiming that he had the authority to decide who would receive salvation.

Jesus must have known that his words would shake up the Pharisee onlookers because they firmly believed that only God can forgive sins. They concluded that Jesus had blasphemed God. Jesus defended himself by launching a frontal attack on the Pharisees: "'But that you may know that the Son of Man has authority on earth to forgive sins ….' He said to the paralyzed man, 'I tell you, get up, take your mat and go home.' Immediately he stood up in front of them, took what he had been lying on and went home praising God." (Luke 5:24–25, NIV)

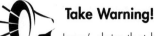

Take Warning!

Jesus' claim that he'd forgiven the paralytic's sins does not mean that Jesus believed that the man's disability represented some sort of punishment for his sin—a common notion in ancient Israel (reaffirmed by the Pharisees in John 9:34). Jesus challenges the connection between sin and illness or injury in Luke (13:1–5) and John (9:1–3).

Miracles, Wonders, and Signs

The English Bible translations that you and I read use three words to describe the extraordinary things Jesus did during his ministry: miracles, wonders, and signs. Three words are necessary, because they translate from three different Greek words, each with a subtly distinctive meaning:

- *Miracle* is typically used to translate a Greek word that means "miraculous power" or "that which is done with miraculous power." It can also imply power and strength, or a mighty work. Consequently, it includes the concept that performing miracles requires the kinds of powers possessed only by God.

- *Wonder* is used to translate a Greek word that means "wonder," an "object of wonder," or "something (an omen, for example) that foretells a coming event." It communicates the impact of a truly miraculous event on the mind and imagination of a witness, and also conveys the idea that the miracle worker has shown that he satisfies some sort of prophesy.

- *Sign* is used to translate a Greek word that expresses the concept of "signal" or "indication." It expresses more strongly the notion that the performer of a miraculous act fulfills a prophesy or prediction.

Scripture often links the two related words together: "signs and wonders." Acts 14:3, NIV, illustrates the related meanings of "signs and wonders": "So Paul and Barnabas spent considerable time there [in Iconium], speaking boldly for the Lord, who confirmed the message of his grace by enabling them to do miraculous signs and wonders."

Miracles and the Messiah

The devout Jews in the Holy Land had numerous expectations about the promised Messiah (see Chapter 13). One of them was that the Messiah would have the power to cast out demons and perform significant healings.

Many Jews believed that Bible verses such as Isaiah 29:18, NIV, meant that one sign of the arrival of the authentic Messiah would be his superlative skills as a healer: "In that day the deaf will hear the words of the scroll, and out of gloom and darkness the eyes of the blind will see." Deafness and blindness are largely irreversible conditions today—and were wholly permanent during the first century. Simply put, the Messiah would be able to effect impossible healings that were beyond any other healer. Isaiah 35:6, NIV, goes on to add, "Then will the lame leap like a deer, and the mute tongue shout for joy."

Jesus' many healings—performed throughout ancient Israel and witnessed by hundreds (perhaps thousands) of people—left no doubt that he met (and exceeded) these prophetic expectations.

Matthew recounts the healings of two pairs of blind men, who though sightless, somehow knew that Jesus was the Messiah. The first pair (see Matthew 9:27–29) call Jesus "Son of David." The second pair (see Matthew 20:29–34) call Jesus "Lord, Son of David." Matthew uses these almost identical healing double-headers as literary bookends in his Gospel. The first twin healing seems to define the specific point in Jesus' ministry when ordinary people began to feel confident that Jesus was in fact the promised Messiah. Although Matthew records that Jesus performed earlier healings, they apparently provided the signs and wonders that testified to Jesus' special abilities and made onlookers think that he might be the anticipated Son of David.

Get Wisdom

Theologians call Jesus' requests not to tell anyone who he was the "Messianic Secret." This seems to be a special emphasis in the Gospel of Mark; he records Jesus admonishing his followers to keep silent six times.

It's interesting that Jesus "warned them sternly, 'See that no one knows about this'" after the healing. (Matthew 9:30, NIV) Theologians have advanced many explanations for Jesus' desire for secrecy, but I like the simplest one best: Jesus knew that his ministry would change dramatically after the word got out—not necessarily for the better. I also noted one of Jesus' "tell-no-one" commands previously in Chapter 13.

The second double healing in Matthew signals that the days of Jesus' public ministry had come to an end. Immediately afterward, Jesus rode triumphantly into Jerusalem. Less than a week later he was crucified.

Jesus' Unusual Miracle-Working Style

Scholars note that Jesus' approach to performing miracles had its own unique style, that he was a distinctively different kind of miracle worker:

◆ Unlike the other Jewish healers of his day, Jesus could cure an ailment without invoking God's name or even praying—he seemingly healed on the basis of his own authority.

◆ He performed miracles without much fanfare, often unpretentiously, even anonymously.

◆ He performed miracles in a remarkably unfussy way, usually by speaking a few words or making a simple gesture—and sometimes at a distance, with no words or gestures at all.

But even these minimalist actions may have been unnecessary, because Jesus virtually broadcast healing power to all around him.

Jesus the Power Healer

Jesus didn't need to do anything for people to take advantage of his healing power. As Matthew 14:36, NIV, reports "and all who touched him were healed."

Perhaps the most well known "power healing" is reported in Mark 5:25–29—the story of the woman who had been bleeding for 12 years. She moved behind Jesus in a crowd, touched his cloak, and was immediately healed. Jesus then noticed that he had, without any action on his part, delivered a jolt of curative power.

Large groups of people could take advantage of Jesus' healing power, as demonstrated in Luke 6:17–19, NIV: "A large crowd of his disciples was there and a great number of people from all over Judea, from Jerusalem, and from the coast of Tyre and Sidon, who had come to hear him and to be healed of their diseases … and the people all tried to touch him, because power was coming from him and healing them all."

Power healing represents one of the most miraculous (and mysterious) aspects of Jesus' healing abilities—a capability that strikes many Christians as thousands of years ahead of its time, and which would fit nicely in a contemporary science fiction story. This further separates Jesus from other healers in ancient Israel.

Healing and Faith

The *Synoptic Gospel* (Matthew, Mark, and Luke) reports of Jesus' healings frequently have him say "… your faith has healed you," or something similar. One of many examples is Mark 5:34. These healings happened during Jesus' ministry, long before there were early Christians who had faith in Jesus as Lord and Savior. So the obvious question is what kind of "faith" was Jesus talking about? It seems to be the belief that Jesus of Nazareth—the rabbi, the prophet, the likely Messiah—had the power to heal virtually any malady.

However, there's no indication that having this kind of faith was a prerequisite for receiving Jesus' help. The invalid in the pool at Bethesda (see John 5:1–9) seemed not to have any preconceived belief that Jesus could help him. (Jesus even asked him "Do you want to get well?") Scholars believe that it was the widespread belief that Jesus could cure that made other sick or disabled people push through the crowds and keep asking to be healed.

Healing and Restoration

The ancient Hebrew "purity laws" forbade imperfect sacrifices to God (see Deuteronomy 15:21) and imperfect priests to offer them. The Hebrew Scriptures spelled out detailed "cleanliness" requirements for temple priests, "the descendants of Aaron." Here, for example, is Leviticus 21:16–20, NIV:

> The LORD said to Moses, "Say to Aaron: 'For the generations to come none of your descendants who has a defect may come near to offer the food of his God. No man who has any defect may come near: no man who is blind or lame, disfigured or deformed; no man with a crippled foot or hand, or who is hunchbacked or dwarfed, or who has any eye defect, or who has festering or running sores ….'"

Many scholars believe these rules trickled down to the ordinary populace and that the temple leaders established rules that banished the chronically ill and disabled from all but a few temple precincts. When Jesus healed the sick, he also restored them to full status as Jews—and symbolically to full citizenship in the Kingdom of God.

Reading Between the Lines

Most Christians come away inspired when they read the miracle stories, but few take the trouble to look inside and see what else can be found "between the lines." These extras can be really interesting. You'll find them easy to spot, once I point you in the right direction.

The Gospel Spin

The three Synoptic Gospels—Matthew, Mark, and Luke—offer similar views of Jesus' miracles, signs, and wonders. But the accounts are not identical. Each writer put a distinctive spin on the healing stories. Scholars analyze the differences among the Gospels to identify the specific emphasis intended by each of the three authors.

When Mark reports the miraculous healings, he often emphasizes that Jesus has made use of powers that belong to God—and has consequently demonstrated that he is the promised Messiah. As I noted earlier, Jesus often tells those he's cured and onlookers to keep the Messianic Secret—which no one does. This seems to be a literary device Mark used to further make the point that people quickly recognized Jesus as the Messiah.

Matthew, more than the other Gospels, emphasizes that Jesus' compassion and mercy were key motivations for the healing he performed. To show you what I mean, compare the second healing of two blind men as told by Matthew (9:35–36) with the parallel story of Jesus restoring Bartimaeus' sight told by Mark (10:46–52). Matthew zeros in on Jesus' compassion, while Mark notes Bartimaeus' belief in the Messiah's ability to heal. (Mark also leaves out the second blind man.)

Luke's Jesus often stresses the holistic link between healing, salvation, forgiveness, and restoration to community. (Many first-century Jews saw healing as a physical analogy to forgiveness from sins.) For example, in the story of Jesus healing the ten lepers (see Luke 17:11–19), only one of the ten—a non-Jewish Samaritan—returned to praise God. He threw himself at Jesus' feet and thanked him. Jesus said to the man, "Rise and go; your faith has made you well." (Luke 17:19, NIV) Because Jesus said this long after the man had been healed—and because "your faith has made you well" can also be translated as "your faith has saved you"—many scholars believe that the Samaritan received salvation in addition to a cure for leprosy.

The lesson in this linkage is easy to interpret: Jesus the miracle worker also has the power to forgive sins and restore your relationship with God.

What About the Gospel of John?

Well, John seems to use stories of miraculous healings to emphasize Jesus' uniqueness—that he has the power to heal in ways far-beyond the other healers in ancient Israel. For example, none of them could restore the sight of someone born blind; Jesus could (see John 9:1–7). And no one else would even think of resuscitating a man dead for three days; Jesus would (see John 11:43–44).

Look for the Symbolism

Many of the healings described in the Gospels are simply that—healings. But some of the reports are laden with symbolism that invites the reader to expand their interpretation of the stories. For example, John describes the feeding of the 5,000 in John 6:1–13. But then, in 6:26–36, we learn that the feeding of the multitudes is also a symbolic act. This is because Jesus is the "true bread" who came down from heaven—bread that gives life to the world.

Take Warning!

It's possible to read bizarre meanings into the healings—meanings that aren't in the Gospels. You'll often find this kind of eisegesis (the inappropriate process of "reading meaning into" a Biblical passage) in weak Bible studies. I remember one study that claimed (incorrectly!) that Jesus' talk about forgiveness during some healings was a warning that a lack of forgiveness would be punished with serious disease. Consider carefully when someone tries to extract a life-lesson from one of Jesus' healings.

A Short Course on Miracles

I'll end this chapter with a section on miracles because this and the following two chapters are about Jesus' many miracles. Feel free to skip this material if you have all the information you need on the topic.

The first thing you should know about miracles is that it's impossible to prove that they happen—or that they don't happen. Consequently, it's futile to argue about miraculous events, because the debate between believer and unbeliever quickly turns into an intellectual stalemate.

A doubter will typically examine the Gospel record of the various healing miracles that are credited to Jesus, and then say such things as:

◆ The Gospel writers got the details wrong.

◆ Most of Jesus' patients had psychosomatic or minor ailments that seemed more serious than they were—and got better because they *thought* that Jesus healed them.

◆ Jesus used the same trick as some modern faith healers—the flashy "healing" of an accomplice who isn't sick at all.

◆ Jesus was an expert physician who used herbs and folk cures to heal not-so-sick people with simple medicines.

Skeptics find these so-called "logical explanations" more credible than the notion that Jesus, fully God and fully man, was a kind of medicinal dynamo who broadcast healing power.

A Christian need merely reply: "I understand how you feel. It can be difficult to accept that Jesus used the power of God to heal people in ancient Judea, Galilee, and Samaria, but I believe that's exactly what happened. You can't prove I'm wrong."

What's a Miracle?

One of the most popular definitions of a *miracle* is credited to David Hume, an eighteenth-century Enlightenment philosopher, economist, and historian who vehemently argued that miracles don't happen. According to Hume, "A miracle is a violation of the laws of nature."

You'll note that Hume, who may have been an atheist, didn't specify the cause of the "violation." Other definitions of "miracle" that build upon Hume's usually go on to say that God intervened to change the usual way that nature works.

def•i•ni•tion

The English word **miracle** is from the Latin word *miraculum*, which means "something wonderful." The contemporary meaning is an event that can't be explained by the laws of nature and consequently is held to be supernatural and/or an act of God.

Science to the Rescue

To unbelievers, science is a kind of magic elixir, a super weapon that will once and for all win the battle over Jesus' miracles that has raged for the past two millennia.

Alas, it doesn't do any good for a skeptic to claim that those "first-century simpletons" merely assumed they were witnessing miracles because they didn't have science to explain how apparently miraculous things happen within the laws of nature. You see, science describes *what* routinely happens in nature; a miracle, by definition, is a *non*routine natural event, and outside the purview of science. If anything, the scientific method lets us sharpen our ideas of which events we should consider miraculous, because science helps to delineate the scope of natural events by discovering the laws of nature.

The bottom line: most Christians assert that the Gospel miracles happened, nonbelievers (and some Christian skeptics) insist that they did not.

The battle goes on!

Miracles Happen Rarely

A simple but important truth about miracles makes a useful alternative definition: miracles are things that happen rarely. We don't expect to witness lots of people walking on water or numerous people blind from birth inexplicably receiving their sight. The rarity of these events is one of the reasons we consider them miraculous.

If a supposed miracle were to happen too often, both Christians and nonbelievers would challenge the reality of the "law of nature" that was allegedly being violated. For the same reason, if God performed the same miracle over and over again, Christians would begin to assume that God had made changes to a previously accepted law of nature.

Get Wisdom

Some doubters claim that the Gospel reports of Jesus' major miracles are theologoumenons—inventions to show that Jesus provided the signs and wonders expected of the promised Messiah. However, most of these unbelievers acknowledge that healing has been a core aspect of Christianity since the first century. This indicates that early Christians believed that Jesus was an effective healer, and that the Gospel healing stories were based on a robust oral tradition.

These notions about miracles go back thousands of years. The fact that Jesus' contemporaries saw his healings as miraculous signs or wonders meant that astonishing cures—the blind seeing, the lame leaping, lepers healed—happened infrequently, if at all. Onlookers back then were probably just as skeptical as doubters would be today. The chief difference was that in the first century people were far more willing to attribute miraculous events to God.

Do Miracles Happen Today?

Some Christians say *yes*, while others argue that miracles stopped happening after the end of the Apostolic age. One of the biggest areas of controversy involves healings. It's hard to find a Christian who hasn't heard about a "miraculous cure"—often of a close friend or relative.

Were these genuine healings or merely coincidences—events when the patients recovered on their own without God's intervention? Are there Christians who have the power to bring healing with the help of God? Do Christian healing rituals—such as laying on of hands and anointing—actually work?

I won't even try to answer these questions here. What I will do is offer three tests based on passages of Scripture that can be used to validate genuine healing miracles:

- Jesus' healing miracles all glorified God. And Paul noted that people with the gift of healing are appointed to the church (see 1 Corinthians 12:28). Be wary of any modern miracle worker who steals the limelight. Also, note that Christians assert that no one today can heal in his or her own authority, like Jesus did.

- Jesus warned that the time would come when false prophets will "appear and perform great signs and miracles to deceive even the elect—if that were possible." (see Matt. 24:24, NIV) Be wary of false prophets who may have powers to heal that are not from God.

- When Jesus healed 10 lepers (see Luke 17:14) he sent them to the priests for examination. In Old-Testament Israel the priests had the responsibility for diagnosing leprosy (see Leviticus 13:2–8). Simply put, Jesus urged that his miraculous healing be confirmed by experts. The same approach makes sense today: purported healings shouldn't be considered miracles until verified by appropriate medical experts.

These tests don't presume that miracles don't occur today; rather, they reflect the sad truth that many so-called miraculous events are fraudulent or overstated. If an event is truly an act of God, it will pass easily through these gates.

The Least You Need to Know

- Twenty of Jesus' 36 miracles recorded in the Gospels are healings: immediate cures of various illnesses or resuscitations of dead people.

- Jesus healed people out of compassion and to establish his credentials as the promised Messiah.

- Jesus was a unique healer—a genuine miracle worker—who could heal any disease or birth defect, even blindness at birth, which other Jewish healers of the day couldn't accomplish.

◆ Jesus healed on the basis of his own authority; the various Gospel reports show that he never performed a healing in God's name or even prayed before beginning.

◆ Jesus often asked the people he helped not to tell anyone they recognized him as the promised Messiah (scholars call this the Messianic Secret).

◆ Miracles are events that can't be explained by the laws of nature, and are thus credited to supernatural causes, typically acts of God.

Chapter 15

The Mystery of Jesus' Power Over Demons

In This Chapter

- Jesus often exorcised demons
- Jesus could cast out demons under his own authority
- Jesus proved he ruled the spiritual realm
- The first victories in his spiritual war with Satan
- More evidence that Jesus is the Son of God

Christians teach that Jesus had the power to cast out demons from possessed people by simply ordering them to go. The handful of exorcisms described in the three Synoptic Gospels are among the most mystery-filled stories in the New Testament—some because of the demonic challenge Jesus faced, others because of the noteworthy events that surrounded the actual casting out of the demons.

In this chapter, I'll share interesting details about each of the reported exorcisms with an eye toward giving "the rest of the story." Because the

Gospel reports are chock full of important information, I've included a complete set of relevant verses about each exorcism (from a single Gospel).

Jesus of Nazareth: A Demon's Worst Nightmare

If you read the Old Testament, you won't find prophecy or prediction about the promised Messiah's ability to drive out demons. Hebrew Scriptures make clear that the "Son of David" will sit on David's throne and reign over Israel and the nations, but it doesn't go on to say that the Messiah will have power over evil spirits.

In fact, the Old Testament says little about demons, except that evil spirits were sent by God to torment wrongdoers (see, for example, 1 Samuel 16:14).

And yet, as you'll see later in this chapter, the demons that Jesus cast out recognized him immediately as the Son of God. Moreover, at least some first-century Jews believed that the Messiah would bring an end to Satan's kingdom. And the onlookers who watched Jesus's successful exorcisms wondered if he was the Son of David (see Matthew 12:23).

Most important of all, Jesus clearly believed that controlling unclean spirits was an important role. He saw his power over demons as a sign that his ministry had inaugurated the reign of the kingdom of God in a new and unexpected way (see Luke 11:20).

Jewish exorcists apparently cast out demons in the Holy Land before and after Jesus arrived on the scene (see Acts 19:13). But unlike them, Jesus never needed incantations or prayers, nor did he appeal to any outside authority. He commanded demons to leave and they did. Jesus did however acknowledge that he cast out demons by the finger of God, a vivid figure of speech for God's power (see Luke 11:20), which Jesus possessed by virtue of his divinity.

Get Wisdom

To understand why Jesus' ability to drive out demons on his own authority astonished people, consider the story of the unnamed exorcist (see Mark 9:38–40). He cast out demons in Jesus' name (until the Apostles intervened, because he wasn't one of Jesus' recognized followers). Invoking God's name was the standard exorcism procedure; a process well known to onlookers. "The crowds were amazed, and were saying, 'Nothing like this has ever been seen in Israel'." (Matthew 9:33, NIV)

Jesus delegated specific authority to his followers to cast out demons in his name (see Matthew 10:1,8), but they were not as powerful exorcists as Jesus and experienced one significant reported failure (a small boy, as you'll see later in this chapter). Jesus provided two explanations for their lack of success:

◆ The Apostles lacked sufficient faith (see Matthew 17:14–20).

◆ Casting out that kind of demon required lots of preliminary prayer (see Mark 9:14–29).

The ABCs of Demons

The Gospels of Matthew, Mark, and Luke use three terms to label evil spirit beings who have the power to possess people: "demon," "unclean spirit," and "evil spirit." Demon is a transliteration of the Greek word *daimon*, which means "a spiritual being of a lower order" (somewhere between the gods and humankind)—not necessarily evil.

In Scripture, *demon* means an evil spirit and *angel* a good spirit. A *demoniac* is an individual inhabited by one or more demons that cause illness, bizarre demeanor, and destructive behavior.

When Jesus dealt with a demon, he typically rebuked (scolded) it first, then ordered it to shut up, then finally cast it out—ordered it to leave the demoniac. On occasion, he ordered it never to return. As I've noted, no other exorcist—before or since—had this level of direct authority over evil spirits.

> **Walking with the Wise**
>
> There are two equal and opposite errors into which our race can fall about the devils. One is to disbelieve in their existence. The other is to believe, and to feel an excessive and unhealthy interest in them. They themselves are equally pleased by both errors ....
> —C. S. Lewis, in the preface to *The Screwtape Letters*

It's probably true that most of what the typical Christian knows about demons comes from movies like *The Exorcist*. Demons are popular villains in Hollywood. The Gospel writers don't say much by way of explanation—they assume their readers are well informed about demons, which suggests that most people in the first century ...

◆ Believed demons existed and that they could be dangerous.

◆ Understood them as spiritual beings.

- Understood their powers over people.

- Probably had different explanations about how a person might be taken over by a demon.

- Believed that exorcists could cast out demons.

- Appreciated that there were different kinds of demons and that some were resistant to exoricisms.

Are Demons Metaphors for Mental Illness?

Several of the demonized people described in the Gospels displayed behaviors that resemble the symptoms of mental and neurological diseases. For example, the boy who threw himself to the ground (see Mark 9:16–29, and later in this chapter) might have had epilepsy. Consequently, some skeptics who doubt that demons exist argue that Jesus actually healed mental illness rather than cast out demons. (They often go on to claim that the concept of demons was invented to provide a language for talking about mental illness long before it was understood).

A boy who might or might not have had epilepsy is one thing, but it's much harder to make the mental-illness case for the Gerasene Demonic (see Mark 5:1–20, and later in this chapter), where the legion of cast-out demons subsequently possessed a herd of pigs.

Jesus Drives Out an Evil Spirit at Capernaum

They went to Capernaum; and when the sabbath came, he entered the synagogue and taught. … Just then there was in their synagogue a man with an unclean spirit, and he cried out, "What have you to do with us, Jesus of Nazareth? Have you come to destroy us? I know who you are, the Holy One of God." But Jesus rebuked him, saying, "Be silent, and come out of him!" And the unclean spirit, convulsing him and crying with a loud voice, came out of him. They were all amazed, and they kept on asking one another, "What is this? … He commands even the unclean spirits, and they obey him." At once his fame began to spread throughout the surrounding region of Galilee. (Mark 1:21–28, NRSV)

Here we have the story of a not-very-bright demon, who went out of his way to challenge Jesus—and attract his attention—when he'd finished teaching a lesson at a synagogue in Capernaum.

Several aspects of what happened are noteworthy:

◆ The demon knew who Jesus was—probably the only being in the church who did that early in Jesus' ministry.

◆ The demon was obviously frightened and knew that Jesus had the power to destroy evil.

◆ The bystanders were astonished by Jesus' authority to command, and cast out, demons—a typical reaction.

◆ Although the onlookers talked about the exorcism, they seemingly did not put the pieces together and acknowledge Jesus as the promised Messiah.

> **Get Wisdom**
>
> Capernaum was an important trading city near Lake Gennesaret, the fishing grounds where Paul and several other Apostles had worked. Jesus apparently spent so much time there—possibly at Peter's home—that Mark 2:1 has Jesus coming "home" to Capernaum.

Jesus Heals the Gerasene Demonic

Then they arrived at the country of the Gerasenes, which is opposite Galilee. And as he [Jesus] stepped out on land, there met him a man from the city who had demons; for a long time he had worn no clothes, and he lived not in a house but among the tombs. When he saw Jesus, he cried out and fell down before him, and said with a loud voice, "What have you to do with me, Jesus, Son of the Most High God? I beseech you, do not torment me." For he had commanded the unclean spirit to come out of the man. (For many a time it had seized him; he was kept under guard, and bound with chains and fetters, but he broke the bonds and was driven by the demon into the desert.)

Jesus then asked him, "What is your name?" And he said, "Legion"; for many demons had entered him. And they begged him not to command them to depart into the abyss. Now a large herd of swine was feeding there on the hillside; and they begged him to let them enter these. So he gave them leave. Then the demons came out of the man and entered the swine, and the herd rushed down the steep bank into the lake and were drowned. … Then people went out to see what had happened, and they came to Jesus, and found the man from whom the demons had gone, sitting at the feet of Jesus, clothed and in his right mind; and they were afraid. … The man from whom the demons had gone begged that he might be with him; but he sent him away, saying, "Return to your home, and declare how much God has done for you." And he went away, proclaiming throughout the whole city how much Jesus had done for him. (Luke 8:26–39, RSV)

This is the most complex of the Biblical exorcism stories, the one that would make a great movie filled with special effects. Jesus confronts a naked man who lives in the local cemetery—a man strong enough to break the chains that local townsfolk used to imprison him and wander into the wilderness.

Jesus had apparently recognized the man as a demoniac before he saw him, and had begun to cast out the evil spirit—who reacts angrily when he finally comes face to face with "Son of the Most High God."

The demon identifies himself as "Legion," meaning that countless evil spirits have taken up residence inside the demoniac. In a curious twist, Jesus allows the demons to flee to a herd of pigs, but then the pigs rush into the lake (the Sea of Galilee) and drown.

There are several interesting aspects to this story:

- The "country of the Gerasenes" was a Gentile region of the Holy Land—which explains the nearby herd of pigs.

- The exorcism transformed the demoniac from someone living more like an animal than a man, into a functioning person, fully clothed, capable of rational thought, and with his own identity restored.

- The man was probably not Jewish, making him an especially valuable witness to other Gentiles in his home city.

- Although Jesus had invited other healed people to follow him, this man's unique testimony seems to be reason that Jesus didn't allow him to become a follower. Instead, Jesus gave him a special commission in his own community.

Get Wisdom

Many scholars have pointed out the story of the Gerasene Demonic can also be read as an anti-Roman parable. "Legion," of course, was the largest military unit of the Roman army (anywhere from 3,000 to 6,000 men). And the symbol on the banner of the Legion that occupied Judea was apparently a boar (a male wild pig). Jesus triumphed by sending the thousands of demon-infested pigs to watery deaths.

Jesus Heals the Syrophoenician Woman's Daughter

Jesus left that place and went to the vicinity of Tyre. He entered a house and did not want anyone to know it; yet he could not keep his presence secret. In fact, as soon as she heard about him, a woman whose little daughter was possessed by an evil spirit came and fell at his feet. The woman was a Greek, born in Syrian Phoenicia. She begged Jesus to drive the demon out of her daughter.

"First let the children eat all they want," he told her, "for it is not right to take the children's bread and toss it to their dogs."

"Yes, Lord," she replied, "but even the dogs under the table eat the children's crumbs." Then he told her, "For such a reply, you may go; the demon has left your daughter." She went home and found her child lying on the bed, and the demon gone. (Mark 7:24–30, NIV)

In this Gospel report we learn almost nothing about exorcisms—other than Jesus can cast out demons at a distance, virtually instantly. But, we run headfirst into one of Jesus' hardest sayings (see Chapter 17).

The text seems to say that Jesus called this worried Gentile mother a "dog." When she begged him to remove a demon from her sick daughter, Jesus replied, "First let the children eat all they want, for it is not right to take the children's bread and toss it to their dogs."

There's little argument among scholars about the first half of the verse. Jesus plainly meant that the children of Israel are to receive God's love and care first—including the casting out of demons. So far, so good. But then, Jesus says it's wrong to toss these things to their "dogs"—which many people read as a slur against the woman.

Jesus' answer has puzzled Christians, baffled pastors, and discouraged apologists for many centuries. The statement is a favorite of Christianity's opponents who hold it up as evidence that "the real" Jesus was intolerant, unkind, uncharitable—and certainly not divine in the way he loved strangers.

Although we may never really explain this mystery, I've found an answer that satisfies me in early translations of the Bible: Here's how the King James Version translates the phrase: "Let the children first be filled: for it is not meet to take the children's bread, and to cast it unto the dogs." (Mark 7:27, KJV) And here's the much newer, but related, Revised Standard Version: "Let the children first be fed, for it is not right to take the children's bread and throw it to the dogs." (Mark 7:27, RSV) Both suggest to me that Jesus' reply was meant as an inside-out question to the woman: Wouldn't it be *wasteful* at this stage of his ministry to shift his healing work to a part of the world where people didn't grasp its purpose?

The woman's witty reply pleased Jesus for several reasons:

◆ She demonstrated her own faith.

◆ She clearly understood the challenges of his ministry.

◆ She proved that news of Jesus' signs and wonders had spread far beyond ancient Israel—and had had a powerful impact on some Gentiles.

And so, Jesus promptly healed the woman's daughter.

Because of the story's ultimate happy ending, it's sometimes used to show that persistence in petitioning God is important, and that Jesus intended to bring salvation to both Gentiles and Jews. While both of these are important Christian teachings, I don't find them in this curious tale as easily as some others do.

Think about the Syrophoenician woman. Perhaps you'll come up with your own interpretation of this long-standing Christian mystery. As for me, I'm satisfied with the interpretation I told you about earlier in this section.

Jesus Heals a Boy After the Apostles Failed

"Teacher, I brought you my son; he has a spirit that makes him unable to speak; and whenever it seizes him, it dashes him down; … I asked your disciples to cast it out, but they could not do so." He answered them, "You faithless generation, how much longer must I be among you? … Bring him to me."

And they brought the boy to him. When the spirit saw him, immediately it convulsed the boy, and he fell on the ground and rolled about, foaming at the mouth. Jesus asked the father, "How long has this been happening to him?" And he said, "From childhood. It has often cast him into the fire and into the water, to destroy him; but if you are able to do anything, have pity on us and help us."

Jesus said to him, "If you are able!—All things can be done for the one who believes." Immediately the father of the child cried out, "I believe; help my unbelief!" When Jesus saw that a crowd came running together, he rebuked the unclean spirit, saying to it, "You spirit that keeps this boy from speaking and hearing, I command you, come out of him, and never enter him again!" … [later] his disciples asked him privately, "Why could we not cast it out?" He said to them, "This kind can come out only through prayer." (Mark 9:17–29, NRSV)

This story offers one of the most gripping scenes in Scripture:

- A boy suffering the symptoms of a potentially lethal demonic possession

- A team of disciples trying—and failing—to exorcise the demon

- Onlookers racing to and fro

- A distraught father who believes that Jesus can help his son—but is not *absolutely* sure

- Jesus trying to avoid a crowd of people who wanted to see what the fuss was about

- Jesus performing a challenging exorcism in the middle of a busy street

- And all of the tumult punctuated a by series of important lessons about faith

To get a full picture of these chaotic events, you need to read the reports in the three Synoptic Gospels, because each telling provides a different perspective: Matthew 17:14–19, Mark 9:14–29, and Luke 9:37–45. Mark's account provides a morsel of new information about demons: specifically that there are different kinds of evil spirits, some easier to cast out than others.

Jesus noted that driving away this particular demon required prayer—although he was merely providing advice for his disciples. There's nothing to suggest that Jesus himself needed to pray during an exorcism. But ultimately, this story teaches Christians more about faith than about demons:

- The disciples had been given authority by Jesus to expel evil spirits from demoniacs, but a stronger-than-usual demon shattered their confidence in the power of God.

- When the disciples lost faith in themselves they also lost faith in Jesus; praying for his (or God's) help in casting out the demon seems like something they should have remembered to do.

- Jesus' initial reply to the father's hesitant request for help—"If you are able!"—is one more example of Jesus' frustration that people around him "don't get it."

- The father of the boy provides a particularly poignant illustration of the doubt-riddled faith that most believers have; we know in our minds that Jesus' promises are true—but perhaps God can do something more to solidify the faith we feel in our hearts?

Jesus Drives a Demon Out of a Mute Man

Then a blind and dumb demoniac was brought to him, and he healed him, so that the dumb man spoke and saw. And all the people were amazed, and said, "Can this be the Son of David?" But when the Pharisees heard it they said, "It is only by Beelzebub, the prince of demons, that this man casts out demons." (Matthew 12:22–24, RSV)

Take Warning!

Don't attempt to use any of these Biblical stories as instruction manuals to diagnose demonic possession or to perform an exorcism; that wasn't their intent.

By all accounts, this was a routine casting out for Jesus; the Bible tells us nothing more than the man could see and talk after Jesus eliminated the evil spirit. Nonetheless this is one of the most momentous of Jesus' exorcisms, because it led directly into the so-called "Beelzebub controversy" that created the mystery of the Unforgivable Sin. See Chapter 18 for the fascinating story.

Jesus Exorcises a Crippled Woman on the Sabbath

Now he was teaching in one of the synagogues on the sabbath. And just then there appeared a woman with a spirit that had crippled her for eighteen years. She was bent over and was quite unable to stand up straight. When Jesus saw her, he called her over and said, "Woman, you are set free from your ailment." When he laid his hands on her, immediately she stood up straight and began praising God.

But the leader of the synagogue, indignant because Jesus had cured on the sabbath, kept saying to the crowd, "There are six days on which work ought to be done; come on those days and be cured, and not on the sabbath day."

But the Lord answered him and said, "You hypocrites! Does not each of you on the sabbath untie his ox or his donkey from the manger, and lead it away to give it water? And ought not this woman, a daughter of Abraham whom Satan bound for eighteen long years, be set free from this bondage on the sabbath day?" When he said this, all his opponents were put to shame; and the entire crowd was rejoicing at all the wonderful things that he was doing. (Luke 13:10–17, NRSV)

The exorcism aspect of this story is quite simple: Jesus on his own decides to free a crippled woman from the spirit that's held her in bondage. He also laid hands on her, perhaps to complete the healing (after all, she'd been bent over for 18 years).

But then, the story goes in a different direction: Jesus uses the event to teach a lesson about *legalism* based on a broader theme of freedom. Jesus' ministry was about freedom—freedom from sin, freedom from the evil forces that had waylaid God's Creation, and also freedom from the legalism that stood in the way of the Kingdom of God.

def•i•ni•tion

Legalism is a fixation on the letter of the law that ousts mercy and charitable behavior, often causes more damage than good, and ultimately offends (rather than pleases) God. The Pharisees became legalistic because they believed that rigorous obedience to the ritual laws of Judaism was the route to salvation—a doctrine that Jesus reshaped during his ministry. It's important to obey God's moral laws but also not to ignore the call to show agape to others.

The Pharisees understood that they could work as required on the Sabbath to care for their animals, but they claimed—hypocritically, as Jesus pointed out—that it was somehow unlawful to work to heal a woman. Jesus didn't see things this way and apparently neither did the crowd of onlookers in the synagogue who witnessed the exorcism and the subsequent debate.

The Least You Need to Know

- The three Synoptic Gospels provide several examples of Jesus casting out demons under his own authority—without rituals, prayer, or calling on God.

- A demon (also called an unclean spirit or an evil spirit) is an evil spiritual being of a lower order (somewhere between the gods and humankind).

- A demoniac is an individual inhabited by one or more demons that cause illness, bizarre demeanor, and destructive behavior.

- The exorcism stories in the Bible typically teach little about demons, but much about Jesus' power, faith, the Kingdom of God, and the challenge of legalism.

Chapter 16

The Mystery of Jesus' Power Over Nature

In This Chapter

- ◆ Nine miracles that demonstrate Jesus' power over nature
- ◆ One-of-a-kind events that show his complete control over Creation
- ◆ Further evidence that Jesus is the promised Messiah
- ◆ Why did onlookers became fearful?

Jesus' nature miracles are the foundations of some of the most exciting stories found in the New Testament. Matthew, Mark, Luke, and John must have felt the same way, because they provided an unusual amount of detail—more than enough for us to visualize the scenes and imagine what happened.

I'll review each of Jesus' nature miracles in this chapter. As in Chapter 15, I'll start off with a Biblical account of each miracle, and then point out the especially interesting aspects.

The Man Who Calmed Storms

If we knew nothing more about Jesus of Nazareth than he had the power to calm storms by rebuking them, we'd have solid evidence of his divinity. No other so-called wonder workers have claimed this kind of power over nature. Such an event is truly a miracle: God intervening in the laws of nature. We can't even begin to come up with a logical explanation for a storm immediately reacting to a few spoken words.

Christians assert that the only sensible responses are to …

- Believe the Gospel reports and acknowledge that Jesus possessed divine powers.
- Reject the reports and insist that the miracles never happened.

I find it interesting that mainstream scholars seem to split along these lines. To paraphrase a leading theologian: A large number of scholars accept that Jesus performed … healings and exorcisms. But a much smaller group is willing to believe that Jesus really performed the nature miracles. The skeptics don't view the Gospel stories as historical reports, but rather as "metaphorical narratives" that teach important concepts about Jesus and his ministry.

Surprisingly, most ordinary Christians don't agree. A recent public opinion study found that 70 percent of American adults (a mix of Christians and nonbelievers) believed that Jesus turned water into wine. And roughly the same number of adult Americans accept as true that Jesus fed the 5,000 with two fish and five loaves of bread. Other surveys repeatedly discover that significant majorities of Christians believe that the key nature miracles really happened.

A High *Yikes!* Factor

When we look back, we find the nature miracles intriguing and fun to imagine. But that's because we lack the close-up view that onlookers experienced. The people in the boat when Jesus calmed the storm (see the account later in this chapter) felt fear because they'd never witnessed such a display of raw power exercised by a person. They recognized that Jesus was unique, but knew little else about him. What was going to happen next? Could they really trust a man who possessed such extraordinary powers? Would Jesus somehow turn his might against them?

The point is that *nothing* else Jesus did—even his dramatic resuscitation of Lazarus—revealed the depth of his powers quite like his nature miracles.

Was Jesus a Reluctant Miracle Worker?

The Gospel reports of the nature miracles hint that Jesus wasn't especially eager to perform several of them. When I read the accounts of the wedding at Cana or the first storm that Jesus calmed (both are in this chapter), I come away thinking that Jesus would have been happier to be left alone. This is in direct contrast to many accounts of his healings and exorcisms, which depict Jesus eagerly curing people and casting out demons.

Are there reasons for his different attitudes? I've come up with two: First, I believe that Jesus enjoyed performing miracles that truly helped people in serious need. Second, I believe that Jesus preferred to offer signs and wonders that matched old-testament prophecies. Healings and exorcisms accomplish both of these goals; several of the flamboyant nature miracles achieve neither.

> **Scripture Says**
>
> Men of Israel, listen to these words: This Jesus the Nazarene was a man pointed out to you by God with miracles, wonders, and signs that God did among you through Him, just as you yourselves know. (Acts 2:22, HCSB)

Okay ... But How Do You Explain the Cross?

Imagine how the Apostles hiding in Jerusalem must have felt: A man who had the power to control nature—a man who could calm storms and turn an armful of food into a dinner for 5,000 men—did not ward off a few Temple soldiers or stop a small Roman crucifixion team. The miracles and a shameful execution don't seem to go together—at least not during the days before Jesus' Resurrection.

It's no wonder that the disciples never really understood Jesus' repeated declarations that he must suffer, die, and be resurrected (see, for example, Luke 9:22).

Jesus Turns Water into Wine

On the third day a wedding took place in Cana of Galilee. Jesus' mother was there, and Jesus and His disciples were invited ... as well. When the wine ran out, Jesus' mother told Him, "They don't have any wine."

"What has this concern of yours to do with Me, woman?" Jesus asked. "My hour has not yet come."

"Do whatever He tells you," His mother told the servants. Now six stone water jars had been set there for Jewish purification. Each contained 20 or 30 gallons. "Fill the jars with water," Jesus told them. … "Now draw some out and take it to the chief servant." And they did. When the chief servant tasted the water (after it had become wine), he did not know where it came from—though the servants who had drawn the water knew. He called the groom and told him, "Everybody sets out the fine wine first, then, after people have drunk freely, the inferior. But you have kept the fine wine until now." Jesus performed this first sign in Cana of Galilee. He displayed His glory, and His disciples believed in Him. (John 2:1–11, HCSB)

The Hebrew Scriptures used many metaphors to describe the kingdom of God. One key figure of speech is abundant wine. For example, "Hear this! The days are coming … when the mountains will drip with sweet wine, and all the hills will flow with it." (Amos 9:13, HCSB) Consequently, the idea that the Messiah would make wine fine wine probably resonated with the disciples and strengthened their newfound belief.

Another resonance pointed out by many scholars is that Jesus' first recorded miracle (at least in the Gospel of John) was turning water into wine, whereas Moses' first miracle when he challenged Pharaoh was turning water into blood. Many first-century Jews saw a linkage between Moses (who freed the children of Israel from slavery in Egypt) and the promised Messiah (who would free Israel from Roman oppression; see Chapter 13).

A frequent question asked about this story is why Jesus insulted his mother by calling her *woman*, a seemingly harsh form of address. One credible explanation is that the Greek language doesn't have the adjective *dear*, so that the literally translated phrase fails to communicate that Jesus said something like, "Dear Woman."

Jesus' First Fishing Miracle

Jesus was standing by Lake Gennesaret. He saw two boats at the edge of the lake; the fishermen had left them and were washing their nets. He got into one of the boats, which belonged to Simon, and asked him to put out a little from the land. Then He sat down and was teaching the crowds from the boat. When He had finished speaking, He said to Simon, "Put out into deep water and let down your nets for a catch."

"Master," Simon replied, "we've worked hard all night long and caught nothing! But at Your word, I'll let down the nets." When they did this, they caught a great number of fish, and their nets began to tear. So they signaled to their partners in the other boat to come and help them; they came and filled both boats so full that they began to sink. When Simon Peter saw this, he fell at Jesus' knees and said, "Go away from me, because I'm a sinful man, Lord!" For he and all those with him were amazed at the catch of fish they took, and so were James and John, Zebedee's sons, who were Simon's partners. "Don't be afraid," Jesus told Simon. "From now on you will be catching people!" Then they brought the boats to land, left everything, and followed Him. (Luke 5:1–11, HCSB)

It's no surprise that fishing miracles are part of the mix. The 12 original Apostles included 7 Galilean fishermen who Jesus transformed into "fishers of men": Simon Peter; Andrew, Simon Peter's brother; James and John (the sons of Zebedee); Nathaniel; Philip; and Thomas (called Didymus).

Get Wisdom

Lake Gennesaret is not a separate body of water, but rather a lake-like cove near the northwestern corner of the Sea of Galilee.

Jesus' purpose in performing this miracle seems to be to convince a large group of almost-Apostles to follow him. And so, after a night of futile fishing, Jesus urges Peter to cast his net into deeper waters. (First-century fishermen may have fished at night because their crude nets were too visible in the water during the day.)

Peter reluctantly agrees and he and his partners promptly catch two boatloads of fish—enough to fill the boats to the point of nearly sinking them. Peter immediately realized that netting such a large number of fish was truly miraculous and that Jesus was responsible.

Peter's immediate reaction was fear—not so much at the shock of the miracle, but at the realization that Jesus had further demonstrated his ability to control nature, more evidence that he is truly "Master" and "Lord." Peter suddenly felt unworthy in Jesus' presence and possibly also afraid of his unique power.

Over the years, many Christians have seen lots of symbolism in the story. Some say the nets are the Gospel messages that catch nonbelievers who are floundering in the deep waters of sin (or who live far from shore in remote parts of the world). Others claim that the two fishing boats signal that Jesus brings salvation to both Jews and Gentiles. If you're comfortable with symbols—enjoy! Otherwise, extract the straight-forward teaching from this and the other nature miracles: they demonstrate that Jesus had dominion over God's Creation, providing powerful evidence of his divinity.

Jesus' Post-Resurrection Fishing Miracle

Simon Peter, Thomas …, Nathanael from Cana of Galilee, Zebedee's sons, and two others of His disciples were together. "I'm going fishing," Simon Peter said to them. "We're coming with you," they told him. They went out and got into the boat, but that night they caught nothing. When daybreak came, Jesus stood on the shore. However, the disciples did not know it was Jesus.

"Men," Jesus called to them, "you don't have any fish, do you?" "No," they answered. "Cast the net on the right side of the boat," He told them, "and you'll find some." So they did, and they were unable to haul it in because of the large number of fish.

Therefore the disciple, the one Jesus loved, said to Peter, "It is the Lord!" When Simon Peter heard that it was the Lord, he tied his outer garment around him (for he was stripped) and plunged into the sea. But since they were not far from land …, the other disciples came in the boat, dragging the net full of fish. When they got out on land, they saw a charcoal fire there, with fish lying on it, and bread. "Bring some of the fish you've just caught," Jesus told them. So Simon Peter got up and hauled the net ashore, full of large fish—153 of them. Even though there were so many, the net was not torn. (John 21:2–11, HCSB)

Scholars have argued about the significance of this post-resurrection miracle for centuries. What does it mean? Why did Jesus perform it? Why did John include it in his Gospel?

For starters, the fishermen disciples didn't recognize Jesus. Is this merely the result of the poor visibility and dim light, or does it signal (as some scholars claim) that Peter and his partners had somehow pushed Jesus to the backs of their mind after his death and resurrection?

Get Wisdom

The Sea of Galilee is actually a large lake, 14 miles long and 6 miles wide, roughly 60 miles north of Jerusalem. The "Sea" is fed by the Jordan River.

If this second possibility seems odd, keep in mind that the resurrected Jesus had told the Apostles to wait for him in Galilee (see Matthew 28:10). By going fishing, they had resumed their old lives, rather than becoming "fishers of men" (see Matthew: 4:19, KJV). Jesus may have appeared on the shore to deliver a refresher course in Christian discipleship.

The account's unusual specificity about the number of fish the disciples caught that morning—exactly 153—has encouraged many Christians over the years to apply numerological approaches to extract meaning from the number. Does 153 somehow signal the date of the Second Coming? Is it a clue to the number of people Jesus will ultimately save? Does it denote the number of species of fish in the Sea of Galilee? Or does it simply mean (this is the explanation I like best) that they caught a big mess of fish—more than enough for a good breakfast?

Jesus Calms a Storm at Sea

> As He [Jesus] got into the boat, His disciples followed Him. Suddenly, a violent storm arose on the sea, so that the boat was being swamped by the waves. But He was sleeping. So the disciples came and woke Him up, saying, "Lord, save us, we're going to die!" But He said to them, "Why are you fearful, you of little faith?" Then He got up and rebuked the winds and the sea. And there was a great calm. The men were amazed and asked, "What kind of man is this?—even the winds and the sea obey Him!" (Matthew 8:23–27, HCSB)

The ancient Jews were not a seafaring people. They lived in the desert and considered most bodies of deep water dangerous wildernesses—the dwelling places of dark powers, such as the Leviathan, a thrashing armored sea monster (see Job 41:10).

The fishermen who worked on the Sea of Galilee would have considered the a storm on the lake—"a roaring sea"—nature at its most fearful and least controllable. Consequently, when Jesus calmed the storm, he simultaneously demonstrated his control over nature *and* the dark forces that might live in deep waters.

The disciples in the boat are fearful because they haven't fully worked out who Jesus is; they understand his power, but not his identity or his purpose. As a result, their faith is flimsy.

Take Warning!

Countless Christians have heard sermons that claim Jesus calmed the storm so that we'll take heart and let him calm the storms that rage in our lives—the death of loved ones, our serious illnesses, our grave disappointments, and the like. While Christians are advised to turn problems over to God, that's not the core point this story was meant to teach. Far more important is the take-away that Jesus, the Son of God, has come among us to usher in the Kingdom of God and that no force—nature or dark power—can stop what he has begun.

Jesus Feeds Multitudes

After this, Jesus crossed the Sea of Galilee … and a huge crowd was following Him because they saw the signs that He was performing on the sick. So Jesus went up a mountain and sat down there with His disciples.

Now the Passover, a Jewish festival, was near. Therefore, when Jesus looked up and noticed a huge crowd coming toward Him, He asked Philip, "Where will we buy bread so these people can eat?" He asked this to test him, for He Himself knew what He was going to do. Philip answered, "Two hundred denarii worth of bread wouldn't be enough for each of them to have a little."

One of His disciples, Andrew, Simon Peter's brother, said to Him, "There's a boy here who has five barley loaves and two fish—but what are they for so many?" Then Jesus said, "Have the people sit down." There was plenty of grass in that place, so they sat down. The men numbered about 5,000. Then Jesus took the loaves, and after giving thanks He distributed them to those who were seated—so also with the fish, as much as they wanted.

When they were full, He told His disciples, "Collect the leftovers so that nothing is wasted." So they collected them and filled 12 baskets with the pieces from the 5 barley loaves that were left over by those who had eaten.

When the people saw the sign He had done, they said, "This really is the Prophet who was to come into the world!" Therefore, when Jesus knew that they were about to come and take Him by force to make Him king, He withdrew again to the mountain by Himself. (John 6:1–13, HCSB)

This is the only one of Jesus' miracles (other than the Resurrection) that is recorded in all four Gospels. I've always felt that the accounts in Matthew, Mark, and Luke don't do it full justice. They provide fairly low-key descriptions of what Jesus accomplished—even though there were probably more than 10,000 people in the hungry crowd. What's more, you can come away from the Synoptic Gospels believing that the people who were fed had no idea that a continuing miracle was happening around them.

Get Wisdom

Two hundred denarii was equivalent to eight months' wages for a working man in ancient Israel.

The picture changes when you read John's account. The people who ate the bread and fish immediately understood the significance of Jesus' miracle: once again, Jesus had echoed what Moses had done when he fed the children of Israel in the Sinai Desert. The devout Jews who ate bread and fish made the connection: Jesus was the promised Messiah who would sit on David's throne and lead them out from under the brutal Roman occupation and restore Israel to its former abundance. Of course they wanted to crown Jesus king!

The feeding of the 5,000 is so well known that many Christians forget that Jesus also fed a multitude of 4,000. This miracle is reported in only two Gospels: Matthew 15:29–39 and Mark 8:1–9. The stories about the 4,000 make the same point as those about the 5,000: Jesus the Messiah will restore Israel's freedom and end her perceived exile under the oppressive Roman occupation.

Jesus Walks on Water and Calms Another Storm

> During the fourth watch of the night [about three o'clock in the morning] Jesus went out to them, walking on the lake. When the disciples saw him walking on the lake, they were terrified. "It's a ghost," they said, and cried out in fear.
>
> But Jesus immediately said to them: "Take courage! It is I. Don't be afraid." "Lord, if it's you," Peter replied, "tell me to come to you on the water." "Come," he said. Then Peter got down out of the boat, walked on the water and came toward Jesus. But when he saw the wind, he was afraid and, beginning to sink, cried out, "Lord, save me!" Immediately Jesus reached out his hand and caught him. "You of little faith," he said, "why did you doubt?" And when they climbed into the boat, the wind died down. Then those who were in the boat worshiped him, saying, "Truly you are the Son of God." (Matthew 14:25–33, NIV)

This story, one of the best known in the New Testament, actually reports *two* miracles—walking on water and calming the storm—although the second is often ignored. Many scholars consider the second a much greater revelation of Jesus' power (for the reasons I wrote about earlier). The events happened immediately after the feeding of the 5,000, when the disciples were returning to Bethsaida on the northwestern shore of the Sea of Galilee.

In John's version of the story, the disciples in the boat were sufficiently impressed to recognize Jesus as the "Son of God," the first record of them using this title. (see John 6:16–21) By contrast, in Mark's account (see Mark 6:45–52), the disciples are amazed but don't seem to understand the meaning of the miracles Jesus has done (Mark attributes this to hardness of heart).

Peter's failure to emulate Jesus seems a straightforward lesson about the destructive influence of doubt when Christians attempt to tap into Jesus' power.

Although the great majority of Christians believe that Jesus walked on water, a much smaller percentage of modern theologians accept the account in John as historical fact. One reason is that walking on water, while astonishing, seems more magician-like than Messiah-like. A second reason is that the original Gospel accounts, written in Greek, can be translated: "Jesus walked along the shoreline near the sea." Of course, this alternative doesn't mesh with Peter's failed attempt to do what Jesus had done.

I much prefer the counter argument that Jesus *did* walk on water and achieved two purposes:

 ◆ He demonstrated his complete authority over nature—as it behaved in the first century, and continues today.

 ◆ He provided a glimpse into what the New Creation will be like when all of humanity will have dominion over nature, and we too will be able to walk across a stormy sea.

Jesus Curses a Fig Tree

> The next day when they came out from Bethany, He was hungry. After seeing in the distance a fig tree with leaves, He went to find out if there was anything on it. When He came to it, He found nothing but leaves, because it was not the season for figs. He said to it, "May no one ever eat fruit from you again!" And His disciples heard it. (Mark 11:12–14, HCSB)

And the next day …

> Early in the morning, as they were passing by, they saw the fig tree withered from the roots up. Then Peter remembered and said to Him, "Rabbi, look! The fig tree that You cursed is withered." Jesus replied to them, "Have faith in God." (Mark 11:20–22, HCSB)

I recall participating in two different Bible studies that examined these verses. Both times, the environmentalists and gardeners in the group became exasperated with Jesus. "It made no sense for Jesus to zap the poor fig tree for having no figs out of season," they complained. "After all, the tree didn't do anything wrong; it merely behaved like a fig tree."

This sounds like another of Jesus' hard sayings (see Chapter 17) but it turns out, Jesus was not being unfair. Before I explain why, you need to understand the chronology of this nature miracle. Jesus cursed the fig tree during the middle of one day (Mark 11:12–14). Peter noticed the tree was withered the next morning (Mark 11:20–22).

What happened in between? Actually, a rather momentous event—Jesus expelled the money changers from the Temple (see Mark 11:15–18).

As countless theologians have noted, the fig tree was a symbol of Israel. Jesus withered the tree to prophesy the soon-to-come destruction of Jerusalem for focusing on outward acts of piety but not yielding the real fruit that faith in God should produce.

Okay—but why zap an innocent fig tree to make a theological point? Because the fig tree in question *wasn't* innocent. Botanically speaking, figs aren't fruit; they're the *flowers* of a fig tree. A fig tree that has leaves will also have small bud-like figs that are bitter, but edible. A tree that doesn't have these buds will never bear full-size figs later during the year. That was the condition of the fig tree Jesus cursed. He expected to find small figs, but "he found nothing but leaves." Consequently, the tree was a perfect metaphor for outward acts (the leaves) that don't yield fruit (the mini-figs).

The Coin in a Fish's Mouth (a Possible Nonmiracle)

> When they came to Capernaum, the collectors of the half-shekel tax went up to Peter and said, "Does not your teacher pay the tax?" He said, "Yes." And when he came home, Jesus spoke to him first, saying, "What do you think, Simon? From whom do kings of the earth take toll or tribute? From their sons or from others?" And when he said, "From others," Jesus said to him, "Then the sons are free. However, not to give offense to them, go to the sea and cast a hook, and take the first fish that comes up, and when you open its mouth you will find a shekel; take that and give it to them for me and for yourself." (Matthew 17:23–27, RSV)

Surprisingly, the story of the coin in the fish's mouth is often included on lists of Jesus' nature miracles. I say surprisingly, because one the one hand, it's a rather minor miracle, and on the other hand, it seems seriously out of character for Jesus to perform a miracle for his own benefit.

Many scholars believe there was no miracle at all. "Find money in a fish's mouth" was an idiomatic expression of the day (in the Aramaic language) that meant, a freshly hooked fish could easily be sold in the marketplace. Simply put, Jesus may have told

Peter to use the earnings from one of the fish he caught to pay their tax. Did Jesus perform a miracle or not? That's a mystery in its own right.

The Least You Need to Know

- Jesus performed nine miracles that spectacularly demonstrated his power over nature.

- None of the other miracles Jesus performed revealed the depth of his powers to the extent of his nature miracles.

- People who witnessed these miracles were usually frightened as well as amazed.

- The overwhelming majority of Christians believe that Jesus turned water into wine, walked on the Sea of Galilee, calmed storms, and fed the multitudes—even though some contemporary theologians are skeptical.

- The accounts of the nature miracles suggest that Jesus performed many of them reluctantly—possibly because his healings and exorcisms more closely fit prophecies about the promised Messiah.

- Many onlookers came away convinced that Jesus was the Messiah—the thousands who ate the multiplied loaves and fishes wanted to crown him king.

The Mystery of Jesus' Hard Sayings

In This Chapter

- ◆ Jesus' difficult-to-understand—or accept—sayings
- ◆ Some "hard sayings" are merely mistranslated
- ◆ Others happened when Jesus used hyperbole or irony
- ◆ Still others are Jesus' challenges to bad behavior
- ◆ A few represent genuine Christian mysteries

Over the centuries, countless Christians have gasped when they reached Luke 14:26 in their Bibles. This is the verse where Jesus seems to urge each of his disciples to *hate* his father, mother, wife, and children. The Greek word in Luke 14:26 is *miseo*—a variant of the primary word *misos*, which means "to detest." Consequently, we can't blame the Bible translators for getting Jesus' statement wrong.

Here we have one of the hardest of Jesus' hard sayings. Can Jesus be serious? What happened to his admonitions to love people? Doesn't the fifth Commandment require the disciples to honor their fathers and mothers?

I'll answer these—and related—questions in this chapter. My goal is to help you make as much sense as you can of Jesus' bewildering statements.

I'll follow the same approach with each hard saying. I'll present the relevant verses of Scripture so you can decide for yourself what Jesus might have meant. Then I'll give you an alternative reading that softens the teaching, along with an explanation (when appropriate) of language-related issues that have caused confusion and misinterpretation.

Hard to Interpret, Hard to Accept

As you'll see in the sections that follow, many of Jesus' hard sayings are hard to interpret because Jesus' original Aramaic words are difficult to translate, or because Jesus used idioms we don't understand today, or because Jesus used figurative language that we shouldn't take literally. These sayings become less hard when we knock down the language obstacles.

Other hard sayings are of a different nature. We don't like them even when we understand them. A great example is Jesus' instruction to give away everything we possess (see Luke 14:33). This is a thoroughly frightening prospect to many (perhaps most) Christians. It certainly is to me!

Still other sayings are hard to accept because they seem wholly *un-Jesus-like*—for example, his Luke 14:26 directive to hate parents and siblings that I mentioned earlier.

Some scholars have come up with alternative interpretations that soften Jesus' hard-to-receive statements; unfortunately, many are based on opinion and are little more than guesswork. In this chapter, I've presented the alternatives that I find sensible. But keep in mind that every Christian must ultimately come up with his or her own interpretation of what Jesus said.

Get Wisdom _____

I've covered three of Jesus' particularly hard sayings in other chapters:

- The Healing of the Syrophoenician woman's daughter—when Jesus seemed to call the woman a dog (see Chapter 15)

- The Cursing of the Fig Tree—when Jesus blamed a fig tree for not having fruit out of season (see Chapter 16)

- The Sin Against the Holy Spirit—what is the unforgivable sin that Jesus said the Pharisees had committed? (see Chapter 18)

Eat My Flesh; Drink My Blood

> Jesus said, "I am the bread of life. Your fathers ate the manna in the wilderness, and they died. This is the bread that comes down from heaven so that anyone may eat of it and not die. I am the living bread that came down from heaven. If anyone eats of this bread he will live forever. The bread that I will give for the life of the world is My flesh." At that, the Jews argued among themselves, "How can this man give us His flesh to eat?"
>
> So Jesus said to them, "I assure you: Unless you eat the flesh of the Son of Man and drink His blood, you do not have life in yourselves. Anyone who eats My flesh and drinks My blood has eternal life, and I will raise him up on the last day, because My flesh is real food and My blood is real drink. The one who eats My flesh and drinks My blood lives in Me, and I in him. Just as the living Father sent Me and I live because of the Father, so the one who feeds on Me will live because of Me. This is the bread that came down from heaven; it is not like the manna your fathers ate—and they died. The one who eats this bread will live forever." He said these things while teaching in the synagogue in Capernaum.
>
> Therefore, when many of His disciples heard this, they said, "This teaching is hard! Who can accept it?" (John 6:48–60, HCSB)

It's fascinating that many of Jesus' disciples had difficulty understanding this hard saying—enough for John to take note of the problem. The confused disciples seem to have fallen into the trap of assuming that Jesus meant his words literally—a significant misinterpretation. Jesus was *not* advocating cannibalism. Scholars point out that Jesus spoke in the present tense: you who are eating my flesh abide in me. (We can be certain that no one in the synagogue was literally eating Jesus' body.) And nothing that Jesus said before (or after) abolished the long-standing Jewish prohibitions against consuming blood (see Leviticus 7:26–27)—a law reaffirmed by Paul in Acts 15:20–29.

The bottom line: Jesus used *body* and *blood* as figures of speech.

Look at the Context

One of the first things to do when you come across a hard saying is to look at the context of the statement. In this case, Jesus was teaching in the synagogue at Capernaum soon after he miraculously fed the multitudes with real bread (see Chapter 16). He wanted to help the disciples—and uncommitted Jews—understand what they had seen.

Take Warning! _____

Understanding the context is essential when you interpret any passage in Scripture. The Bible is tightly written, and an isolated phrase may not mean what it seems to mean when given a cursory reading. An excellent example is "For where two or three are gathered together in My name, I am there among them." (Matthew 18:20 HCSB) These words, spoken by Jesus, are sometimes used to justify worshiping at home rather than in church. But if you read the preceding verses (16 through 19), you'll see that Jesus was talking about the number of witnesses necessary to prove that a fellow believer has sinned against you.

The onlookers to the miracle would have envisioned Jesus as the new Moses and the bread fed to the crowd as equivalent to the manna fed to the Israelites in the wilderness. But Jesus wanted to communicate that he offered much more than mere food to his followers. Specifically, he brought eternal life to those who took in his teachings in faith.

Actually, *eat* is not far away from a figure of speech that we commonly use today in a similar way. Now that I've presented an alternative interpretation of John 6:48–60, I'd like you to *chew on it*.

Did Jesus Have the Lord's Supper in Mind?

Some Christians assert that this passage is related to Jesus' later command to remember him in the Lord's Supper, or Communion. Others deny the linkage, and point out that Jesus was not talking about his eventual death but rather was conveying the essence of his ministry and the power of his teachings.

The second view seems more logical to me, considering that Jesus gave the onlookers at Capernaum a detailed explanation—albeit a lecture full of metaphors and analogies—designed to convince them that anyone who "ate up" and "drank in" his messages would abide in him and have eternal life.

Scripture Says

Paul wrote about the Lord's Supper in 1 Corinthians 11: "… on the night when He was betrayed, the Lord Jesus took bread, gave thanks, broke it, and said, 'This is My body, which is for you. Do this in remembrance of Me.' In the same way He also took the cup, after supper, and said, 'This cup is the new covenant in My blood. Do this, as often as you drink it, in remembrance of Me.' For as often as you eat this bread and drink the cup, you proclaim the Lord's death until He comes." (1 Corinthians 11:23–26, HCSB)

Dangerous Body Parts

> If your hand causes you to stumble, cut it off; it is better for you to enter life maimed than to have two hands and to go to hell, to the unquenchable fire. And if your foot causes you to stumble, cut it off; it is better for you to enter life lame than to have two feet and to be thrown into hell. And if your eye causes you to stumble, tear it out; it is better for you to enter the kingdom of God with one eye than to have two eyes and to be thrown into hell .... (Mark 9:43–47, NRSV)

What sinner doesn't have eyes, hands, or feet that lead him or her into sinful behavior? Christianity teaches that you, I, and everyone we know are among the afflicted. And yet, few believers take Jesus' advice literally—even though it was spoken directly and emphatically. Why? Because we recognize that Jesus was using hyperbole to make the point that we should eliminate the factors in our lives that encourage us to sin. Hyperbole is extreme exaggeration for the purpose of making a point; for example, "you've kept me waiting an eternity." Because hyperbole is often impossible (no one lives for an eternity, much less waits for one), a statement that uses hyperbole cannot be taken literally.

Scholars note that hyperbole was commonly used by first-century rabbis and was often used by Jesus.

You and I routinely use hyperbole in our conversations with other people:

◆ I woke up with a *thousand* aches and pains.

◆ I sat down at the dinner table hungry enough to *eat a horse*.

◆ I'd *swim the ocean* to go out with her.

◆ Your gift *tickled me to death*.

◆ I *cracked up* when you told your funny story.

We don't intend our exaggerations to be taken literally, and neither did Jesus when he said, "Woe to you, scribes and Pharisees, hypocrites! For you have ... neglected the weightier matters of the law: justice and mercy and faith. ... You strain out a gnat but swallow a camel!" (Matthew 23:23–24, NRSV)

Jesus knew that the Pharisees didn't eat bugs and dromedaries. His point was that their legalism (see Chapter 15) enforced tiny details of law while ignoring the most important principles: justice, mercy, and faith.

Jesus also said, "Why do you see the speck in your neighbor's eye, but do not notice the log in your own eye?" (Matthew 7:3, NRSV) To explain Jesus' hyperbolic language, the "log" in your eye represents the seriously sinful behavior you ignore—at the same time you complain about a minor sin (the "speck") your neighbor commits.

Hate Your Father and Mother

> Jesus said, "Whoever comes to me and does not hate father and mother, wife and children, brothers and sisters, yes, and even life itself, cannot be my disciple. Whoever does not carry the cross and follow me cannot be my disciple." (Luke 14:26–27, NRSV)

Yikes! Did Jesus really mean this? Well, no and yes. For starters, the idea that Jesus really wants people to hate their parents doesn't compute. It counters everything the Gospels teach us about Jesus—and many of the other things he said during his ministry.

However, the Greek word for *hate* can also be translated as "love less," a term of comparison. Consequently, a common alternative interpretation of these verses holds that Jesus urged his followers to make their dedication to God's kingdom the single most important thing in their lives—to place their faith ahead of even their family members.

Although this is a softer interpretation, it still begins to fall into the category of a saying we'd rather not hear. So let me give you alternatives to the alternative. It's also possible that Jesus wanted to warn his disciples about the cost of discipleship. In that event, the passage may mean something like: Be single-minded about following me. Don't be half-hearted when I call. Strive to make authentic discipleship the central focus of your life. But don't be surprised if your parents, spouse, kids, or siblings complain about your priorities. Chances are you'll end up crucified—metaphorically, at least. Sorry guys … but that's the way it is.

Finally, Jesus may have meant Luke 14:26–27 to be ironic. Irony uses incongruity—possibly even an obvious contradiction—to make a point. Saying, "It sure is a beautiful day today" during an intense thunderstorm is an example of irony.

An ironic reading of Luke 14:26–27 goes something like this: "Look at my new Bible study partner. She's so committed to being a disciple, she must have *hated* her old life. And she spends so much time working at church that she must *detest* her husband and family."

A Hundredfold Reward for Following Jesus

> Jesus said, "Truly I tell you, there is no one who has left house or brothers or sisters or mother or father or children or fields, for my sake and for the sake of the good news, who will not receive a hundredfold now in this age—houses, brothers and sisters, mothers and children, and fields, with persecutions—and in the age to come eternal life." (Mark 10:29–30, NRSV)

Whoa! Follow Jesus and receive a hundred houses? Or a hundred mothers? Those seem highly unusual rewards for being a faithful disciple. What was Jesus thinking? Did he expect Peter—who was on the receiving end of the promise—to take his words literally?

The context of this saying is important. Peter had just reminded Jesus that the Apostles had given up everything to follow him. Peter wanted to know: What's in it for us?

Jesus' reply drips with irony. To paraphrase his hard saying: The Apostles who follow me will be *rewarded* with persecutions. Oh, and as leaders of the church you'll also be *given* houses, fields, and families of people to take care of. But—and this is a big but—following me is worth it, because you'll have eternal life in the age to come.

Give Up Everything

> For which of you, intending to build a tower, does not first sit down and esti-mate the cost, to see whether he has enough to complete it? … Or what king, going out to wage war against another king, will not sit down first and consider whether he is able with ten thousand to oppose the one who comes against him with twenty thousand? … So therefore, none of you can become my disciple if you do not give up all your possessions. (Luke 14:28–33, NRSV)

Ouch! I remember wincing the first time I read these verses. They seem to suggest that every Christian should live in abject poverty. That seems to be the literal meaning of the final sentence. Perhaps you reached the same conclusion, too.

Well, take a deep breath and read the entire passage slowly once again. When you've done that, read it one more time. Notice that the third sentence has a different struc-ture than the first two. The difference is the key to the alternative interpretation of what Jesus wanted to communicate.

The earlier sentences talk about estimating the future costs of one's decisions. Consequently, a sensible reading of the final sentence is that Jesus is urging his followers to take the time to fully understand the *future* cost of discipleship.

The alternative reading of the hard saying is much softer: Jesus is not asserting that you must give everything away to become a disciple. Rather, he's warning his followers that when they become authentic disciples, they will *want* to give up the things they covet today. Consequently, discipleship ultimately means a loss of possessions. This seems to be exactly what happened in first-century Christianity (see Acts 4:34–35).

Get Wisdom

Medieval theologians taught that Jesus' hard sayings were "evangelical counsels"—a form of advice—rather than commands applicable to everyone. Nonetheless, over the centuries, many Christians have honored the literal reading of Luke 14:28–33 and related hard sayings. They took vows of poverty and chastity, joined monastic orders, renounced personal ambition, lived simply, and generally tried to imitate the life of Jesus Christ and his Apostles. Some believers argue today that wealth is incompatible with true Christianity.

No Peace on Earth

Do not think that I have come to bring peace to the earth; I have not come to bring peace, but a sword. For I have come to set a man against his father, and a daughter against her mother, and a daughter-in-law against her mother-in-law; and one's foes will be members of one's own household. (Matthew 10:34–36, NRSV)

Every Christmas season, countless Christmas cards are sent that link Jesus to peace on earth, good will toward men. And the famous words of Isaiah 9:6 give the promised Messiah the titles, Wonderful Counselor and Prince of Peace.

And yet, in this especially hard, hard saying, Jesus seemingly rejects these notions. Worse yet, he promises to bring the kind of discord that will shatter families.

Understanding the context of this statement is essential to interpreting what Jesus meant. He was sending the 12 Apostles on a mission trip to "the lost sheep of Israel." But Jesus anticipated that the new evangelists would run into severe—possibly violent—opposition (see Matthew 10:17).

Jesus recognized that his message had the power to inflame people and invariably start arguments—often among members of the same family. He used the word *sword* as a metaphor for the divisive impact of his teaching.

When Jesus spoke these words, he may well have been thinking of the conflicts within his own family. Mark 3:21 provides a glimpse of the problems Jesus faced at home—his family wondered if he was out of his mind.

Let the Dead Bury the Dead

> To another he [Jesus] said, "Follow me." But he said, "Lord, first let me go and bury my father." But Jesus said to him, "Let the dead bury their own dead; but as for you, go and proclaim the kingdom of God." (Luke 9:59–60, NRSV)

Talk about harsh. How can Jesus not allow a man bury his dead father? Isn't that an essential act under the commandment to honor your father and mother?

The context of this statement has Jesus walking along a road toward Jerusalem. People along the way offer to become disciples, including the unnamed man in these verses. Jesus says, "follow me," but then tacks on an extraordinary condition.

The most common interpretations hold that Jesus' intent was to indicate that doing the work of the Kingdom must take precedence over "ordinary" chores—even burying the dead. If so, this is a hard saying, indeed, because it makes Jesus seem heartless, almost inhuman.

The alternative interpretation is fascinating. It points out that first-century Jews used the expression "bury my father" to mean "take care of my elderly parents until they die." Some scholars point out that the wannabe disciple might also have been concerned about the inheritance he would eventually obtain from his aged father.

Consequently, the man had actually offered to follow Jesus in the future—after his parents were dead and after he'd received his inheritance.

In reply, Jesus urged the man to become a disciple *now* and proclaim the kingdom of God. That's a far more important task than waiting for an earthly inheritance. Jesus went on to note that nondisciples (the "spiritually dead") could take care of his father (bury the dead).

The Camel and the Needle's Eye

> Then Jesus said to his disciples, "Truly I tell you, it will be hard for a rich person to enter the kingdom of heaven. Again I tell you, it is easier for a camel to go through the eye of a needle than for someone who is rich to enter the kingdom of God." When the disciples heard this, they were greatly astounded and said, "Then who can be saved?" But Jesus looked at them and said, "For mortals it is impossible, but for God all things are possible." (Matthew 19:23–26, NRSV)

The usual interpretation is straightforward: wealthy people idolize their possessions, care more about them than salvation, and are the least likely to accept Jesus' teachings. But is this really true? Joseph of Arimathea—the member of the temple counsel who provided Jesus' tomb—was both rich and a follower of Jesus (see Matthew 27:57).

Alternative interpretations of Jesus' statement often claim that the "Needle's Eye" actually existed. You'll hear it described as a small gate in ancient Jerusalem—possibly a small door cut into a large door—that a camel could traverse with difficulty, if its cargo was removed and the animal kneeled. Many a pastor has sermonized that sending a camel through the eye of a needle is a metaphor for prayer (the kneeling) that helps one shed the burden of sin (the cargo)—something that a wealthy person finds especially difficult to do.

In fact, there's no historical evidence that such a gate actually existed. Moreover, if Jerusalem had such a gate, the disciples wouldn't have been astounded by what Jesus said.

This is a case when the customary interpretation is probably correct: Jesus exaggerated to make a point. A camel was the largest everyday animal seen in the Holy Land. And "needle's eye" was a frequently used metaphor for a small opening. Put the figures together, and you've described an impossible situation—something that could never happen.

The context of the hard saying proves the point. Jesus had just chatted with the rich young man who grieved at the thought of losing his possessions to gain eternal life (see Matthew 19:16–22). Jesus knew that love of one's possessions could be a truly fatal impediment to achieving a saving faith in him. And, he saw it as an almost universal problem among the rich.

The disciples were chiefly poor, yet something Jesus said about the rich young man shocked them. First-century Jews believed that wealthy people had been blessed by God—that their riches testified to their righteousness. Moreover, the rich young man claimed that he had followed the chief requirements of the law. Yet despite his apparent righteousness, he would not have eternal life.

The disciples understood their predicament immediately: If a rich (blessed) man would not gain eternal life, what could they (poor men) do to be saved? Jesus explained that mortal men could do nothing, but that God could save them. Simply put, Jesus gave them the first recorded lesson that humanity is ultimately saved by God's grace (see Chapter 6).

The Least You Need to Know

- The Gospels record several statements made by Jesus that Christians find difficult to understand or accept—these are called "hard sayings."

- As a rule, these hard sayings seem "un-Jesus-like" when they are looked at in isolation and interpreted literally.

- Many of Jesus' hard sayings become softer when you understand their context and/or resolve language-related issues.

- Others make sense when you understand that Jesus often used hyperbole and irony when he spoke.

- Still others become clear when you recognize that Jesus was making use of idiomatic expressions unique to first-century Israel.

- It's useful to consider alternative interpretations of Jesus' hard sayings—but recognize that these are based on personal opinion and guesswork.

Chapter 18

The Mystery of the Unforgivable Sin

In This Chapter

- ◆ Jesus described a sin that won't be forgiven
- ◆ What "blaspheming the Holy Spirit" might mean
- ◆ But ... isn't salvation available to every sinner?
- ◆ What theologians have concluded
- ◆ Can you or I commit the unforgivable sin?

Do you like detective novels? Well, let me share an unusual "whodunit" that has remained unsolved for 2,000 years. The victim of the crime is the Holy Spirit. The perpetrators are all identified—a group of Pharisees in ancient Israel. The punishment has been determined—no forgiveness in this world or the world to come. But no one can explain for certain the specific crime that the perps committed.

What is "blasphemy against the Holy Spirit"?

Theological detectives by the thousands have tried to answer this question, but The Case of the Unforgivable Sin remains one of Christianity's thorniest mysteries. We'll reexamine the clues in this chapter.

The Facts of the Case

A relatively long passage—Matthew 12:22–32—lays out the details of the unforgivable sin. I'll tell you the complete story, using Scripture verses from the King James Version of the Bible (which sets the right tone for a detective tale).

It All Began with an Exorcism

> Then was brought unto him [Jesus] one possessed with a devil, blind, and dumb: and he healed him, insomuch that the blind and dumb both spake and saw. And all the people were amazed, and said, Is not this the son of David. (Matthew 12:22–23, KJV)

It happened while Jesus of Nazareth was teaching and preaching in Galilee. The locals asked him to heal a man who was believed to be possessed by a demon—a man both blind and mute. When Jesus succeeded (the man was abruptly able to talk and see) the locals were so impressed that they began to wonder aloud if Jesus could be the Messiah promised in the Hebrew Scriptures.

The Pharisees Claimed Jesus Invoked Beelzebub

> But when the Pharisees heard it, they said, This fellow doth not cast out devils, but by Beelzebub the prince of the devils. And Jesus knew their thoughts, and said unto them, Every kingdom divided against itself is brought to desolation; and every city or house divided against itself shall not stand: And if Satan cast out Satan, he is divided against himself; how shall then his kingdom stand? (Matthew 12:24–26, KJV)

A party of Pharisees from Jerusalem who'd apparently been tagging along after Jesus on his ministry through Galilee immediately disagreed with the idea that Jesus was the promised Son of David, probably because they didn't believe that he met all the requirements (see Chapter 13).

And so, the Pharisees launched an outlandish attack on Jesus that challenged *all* of the exorcisms he'd performed during his ministry. And therein lies a tale.

Get Wisdom

According to Josephus, the first-century Jewish historian, the Pharisees represented one of the four schools of thought of Jewish philosophy. They were considered the leading experts in Jewish law. Modern scholars believe that most Pharisees were sincere in their efforts to apply the Law to everyday life. Consequently, although Jesus spoke harshly to some Pharisees, the group as a whole probably doesn't deserve its reputation as self-righteous, legalistic nit-pickers.

The Pharisees could also drive out demons. They did this by drawing on the power of God; in other words, they drove out demons in God's name. But when Jesus performed exorcisms, he apparently did not have to invoke God through spoken prayer.

The crowd of people who watched Jesus heal the man hadn't heard him call upon God and concluded that Jesus had *personal authority* to cast out demons—a clear sign that he was much more than an ordinary itinerant rabbi.

The Pharisees couldn't deny the obvious success of the healing Jesus had performed, so they challenged the power that had achieved it. They said that Jesus did not have personal authority to expel demons and had not called upon God. Rather, they claimed, he had called upon Beelzebub, the prince of the devils. Jesus understood that this claim was part of a strategy to undermine his credibility among the people of Galilee whom he'd impressed.

Jesus offered an unexpected indirect rebuttal to the Pharisees' claim. He pointed out that the demon in question was obviously part of Satan's household. Had Beelzebub assisted Jesus in casting out the demon, he would have started a ruinous fight in his own "house," and possibly destroyed his "kingdom."

But Jesus didn't stop there. He made two more attacks on the absurd notion that he was somehow in cahoots with Beelzebub.

Get Wisdom

Beelzebub, pronounced *bee-al-zeh-bub* (occasionally Beelzebul), is an alternative form of Ba'al Zebub, another name of the pagan god Ba'al—a false god the Israelites often worshiped when they turned away from God. Some scholars believe that Ba'al Zebub is a scornful, intentionally mocking form of Ba'al, because Zebub is a Hebrew collective noun for things that fly. Thus, Beelzebub is often translated as "Lord of the Flies." When Beelzebub appears in Scripture—sometimes accompanied by the phrase "prince of demons" or "prince of devils"—it may refer to Satan (as in Matthew 12:24–26), or else name a lesser devil.

Jesus Affirms That Only God Casts Out Devils

> And if I by Beelzebub cast out devils, by whom do your children cast them out? therefore they shall be your judges. But if I cast out devils by the Spirit of God, then the kingdom of God is come unto you. (Matthew 12:27–28, KJV)

Jesus' second attack was even more subtle than the first. He reminded the Pharisees that they unthinkingly insulted their "children" (followers) who were able to cast out devils by suggesting that they, too, were calling on Beelzebub. Moreover, if the followers heard these accusations, they'd be furious and denounce the Pharisees who spoke such nonsense.

However—and this is a big *however*—if the Pharisees tried to save face by withdrawing their foolish claim, they'd be forced to acknowledge that Jesus invoked the Spirit of God during every successful exorcism, but without speaking a prayer of invocation. This meant, in turn, that the Pharisees would have to admit that Jesus' personal power over demons attested to the truth of his preaching about the Kingdom of God (see Chapter 15).

Jesus Asserts His Power Over Beelzebub

> Or else how can one enter into a strong man's house, and spoil his goods, except he first bind the strong man? and then he will spoil his house. (Matthew 12:29, KJV)

Jesus' third attack reminded the Pharisees that casting out a demon is like breaking into Satan's house and stealing one of his prized possessions. The idea that Jesus called on Beelzebub is akin to saying that Satan willingly gave up without a fight.

Looking at this verse the other way around, Jesus told the Pharisees that he is stronger than Satan—which explains his personal authority to expel demons.

Jesus Defines the Unforgivable Sin

> He that is not with me is against me; and he that gathereth not with me scattereth abroad. (Matthew 12:30, KJV)

> Wherefore I say unto you, All manner of sin and blasphemy shall be forgiven unto men: but the blasphemy against the Holy Ghost shall not be forgiven unto men. And whosoever speaketh a word against the Son of Man, it shall be forgiven him: but whosoever speaketh against the Holy Ghost, it shall not be forgiven him, neither in this world, neither in the world to come. (Matthew 12:31–32, KJV)

I've separated Matthew 12:30 to give it prominence. This verse is often ignored by Christians when they consider the unforgivable sin. Note that Jesus began his definition with an abrupt—and curious—change of tone. His noticeably sarcastic attacks on the Pharisees gave way to a much more serious comment that suggests a war is raging and that people need to take sides. Presumably the war is between Jesus and Satan, and it's impossible to remain neutral because anyone who doesn't support Jesus supports Satan.

Having made this grim point, Jesus goes on, "Wherefore I say unto you …" ("Therefore," or "And so, I tell you" in more modern translations), and introduces a three-part definition of the unforgivable sin:

- Forgiveness from God is available for every sin and blasphemy—except blasphemy against the Holy Spirit.

- People who seek forgiveness after blaspheming Jesus shall be forgiven.

- Anyone who speaks against the Holy Spirit will not be forgiven.

The third part defines the specific unforgivable sin.

Mark's Version of the Unforgivable Sin

Many Bible scholars believe that Matthew and Luke built their Gospels atop the writings of Mark. The following three verses convey Mark's ending of the story of the unforgivable sin:

> Verily I say unto you, All sins shall be forgiven unto the sons of men, and blasphemies wherewith soever they shall *blaspheme:* But he that shall blaspheme against the Holy Ghost hath never forgiveness, but is in danger of eternal damnation: Because they said, He hath an unclean spirit. (Mark 3:28–30, KJV)

One interesting aspect of the King James Version translation of Mark's version is the idea that the blasphemer is "in danger of eternal damnation," rather than it being a certainty. Also, many modern Bibles translate that phrase "eternal damnation" as "eternal sin"—a common alternative for "unforgivable sin."

def•i•ni•tion _____

The verb **blaspheme**—to revile or disparage a person or thing worthy of high esteem—comes from two Greek words: *blaptein* (to injure) and *pheme* (reputation). Blasphemy is to speak words (or commit deeds) of insult, contempt, or scorn against God.

Where's the Mystery?

Right now, you're probably thinking: the unforgivable sin doesn't seem all that mysterious. Jesus seemed to say that because a spiritual war is underway, anyone who gives Beelzebub (Satan) the credit for a miracle accomplished by the Holy Spirit has blasphemed the Spirit and committed a sin that won't be forgiven.

Maybe so, but keep in mind that the Pharisees didn't "speak against" the Holy Spirit, at least not directly. They didn't openly slander the Holy Spirit by saying that he was Satan. Consequently, we can't learn much from their mistake. Specifically, how do we avoid committing the unforgivable sin?

> **Take Warning!**
>
> Some Christians claim that the Pharisees wrongly equated the Holy Spirit with Beelzebub when they said that Jesus needed Beelzebub's help to cast out demons. This explanation isn't as widely accepted as those I'll present later in the chapter, including the notion that the Pharisees slandered the Holy Spirit by attributing his work to Satan.

Without doubt, the Pharisees blasphemed Jesus when they accused him of calling on Beelzebub. But, he explained that speaking against him will be forgiven.

So we're left with an unresolved conundrum. One the one hand, we're told there's an unforgivable sin. On the other hand, the Gospel verses that introduce it don't provide an easy-to-interpret definition. It's not surprising then, that Christianity's brightest scholars and theologians have tried to fill in the gaps and come up with a credible explanation.

The Implications of "Unforgivability"

The mystery of the Unforgiveable Sin becomes more pressing to resolve when we consider the implications of words or deeds being unforgivable:

◆ Scripture seems to imply that if an unsaved person blasphemes the Holy Spirit, possibly during a lively argument with a would-be evangelist, she/he will never attain salvation—despite all attempts to repent and become a Christian (one strike and you're out).

◆ The verses also seem to imply that if a believing Christian blasphemes the Holy Spirit, his or her salvation will end and can never be restored.

Both of these implications fly in the face of two beliefs that are foundational in various Christian denominations. The first is the majority notion that every sinner who seeks salvation can attain it. The second is the somewhat less popular belief that a saved Christian can't lose his or her salvation (once saved, always saved).

Yikes! I'm Sure I've Done It!

Many pastors report hearing parishioners say things like: "I became terrified when I read about the unforgivable sin, because years ago, when something awful happened in my life, I cursed the Holy Spirit," or "I'm a careless talker and thinker. I worry about saying—or thinking—something bad about the Holy Spirit by accident and losing my salvation." For this reason most Christian counselors are taught to help people cope with fears that they have committed (or might in the future commit) the unforgivable sin.

A common approach is to remind a fearful person that:

◆ Because leading theologians during the past 2,000 years have disagreed as to the nature of the unforgivable sin, no Christian can say for sure that he or she has committed it.

◆ Furthermore, most theologians agree that an offhand blasphemous exclamation that insults the Holy Spirit is not enough of a sin to be considered the unforgivable sin.

◆ As Paul affirms in Romans 2:4, NSRV, "God's kindness is meant to lead you to repentance," which means that any Christian who repents words or deeds is on speaking terms with the Holy Spirit.

◆ Paul expressed his confidence that "he who began a good work in you will carry it on to completion …." (Philippians 1:6, NIV)

The bottom line? Any Christian who cares enough to worry whether he or she has committed the unforgivable sin … *hasn't!*

Different Solutions

So—what is the unforgivable sin? The famed fifth-century theologian, Augustine of Hippo, considered this one of the most difficult questions related to Scripture. He proposed a suggested solution that is still considered a strong possibility today: *final impenitence* (a complete refusal throughout one's lifetime to repent and seek salvation).

Thanks ... But I'll Keep Sinning

If someone perseveres in sin until his or her death, he or she has foreclosed the possibility of salvation. Augustine saw this kind of impenitence against the Holy Spirit as totally frustrating the Spirit's efforts to remit sins. Rejecting the work of the Holy Spirit is equivalent to blaspheming the Holy Spirit, the "unforgivable sin" because the person persisting in sin is preventing forgiveness. Such a person has hardened his or her heart and made the decision to remain a sinner, despite knowledge of the consequences—which puts him- or herself beyond the reach of salvation.

Now it's obvious that this explanation of the unforgivable sin doesn't foreclose the possibility of eventual salvation—since a sinful person can repent late in life, even on his or her deathbed. Thus, Augustine's suggestion is more in tune with Mark's warning of danger than Matthew's statement of total unforgiveability.

Many modern scholars reject this solution because Jesus seemed to be talking about something more than the risk of dying in unbelief—even if exacerbated by a hard heart. He rebuked the Pharisees for their words, not for their unbelief. Moreover, Jesus specifically linked the unforgivable sin to "speaking against" the Holy Spirit.

Take Warning!

The story of the unforgivable sin begins with people watching Jesus perform a miracle. Well, because Jesus is no longer on Earth, it's impossible to witness one of his miracles and attribute his success to the power of Beelzebub. Consequently, some Christians argue that no one can commit the sin today. This is a convenient "explanation," but one that scholars consider exceedingly weak. For starters, Jesus doesn't have to be present for sinners to claim that he is empowered by Satan rather than the Holy Spirit.

Perhaps Only Learned People Can Commit the Sin?

An especially interesting spin on the unforgivable sin alleges that you have to be highly educated in theology to commit it. The Pharisees who blasphemed the Holy Spirit had received the best theological training available anywhere. They clearly knew better when they chose to maliciously attribute the miracle Jesus performed to Beelzebub. Because of their knowledge, what they said represented blasphemy against the Holy Spirit.

This supposed solution lets most of us off the hook, and shifts the danger to people who are highly educated authorities about the work and role of the Holy Spirit—theologians, seminary trained pastors, and other highly experienced clergymen.

As with all proposed solutions, not everyone agrees with this suggestion. The naysayers remind us that Jesus said, "whosoever speaketh against the Holy Ghost, it shall not be forgiven him." (Matthew 12:32, KJV) "Whosoever" includes *everyone*; it encompasses you and me, as well as scholars who've attended universities and seminaries.

The Most Comprehensive Solution

Only Jesus can provide a correct answer to the question, "How do you commit the unforgivable sin?" But the suggestion I find most credible (perhaps you will, too) combines bits and pieces from the suggestions I've described so far.

The unforgivable sin is:

◆ Intentionally, malevolently, and obstinately slandering the Holy Spirit …

◆ By hatefully attributing the obvious work of the Holy Spirit to Satan—despite having full knowledge and conviction of the truth …

◆ In such a way that might injure seekers and give "aid and comfort to the enemy."

I see this last point as an important aspect of the sin that's described in the Bible. Jesus performed miracles to authenticate the claims he made. The Pharisees clearly intended to undermine the successful exorcism he'd performed and—perhaps even more important—to change the minds of the people who'd witnessed what Jesus had done. Consider the long-term damage to them if the Pharisees had succeeded.

But even a sin this significant seems forgivable—unless the people committing it have hearts so hard that they will *never* repent or trust Jesus Christ as savior. In short, they must put themselves beyond God's reach to keep the sin eternal.

Because you and I will probably never face this highly unusual set of circumstances, we can ponder the mystery of the unforgivable sin, but not worry much about committing the sin ourselves.

The Least You Need to Know

◆ The Gospels of Matthew, Mark, and Luke warn that blaspheming the Holy Spirit is an unforgivable sin.

◆ From the first century to today, theologians have struggled to understand the elements of the unforgivable sin.

◆ No one has produced a wholly convincing definition of blaspheming the Holy Spirit.

◆ Countless Christians have unnecessarily worried about committing the sin inadvertently—most scholars agree that if you care about committing it, you *haven't!*

◆ The sin in a nutshell is assisting Jesus' spiritual enemies by hatefully attributing the Spirit's work to Satan—despite knowing that you've malevolently slandered the Holy Spirit.

◆ The sin may be unforgivable because people who commit it have hearts so hard that they cut themselves off from salvation.

Part 4

Other Mysteries of Christianity

The lion's share of the Christian mysteries I've presented so far involve some aspect of Jesus' person, nature, mission, achievements, or ministry. That's what you would expect in a faith called Christianity.

Part 4 expands your horizons and introduces you to the Holy Spirit, and to several fascinating mysteries that are related to Christianity's history, Apostles, and the billions of believers that have made up the church—the body of Christ—during the past two Millennia.

These Christian mysteries involve questions that you've probably asked yourself: why did Christianity grow so large, and why are there so many different denominations?

I promise you an exciting final segment of our journey through Christianity.

Chapter 19

The Mystery of the Holy Spirit

In This Chapter

◆ The Holy Spirit: the most mysterious person of the Trinity

◆ The Spirit's essential roles in the Gospel

◆ How the Holy Spirit brings people to Jesus

◆ Common symbols for the Holy Spirit

◆ The fruit of the Spirit

◆ The gifts of the Spirit

Why is the Holy Spirit so mysterious? Some say it's because mainstream denominations overlook the Spirit in sermons, hymns, and Bible studies. Consequently believers like you and me learn little about the Holy Ghost at worship or in adult-education classes.

This chapter will teach you what you should know about the Holy Spirit. I've designed it to give you a detailed introduction to the third Person of the Trinity—with special emphasis on how the Holy Spirit moves us toward God.

The Cinderella of the Trinity

"The Holy Spirit has long been the Cinderella of the Trinity. The other two sisters may have gone to the theological ball; the Holy Spirit got left behind every time." These words were written by Alister McGrath, a leading theologian and teacher.

One explanation for this seeming neglect is that the study of the Spirit—*pneumatology* to theologians—is more recent (and less developed) than the study of the Father or the Son.

def•i•ni•tion

> The Hebrew Scriptures use *ruach* for God's Spirit, a word that means "wind," "breath," and of course "spirit." When the Jewish Bible was translated into Greek, the Greek word *pneuma* (which means "to breath") replaced *ruach.* Thus, **pneumatology** is the study of the person and works of the Holy Spirit. Jesus also used *paraclete* to label the Holy Spirit, a Greek word that means "comforter," "counselor," "advocate," and "helper."

The Misunderstood Third Person

Ordinary Christians have shown an even greater propensity to ignore the nature and work of the Holy Spirit. A public opinion study conducted at the start of the twenty-first century found that the majority of Christians thought that the Holy Spirit is a symbol of God's power, but *not* a living entity. This is an astonishing display of mis-understanding given Christianity's teachings about the Holy Spirit's work and impor-tance.

For starters, Christianity claims that the Holy Spirit calls people to follow Jesus, and also enables the basic belief in Jesus that blossoms into faith. If it wasn't for the work of the Spirit, many current Christians would still be unbelievers repelled by the apparent "foolishness" (to use the Apostle Paul's word) of the Gospel: Those who are unspiritual do not receive the gifts of God's Spirit, for they are foolishness to them, and they are unable to understand them because they are spiritually discerned. (1 Corinthians 2:14, NRSV)

Theologians point out that the idea that God's Spirit makes stony-hearted people receptive to the Gospel message has its roots in the Old Testament book of Ezekiel: "I will also sprinkle clean water on you, and you will be clean. I will cleanse you from all your impurities and all your idols. I will give you a new heart and put a new spirit within you; I will remove your heart of stone and give you a heart of flesh." (Ezekiel 36:25–26, HCSB)

The Spirit—Simply Put

Many churches publish statements of faith that define how members view the Holy Spirit. Here's a typical example: "We believe that the Holy Spirit is sent by God to be our teacher and comforter. He draws us to Christ and transforms our lives so that we increasingly become like Jesus Christ and live a life pleasing to God." And here's a description of the Holy Spirit that was written for middle-school students: "God the Father sends the Holy Spirit. The Holy Spirit teaches us, lives in us, and helps us grow as Christians."

Take Warning!

Some Christians feel edgy about the third Person of the Trinity because they are overly concerned about committing the "unforgivable sin" of blaspheming against the Holy Spirit. As I explained in Chapter 18, it's highly improbable that you, I, or anyone we know can commit this unique sin.

The Spirit in the Creeds

Christians who recite the Apostle's Creed confess that Jesus "was conceived of the Holy Spirit" and that "I believe in the Holy Spirit." Believers who recite the Nicene Creed say much more: "And we believe in the Holy Spirit, the Lord and Giver of life, who proceedeth from the Father and the Son, who with the Father and the Son together is worshiped and glorified, who spoke by the prophets."

The Nicene Creed was written in 325 and revised in 381. Scholars believe that the words about the Holy Spirit were added to counter the so-called *Pneumatomachi*—combaters of the Spirit who denied the divinity of the Holy Spirit. Interestingly, the Nicene Creed doesn't make the direct statement that the Holy Spirit is God; rather, it asserts that the Holy Spirit does divine things (give life), is worshiped as God, and reveals to us what God wills (this is the meaning of "spoke by the prophets").

Walking with the Wise

Tertullian (died 220) is thought to be the first Christian theologian and apologist to define the Holy Spirit as God. He wrote in a work named *Against Praxeas* that "the Holy Spirit is God ... and is the third degree of the Godhead."

When you read the Creedal statements, remember what I told you in Chapter 3. The Holy Spirit is God, one of the three Persons of the Trinity, of one the same substance or divine essence as the Father and the Son.

The Work of the Holy Spirit

As I also noted in Chapter 3, God acts as a single being, functioning as one force, rather than some sort of divine trio. However, it's convenient for us to envision certain of God's activities as the specific work of Holy Spirit.

Many scholars view the Holy Spirit as the "utility infielder" of the Trinity—the Person that performs an extraordinary variety of works; so many, in fact, that it's easy to lose track of the Spirit's many accomplishments that are memorialized in the Scriptures. Here are some of the Spirit's best-known works:

- The Holy Spirit was responsible for Jesus' conception and thus the Incarnation (see Luke 1:35)

- The Holy Spirit prompted Elizabeth's realization that Mary's unborn baby was the Lord (see Luke 1:41)

> **Scripture Says**
>
> But the Advocate, the Holy Spirit, whom the Father will send in my name, will teach you everything, and remind you of all that I have said to you. (John 14:26, NRSV)
>
> And …
>
> When the Spirit of truth comes, he will guide you into all the truth …. (John 16:13, NRSV)

- Elizabeth was filled with the Holy Spirit (see Luke 1:41)

- The Holy Spirit stimulated Zechariah, John the Baptist's father, to prophesize (see Luke 1:67)

- At Jesus' baptism, the Holy Spirit descended on Him in a physical appearance like a dove (see Luke 3:21–22)

- The Holy Spirit filled Jesus and led him into the desert to be tempted by Satan (see Luke 4:2)

- When Jesus commissioned the Apostles after his resurrection, the Holy Spirit empowered them to forgive sins (see John 20:22–23)

- The Holy Spirit is actively involved in the salvation of sinners made possible by Jesus' atoning death (see 1 Corinthians 6:11)

- The Holy Spirit fills believers' hearts with agape love (see Romans 5:5)

- The Holy Spirit lives in every believing Christian (see Romans 8:9)

◆ The Holy Spirit, in contrast with the old law, gives life (see Romans 8:2)

◆ The Holy Spirit puts appropriate words in a Christian's mouth in times of persecution (see Mark 13:11)

◆ The Holy Spirit communicates instruction from Jesus (see Acts 1:2)

◆ The Holy Spirit convicts the world of sin—helps unbelievers recognize when they are sinning—so that they appreciate the need for a Savior (see John 16:8–9)

◆ The Holy Spirit bears witness with our spirit that we are the children of God—and makes us cry "Abba! Father!" (see Romans 8:15–16)

◆ The Holy Spirit "poured out" itself on the Day of Pentecost, enabling the Apostles to proclaim the Gospel in different languages to the various Jewish visitors in Jerusalem (see Acts 2:1–4).

The Spirit on Pentecost

I've ended my list of the Spirit's works with his outpouring on the Pentecost after the Resurrection because many Christians consider that day the birthday of the church. Christianity claims that God's gift of the Holy Spirit on Pentecost accomplished a fundamental change for humankind. The source of inspiration, of vision, of dreams, of prophecy had been poured out on all flesh as foretold in the Old Testament (see Joel 2:28–29).

The significance of the Holy Spirit's arrival on Pentecost is that the followers of Jesus Christ could now fully believe in him as Lord and Savior. The Spirit could enter all believers as he had the Apostles—to bring faith and understanding.

The Spirit's Work in the Old Testament

Although Jews don't recognize God's Spirit as a distinct person, the Hebrew Scriptures include many examples of the Spirit at work. One example, from 1 Samuel, describes what happened to King Saul: "Now the spirit of the LORD departed from Saul, and an evil spirit from the LORD tormented him." (1 Samuel 16:14, NRSV)

God's Spirit also equipped people to perform special tasks. Numbers 27:18 describes Joshua as Spirit-filled, presumably preparing him to lead the Children of Israel. And accounts in the Book of Judges say "the Spirit of the Lord came upon" Othniel, Gideon, Jephthah, and Samson (see, for example, Judges 15:14) to give them extraordinary skills or powers.

Is the Holy Spirit Jesus' Spirit?

Some theologians hold—and some Christian denominations teach—that the notion that the Holy Spirit is Jesus' Spirit is an essential insight supported by Scripture. They claim that because Jesus has ascended to Heaven, the Holy Spirit has become Jesus' mode of existence now on Earth. In the words of one scholar, "we can't know Jesus apart from the Spirit or other than through the Spirit." Consequently, to experience the Spirit is to experience Jesus, and vice versa.

Scripture Says

Here are two passages from the New Testament that some scholars use as evidence that the Holy Spirit is Jesus' Spirit:

◆ … he [Jesus] breathed on them and said to them, "Receive the Holy Spirit." (John 20:22, NRSV)

◆ When they [Paul and Silas] had come opposite Mysia, they attempted to go into Bithynia, but the Spirit of Jesus did not allow them … (Acts 16:7, NRSV)

I prefer to think of the Holy Spirit simply as "The Spirit," a distinct person of the Trinity, and recognize that all three Persons take part in everything that God does. Even the Apostle Paul wrote ambiguously on the topic: "But you are not in the flesh; you are in the Spirit, since the Spirit of God dwells in you. Anyone who does not have the Spirit of Christ does not belong to him." (Romans 8:9, NRSV)

Symbols for the Holy Spirit

Different Christian traditions have come up with various symbols for the Holy Spirit. Here are four that you've probably seen before:

◆ A dove—probably the most common symbol, because the Holy Spirit descended on Jesus at his baptism in the form of a dove (see Matthew 3:16)

◆ Water—reflecting the Holy Spirit's role in baptism and the teaching that Christians "drink of one Spirit" (see 1 Corinthians 12:13)

◆ Fire or tongues of fire—the form the Holy Spirit took on Pentecost (see Acts 2:3)

◆ The finger of God—Jesus cast out demons by the finger of God (see Luke 11:20) and the Ten Commandments were written on stone tablets by the finger of God (see Exodus 31:18)

Fruit of the Spirit

The fruit of the Spirit are personal characteristics that one can expect to observe when the Holy Spirit has worked to change a person's heart and mind. When talking about false prophets, Jesus noted that: "A good tree cannot bear bad fruit, nor can a bad tree bear good fruit. ... Thus you will know them by their fruits." (Matthew 7:18–20, NRSV)

Paul, in a well-known passage, makes use of this metaphor to describe how the inward working of the Holy Spirit changes Christians: "... the fruit of the Spirit is love, joy, peace, patience, kindness, generosity, faithfulness, gentleness, and self-control." (Galatians 5:22–23, NRSV) Some traditions add modesty and chastity to the list.

> **Take Warning!**
>
> The fruit of the Spirit can take time—a lifetime in fact—to develop. Consequently, one should not use the teaching to "test" whether or not someone is a true Christian. For example, the absence of patience or generosity is not evidence that a person remains unsaved.

Gifts of the Spirit

Christians claim that the Holy Spirit bestows skills, talents, and abilities on Christians. These are called gifts of the Spirit. Some of the best-known gifts are:

- Words of wisdom
- Words of knowledge
- Prophecy
- Discernment
- Faith
- Healing
- Miracle-working
- Leadership
- Service
- Teaching
- Exhortation
- Giving

Everyone may have some abilities in one or more of these areas, but a spiritual gift, or *charism*, represents a significant increase in skill that sets the recipient apart from other people. Consequently, a gift from the Spirit can be perceived as a "burden" because it can propel the recipient's life in unwelcome directions.

The Gifts Have a Purpose

Scholars differ as to the number and nature of the gifts of the Holy Spirit, which is why you see different lists of gifts. But most agree on the following basic principles:

def•i•ni•tion

A **charism** (spiritual gift), comes from a Greek word meaning "grace." Christianity teaches that the gifts of the Spirit are freely given supernatural gifts of God bestowed on Christians after they are saved. The plural of charism is charismata.

♦ Because the gifts of the Spirit are not necessary for the salvation or spiritual improvement of individual believers, the gifts were not given to all Christians.

♦ The gifts of the Spirit were given in the expectation that those who received the gifts will use them in ways that benefit other Christians.

♦ Different gifts will be bestowed at different times in history, depending on the changing nature of God's work on Earth (consequently, some denominations teach that certain gifts were given only during the early years of Christianity).

Identifying Gifts of the Spirit

Many Christians are fascinated with the concept of gifts of the Spirit and want to catalog the specific gifts they've been given. Consequently, tests have been developed (most are variants of so-called personality tests) to identify a person's spiritual gifts. Some churches administer these tests to new members, to help guide their choice of ministry. If you're curious about your specific gifts, tests are also available online (I've listed a few in Appendix B).

Paul enumerates some of the gifts of the Holy Spirit in 1 Corinthians 12:7–11: "To each is given the manifestation of the Spirit for the common good. To one is given through the Spirit the utterance of wisdom, and to another the utterance of knowledge according to the same Spirit, to another faith by the same Spirit, to another gifts of healing by the one Spirit, to another the working of miracles, to another prophecy, to another the discernment of spirits, to another various kinds of tongues, to another the interpretation of tongues. All these are activated by one and the same Spirit, who allots to each one individually just as the Spirit chooses." (1 Corinthians 12:7–11, NRSV)

Paul introduced another metaphor to explain how the varied gifts of the Spirit should work together. In 1 Corinthians 12:12–27 he compares the church to the human body, which has many different parts with different functions. One of the important purposes of this passage is to convince Christians not to be envious of the spiritual gifts bestowed on other believers. Simply put, we can't all be pastors, or prophets, or miracle workers.

The Least You Need to Know

- The Holy Spirit is the most mysterious—and most misunderstood—Person of the Trinity.

- Christianity teaches that the Holy Spirit calls people to Christ, and also enables a fundamental belief in Jesus that leads to faith.

- The Spirit also teaches, comforts, counsels, and convicts us of sinful behavior.

- The Holy Spirit is described in Scripture as both the Spirit of God and the Spirit of Christ.

- The most common symbols of the Holy Spirit are a dove, water, fire or tongues of fire, and the finger of God.

- Christians believe that the Holy Spirit bestows various gifts of the Spirit on believers—and that the inward working of the Spirit changes believers for the better (these improvements are called the fruit of the Spirit).

20

The Mystery of the Suddenly Courageous Apostles

In This Chapter

◆ Jesus' Apostles seemed hopeless leaders

◆ Jesus' crucifixion threw them into fear and despair

◆ The Resurrection changed the Apostles' mindset

◆ The Holy Spirit empowered and emboldened them

◆ They became leaders of the growing church

◆ Most of the Apostles were martyred

Jesus' Apostles weren't a courageous lot: most of them fled after Jesus was arrested and crucified. And all of them went into hiding after he was buried. Neither were they the sharpest hooks in the tackle box—they repeatedly misunderstood his teachings and the purpose of his mission.

Yet a few weeks after his death, the Apostles boldly proclaimed Christianity. The group went on to become the steadfast leaders of the fledgling church—and willing martyrs for their faith. This remarkable change of heart and head represents one of Christianity's most fascinating mysteries. I'll tell you the details in this chapter.

What's an Apostle?

The word *apostle* comes from a Greek word that means, "a person sent on a special mission." An apostle is not a mere messenger or assistant, but is a kind of ambassador who represents the sender and can speak for him. Scripturally speaking, there seem to be two requirements to be considered one Jesus' Apostles.

First, virtually all of the named Apostles in the New Testament saw Jesus after his Resurrection. Second, the true Apostles received direct orders from Jesus to do something.

Paul addresses the first requirement when he defends his Apostleship (see 1 Corinthians 9:1) and the second when he describes his conversion on the Road to Damascus (see Acts 26:16). Mainstream Christians assert that these requirements mean that no new Apostles have been made in almost two millennia.

Scholars presume that Jesus appointed 12 *disciples* to emulate the 12 sons of Jacob who led the 12 tribes of Israel. The Apostles are the new patriarchs who witness Jesus' miracles, testify to the Resurrection, and ultimately lead the church—the community that many Christians see as the new Israel.

def•i•ni•tion

Apostle derives from a Greek word that means "one who is sent out" in the manner of an ambassador. Our English word disciple comes from the Latin word "discipulus," which is the translation of a New Testament Greek word that meant the "pupil, follower, or apprentice of a specific teacher."

In most modern Bible translations, the word "apostle" appears a total of about 10 times in the 4 Gospels. By contrast, "disciple" is used hundreds of times to describe Jesus' devoted followers. The context of the many different mentions suggests that not all of his disciples were committed apprentices. Thus, while all of the Apostles were disciples, not all of the disciples were Apostles.

Disciples are the key supporting cast in the Gospels. We learn many things about Jesus through the eyes of the disciples. It's not too fanciful to think of the Synoptic Gospels as the story of the Apostles' apprenticeship to Jesus.

Two *Formerly* Illiterate Ignoramuses

Let me summarize the story told in Acts 3 and the first verses of Acts 4. Some weeks after Jesus' death, Peter and John went to the Temple in Jerusalem. Peter healed a crippled beggar and took advantage of the onlookers' amazement to preach about

Jesus and urge repentance. The Temple officials, angered by Peter's success—he apparently evangelized 5,000 people—arrested him and John.

At a hearing the next morning, an assembly of rulers, elders, and scribes demanded to know how Peter had accomplished the healing. Peter explained that he healed the beggar by the name of Jesus Christ of Nazareth, whom God had raised from the dead. Acts 4:13, NRSV, goes on: "Now when they [the rulers] saw the boldness of Peter and John and realized that they were uneducated and ordinary men, they were amazed and recognized them as companions of Jesus."

The English translation loses much of the tang of what the officials actually thought. The original Greek says that they recognized Peter and John as "illiterate ignoramuses" who used to hang out with Jesus.

Twelve Ordinary Workingmen

We've all seen paintings and stained-glass windows that depict Jesus' Apostles as first-century supermen. The reality is quite different. Jesus chose 12 ordinary workingmen—most of them Galilean Jews—to proclaim that the kingdom of God had arrived. There was nothing special about them—in intelligence, oratorical skills, or leadership abilities.

"Nothing special" is probably a kinder label than they might have deserved. Again and again, the Gospels show the Apostles as confused, petty, and occasionally reluctant followers. They repeatedly say and do the wrong things (see examples in Chapters 14–17). Worse yet, while Jesus was alive, none of the Apostles—not even Peter—seemed to understand Jesus' ministry or their vital role in carrying it forward.

Who Could Be Slow on the Uptake ...

The Gospels suggest that Jesus recognized his Apostles could be slow on the uptake. Case in point: Matthew 16:5–12. "When the disciples reached the other side [of the Sea of Galilee] ... Jesus said to them, 'Watch out, and beware of the yeast of the Pharisees and Sadducees.' They said to one another, 'It is because we have brought no bread.'

And becoming aware of it, Jesus said, '... How could you fail to perceive that I was not speaking about bread? Beware of the yeast of the Pharisees and Sadducees!' Then they understood that he had not told them to beware of the yeast of bread, but of the teaching of the Pharisees and Sadducees." (Matthew 16:5–12, NRSV)

Simply put, the Apostles were just as likely as modern Christians to misunderstand Jesus' figures of speech—one more proof they were not theologians or scholars.

Although Jesus met two of his disciples on the Road to Emmaus—not any of the designated Apostles—what he said to them could have applied to each of the Twelve: "Oh, how foolish you are, and how slow of heart to believe all that the prophets have declared!" (Luke 24:25, NRSV)

> **Take Warning!**
>
> Don't be confused by the word "heart" that Jesus spoke on the Road to Emmaus. Jesus was actually referring to his disciples' thinking powers. "Slow of heart" means "slow to understand," because in Biblical times, the heart (not the head) was considered to be the site of intellect and reason. The Bible uses the words "heart" and "mind" interchangeably. A good example can be found in Psalms 14:1 (HCSB): The fool says in his heart, "God does not exist." This verse means that a fool doubts God's existence.

Somewhat "Me-Focused" ...

In Chapter 17, I told you about the episode recorded in Mark 10:28–30 when Peter reminded Jesus that the Apostles had given up everything to follow him. Peter wanted to know, "what's in it for us?" Jesus replied to his me-focused question with an ironic answer that meant not at all what you might expect.

Mark 10:35–45 describes another me-centric episode. The two sons of Zebedee ask Jesus to give them places of honor and power in his kingdom. Jesus explains to James and John—and the other Apostles—that to be great they must become servants. There's no indication that any of them took that unexpected message to heart at the time.

And Lacking in Courage!

Over the years, the Apostles have been called fearful, timid, even spineless. Peter, of course, denied Jesus three times (see Matthew 26:69–75). None of the Apostles risked attending the crucifixion except John, "the disciple Jesus loved" (see John 19:26). And, after Jesus was buried, the surviving Apostles—Judas had killed himself—went into hiding, apparently in the "Upper Room," in Jerusalem (see Acts 1:12).

Given the brutality of the Roman occupation, it's probably not fair to call them cowardly—but scholars are confident that Jesus' gruesome death at the hands of the Romans reduced the Apostles to despair and hopelessness. They feared for their own lives enough to disappear and lie low immediately after the crucifixion.

Many scholars presume that some (if not all) of Jesus' Apostles had written off Jesus as a failed Messiah, despite the many miracles they had seen Jesus perform. This is because first-century Jews took for granted that a dead messiah had irreversibly demonstrated his inability to fulfill the prevalent Messianic prophecies. A dead messiah couldn't sit on David's throne and restore Israel to her former glory (see Chapter 13).

What Happened to Peter and John?

Is it any wonder that the rulers, elders, and scribes in the Temple were astonished by Peter's performance and John's boldness? The sight of a Galilean fisherman with the ability to heal and the willingness to challenge authority must have shocked everyone at the hearing. You can picture the leaders—who appreciated the limitations of Jesus' ragtag band of disciples—asking each other, "What happened to Peter and John?"

Imagine the dazed reaction if someone in the room had suggested that Peter and John would go on to write Scripture that would have as much authority as the books of the Old Testament. (Most of the New Testament was written by Apostles, including Paul. The most prominent non-apostle writer is Luke, who wrote the *Gospel of Luke* and *Acts of the Apostles*.)

The Mystery in a Nutshell

What power transformed the Apostles almost overnight?

- ◆ What made them bold?

- ◆ Who put compelling words in their mouths?

- ◆ Where did they get the courage to defy the most powerful Empire in the world?

- ◆ How did they learn to write words that have commanded respect for 2,000 years?

- ◆ When did they become inspired to travel long distances—to places they must have seen as the ends of the earth—to proclaim the Gospel?

- ◆ And, most important of all, what changed their minds about Jesus of Nazareth?

Why did the Apostles start believing that he was the promised Messiah—and that he was still alive—despite being crucified by the Romans?

A One-Two Punch

If you've read the earlier chapters in this book, you know the twin answers to the questions I've asked:

◆ When the Apostles witnessed Jesus' resurrected body, they experienced a faith recharge that renewed their belief—acquired by spending almost three years with Jesus—that he was the promised Messiah. In time, they came to understand that Jesus—the Son of God—had redefined the concept of messiahship in a totally unexpected way.

◆ The Apostles were empowered by the Holy Spirit (see Chapter 19). The Peter and John episode I described earlier happened after Pentecost, when the Holy Spirit came upon the Apostles (see Acts 2:1–4) and "tongues of fire" touched them.

Christians claim that the Holy Spirit took away the Apostles' fear and doubt and gave them the powers and capabilities to fulfill Jesus Christ's commission. Moreover, the Spirit guided and inspired the Apostles as they went on to lead the new church.

The Original Twelve

Scripture doesn't provide extensive detail about the Apostles (for some we know only their names) and describes the martyrdom of only one. However, early apocryphal documents and tradition provide additional information about the Twelve that while not completely reliable, probably presents much that's true. Here are mini-biographies of the Apostles.

Andrew

Andrew, the brother of Peter, was also a fisherman from Bethsaida. He apparently had been a disciple of John the Baptist and heard John describe Jesus as "the lamb of God who takes away the sin of the world!" (John 1:29, NRSV) After that, he told Peter that, "we have found the Messiah" (see John 1:40) and took him to meet Jesus.

Acts 1:13 mentions him as one of the Apostles in the Upper Room during the grim days before Pentecost.

Tradition holds that he died a martyr in Patra (or Patros) in Greece. He may have been crucified on an X-shaped cross that some denominations call the "St. Andrew's cross."

Bartholomew

Scholars point out that Bartholomew means "son of Tolmai," so that he may have had another name. Consequently, some Christians claim he is the Nathanael mentioned in John 1:45–51—a man that Philip invited to meet Jesus. John later mentions that Nathanael hailed from Cana (see John 21:2).

If Bartholomew is Nathanael, his most memorable observation is recorded in John 1:46, NRSV: "Nathanael said to him [Philip], 'Can anything good come out of Nazareth?' Philip said to him, 'Come and see.'"

The last Biblical mention of Nathanael (Bartholomew) lists him among the disciples who ate the fish breakfast that Jesus prepared in Galilee (see John 21:2–13).

Tradition claims that Bartholomew carried a copy of Matthew's Gospel to India and that he died as a martyr in Albanapolis, Armenia (he was flayed to death by knives).

> **Get Wisdom**
>
> Although all 12 Apostles apparently played significant roles in Jesus' ministry, scholars note that he seemed to have an "inner circle" of four especially important disciples: Peter, Andrew (Peter's brother), and James and John (the sons of Zebedee). Peter, James, and John were witnesses to Jesus' Transfiguration (see Matthew 17:1–9).

James, Son of Alphaeus

This James (there are two James in the list of Apostles) is identified as the son of Alphaeus (a man who some scholars believe is the Cleopas who met Jesus on the Road to Emmaus—see Luke 24:18). This James's identity has long been a topic of controversy:

Is he the same person as James the younger (or lesser) mentioned in Matthew 15:40? Is he the same as James the Just, noted for his ascetic practices? Or could he be James, the brother of Jesus, who took over leadership of the early church in Jerusalem (see Galatians 1:19)? There are many advocates for and against each of these possibilities.

Little has been written about James, Son of Alphaeus, but some tradition holds that he preached in the Holy Land, was martyred in Egypt, and that his body was sawed apart.

James, Son of Zebedee

This James is the brother of John, the two Apostles Jesus named "Sons of Thunder," or "Boanerges" (see Mark 3:17), probably in response to their zealous and volatile behavior. James seems to have been a privileged member of the inner circle of Apostles.

James' martyrdom is recorded in Scripture: "About that time King Herod laid violent hands upon some who belonged to the church. He had James, the brother of John, killed with the sword." (Acts 12:1–2, NRSV) Some scholars believe that "killed with the sword" means that James was beheaded.

John, Son of Zebedee

John is the disciple who Jesus loved (see John 21:20) and the brother of James, Son of Zebedee, the other of the "Sons of Thunder" (see James's biographical sketch, above). Jesus entrusted Mary to John at the foot of the cross (see John 21:26–27).

John traveled with Peter on a ministry trip to Samaria: "Now when the apostles at Jerusalem heard that Samaria had accepted the word of God, they sent Peter and John to them. The two went down and prayed for them that they might receive the Holy Spirit." (Acts 8:14–15, NRSV)

Most Christians believe that John is the author of the Gospel of John and three canonical letters. Many, but not all, scholars believe he is the author of the Book of Revelation. Many historians assume that John was exiled to the island of Patmos during the reign of Nero (or possibly Domitian).

Tradition holds that John was freed from Patmos, traveled to Ephesus to preach, and died there sometime later. If so, he was the only of the 12 Apostles to die a natural death.

Judas Iscariot

Judas Iscariot is the Apostle who betrayed Jesus to the Sanhedrin, the supreme council (see John 18:2–3). Scholars are unsure of the meaning of the name "Iscariot." One theory is that it refers to two Judaean towns named Kerioth; another is Judas was from the region of Issachar; a third that his name reflects he was a *sicarii* (a sect of knife-carrying assassins). He is also called Judas, the Son of Simon (see John 6:71).

If Judas was from Judea, he was unique among the Apostles; the other 11 were from Galilee.

According to Matthew 27:3–5, Judas committed suicide after betraying Jesus. He was replaced by Matthias, a new Apostle selected by lot (see Acts 1:23–26).

Matthew

Matthew, also known as Levi, is, like James, a son of Alphaeus. Matthew was a tax collector, a hated occupation in ancient Israel, because virtually all were corrupt.

He is the author of the Gospel of Matthew. Scholars believe that Matthew's chief goal was to convince Jewish readers that Jesus is the promised Messiah. Consequently, he attempted to prove Jesus' ministry fulfilled key prophecies in the Hebrew Scriptures.

Although little is known about Matthew's life and death, most tradition holds that he was martyred in Ethiopia.

> **Walking with the Wise**
>
> Scholars are unsure as to why there are variations in the Apostle's names in the different Gospels. One likely explanation is the Twelve had Hebrew or Aramaic names that were given different translations into Greek by the four Gospel authors.

Peter

Simon, whom Jesus named Peter, was a fisherman from Bethsaida, on the Sea of Galilee. Jesus called Peter to be a "fisher of men" (see Matthew 4:19). Because Peter is named first in all the lists of Apostles, scholars assume he was "first among equals" in the inner-group of Apostles. Peter, too, attended the Transfiguration (see Luke 9:28–36). While there he committed one of his many "foot-in-mouth" gaffes by suggesting that he build shelters (see Luke 9:23).

When Peter proclaimed that Jesus was the Messiah, Jesus said: "And I tell you, you are Peter, and on this rock I will build my church, and the gates of Hades will not prevail against it. I will give you the keys of the kingdom of heaven …." (Matthew 16:18–19, NRSV)

Tradition teaches that Peter was crucified in Rome, hung upside-down on a cross, because he felt unworthy to die in the same way that Jesus had died. Some scholars date Peter's death during the reign of Nero (54–68).

Philip

Philip also hails from the village of Bethsaida on the Sea of Galilee. He had a speaking role in Jesus' miracle of feeding the multitudes (see Chapter 16).

He's also remembered for challenging Jesus: "Philip said to him, 'Lord, show us the Father, and we will be satisfied.' Jesus said to him, 'Have I been with you all this time, Philip, and you still do not know me? Whoever has seen me has seen the Father.'" (John 14:8–10, NRSV)

Very little is known about Philip and many aspects of tradition are muddled, because Philip the Apostle is often confused with a different historic figure, "Philip the Deacon and Evangelist." In any case, Philip may have been martyred in Phrygia and buried at Hierapolis.

Simon the Zealot

Simon (often called Simon the Canaanean) to differentiate him from Simon called Peter, is identified in Luke and Acts as "Simon the Zealot." This implies that he was a member of a radical Jewish political party committed to the honor of God and the purity of religious practices. The zealots were determined to end the Roman occupation of the Holy Land. Tradition holds that he was martyred in Persia—possibly by being crucified.

Thaddeus (Jude)

Thaddeus is another of the Apostles whose name is uncertain. Mark calls him Thaddaeus, but various ancient copies of Matthew name him "Lebbaeus" and "Lebbacus." Luke calls him "Judas, son of James" (the King James Version says "Judas the brother of James"). And John identifies him as Judas (not Iscariot).

In any case Thaddeus is believed to be the author of the Epistle of Jude. The apocryphal "Passion of Simon and Jude" claims that he was martyred in Persia.

Thomas

Both of Thomas's two alternative names are variants of words that mean "twin": T'oma' is Aramaic for twin, and Didymous is Greek for twin.

Thomas gained immortality as "Doubting Thomas" when he requested to feel Jesus' wounds after the Resurrection. The story is told in John 20:24–29. But once Thomas was convinced that the man he knew had risen from the dead, he proclaimed Jesus, "My Lord and my God!"

According to tradition, Thomas preached in Parthia, Persia, and India, and was martyred near Madras, in India. He was supposedly killed with a spear.

The Least You Need to Know

- ◆ The 12 Apostles called by Jesus were ordinary men, most from Galilee, without special skills or training.

- ◆ They were not respected by the Temple elders in Jerusalem, who considered them "illiterate ignoramuses."

- ◆ The Gospels record that they often said and did the wrong thing, and—when Jesus was alive—failed to understand his mission or their roles as his disciples.

- ◆ When he was arrested and crucified, most of the Apostles went into hiding—they were in despair over Jesus' death and fearful for their own lives.

- ◆ After Jesus' death their fear seemed to vanish; they became bold proclaimers that Jesus was the promised Messiah—to the surprise of those who knew them.

- ◆ Christians attribute this dramatic change to the empowerment of the Holy Spirit and to the fact that the Apostles witnessed the risen Jesus.

Chapter 21

The Mystery of Paul's Conversion

In This Chapter

- ◆ A horrific persecutor of Jewish Christians underwent a mysterious transformation

- ◆ Saul encountered Christ while journeying to Damascus

- ◆ Jesus commanded Saul to become the Apostle to the Gentiles

- ◆ Saul's education made him ideal for the job

- ◆ Why Saul changed his name to Paul, and other minor mysteries

Saul of Tarsus, a highly educated Pharisee living in Jerusalem, was on his way to becoming a notable (if infamous) figure in early Christianity—he was the leading persecutor of Jewish Christians in Jerusalem and other cities with large Jewish populations.

But then a mysterious event changed Saul's life—and the future of Christianity. A man who thoroughly despised the new faith went on to articulate many of Christianity's key doctrines in the letters he wrote to churches in Rome and the Province of Asia. These letters represent about one fourth of the New Testament.

I'll tell you about Saul's remarkable conversion on the road to Damascus in this chapter. The event has become a metaphor for sudden, unexpected, radical change.

The Scriptural Story of Saul's Conversion

The Christian Apostle we know as Paul started out as a determined Jewish scholar named Saul. He underwent an extraordinary transformation on the road to Damascus that changed his faith—and eventually his name. (I'll call him Saul until we reach the point in his story that he becomes Paul.) The best way to begin the story of Saul's conversion is to start with the Scriptural witness. Much of the story is told in the book of Acts, a book written by Luke, who traveled with the Apostle during portions of his later journeys. Luke introduces Saul while giving his account of the death of Stephen, the first recorded Christian martyr.

Stephen was arrested and falsely accused of speaking "blasphemous words against Moses and God" and continuously saying "things against this holy place [the Temple] and the law," specifically that "Jesus of Nazareth will destroy this place and will change the [religious] customs that Moses handed on to us." (Acts 6:11–14, NRSV)

> **Get Wisdom**
>
> What did the Apostle Paul look like? Scripture is silent on the point, but the apocryphal *Acts of Paul and Thecla* describes him as a man of moderate stature, with scanty hair, crooked legs, blue eyes, large knit brows, and long nose. These features are emphasized in paintings of Paul, many of which give him a bald head, a prominent nose, and a slender frame.

Stephen gave an impassioned speech (see Acts 7:1–53) that accused the elders and the teachers of the law of "forever opposing the Holy Spirit." The outraged elders dragged Stephen out of the city and began to stone him (see Acts 7:58). The various witnesses to the stoning placed their coats at the feet of a young man named Saul, apparently for safekeeping.

Some scholars argue that Saul was the person in charge of Stephen's execution, although Scripture is silent on this point. In any case, Saul approved of Stephen's stoning (see Acts 8:1).

Saul the Persecutor

The day Stephen died marked the start of persecution, led by Saul, against the Jewish Christians in Jerusalem. He tried to destroy the young church by arresting, jailing, and occasionally executing some Christians—with the intent of encouraging the others to flee from Jerusalem to the countryside of Judea and Samaria (see Acts 8:1–3).

Why was Saul so angry about the Christian communities in Jerusalem and Damascus? When the Apostle told the story of his conversion to King Agrippa, he explained that he was so "furiously enraged by them, I pursued them even to foreign cities." (Acts 26:11, NRSV) Some scholars believe that Saul was truly offended by the idea of a crucified Messiah. He knew that anyone hung on a tree was cursed by God (see Deuteronomy 21:23).

The early persecutions of Christians in Jerusalem must have stopped—or at least abated—for a decade or two after Paul's conversion. According to the book of Acts, Jerusalem was the center of Jewish Christianity. When Luke describes Paul's visit to Jerusalem after his third missionary journey, he writes, "When we arrived in Jerusalem, the brothers welcomed us warmly. The next day Paul went with us to visit James; and all the elders were present." (Acts 21:17–18, NRSV)

Fast Forward to Syria

I'll let Luke tell the story from this point forward:

> Meanwhile Saul, still breathing threats and murder against the disciples of the Lord, went to the high priest and asked him for letters to the synagogues at Damascus, so that if he found any who belonged to the Way, men or women, he might bring them bound to Jerusalem. Now as he was going along and approaching Damascus, suddenly a light from heaven flashed around him. He fell to the ground and heard a voice saying to him, "Saul, Saul, why do you persecute me?"
>
> He [Saul] asked, "Who are you, Lord?" The reply came, "I am Jesus, whom you are persecuting. But get up and enter the city, and you will be told what you are to do." The men who were traveling with him stood speechless because they heard the voice but saw no one. Saul got up from the ground, and though his eyes were open, he could see nothing; so they led him by the hand and brought him into Damascus. For three days he was without sight, and neither ate nor drank. (Acts 9:1–9, NRSV)

When the Apostle himself tells this part of the story later on two other occasions in Acts (see Acts 22:6–11 and Acts 26:12–18), he adds a few key details:

◆ Saul saw the light from Heaven about noon.

◆ Jesus actually appeared to Saul in his glorified body, which convinced him that he had seen the resurrected Jesus.

◆ His companions also fell to the ground when they saw the light, but they couldn't hear the voice clearly enough to understand what Saul heard.

- They were apparently not blinded by the light and could take Saul into Damascus.

- When Jesus asked Saul "Why are you persecuting me?" he also told Saul "It hurts you to kick against the goads."

- Jesus gave Saul some information about his new mission—specifically, that he would open the eyes of the Gentiles and enable them to share in salvation.

Get Wisdom

"Kick against the goads" is from an ancient Greek proverb that warns against futile resistance to authority. An animal (often an ox) that kicked against the farmer's pointed stick would hurt itself more than the pricks the farmer inflicted to guide the animal in a specific direction. Some scholars believe Acts 26:14 suggests that Saul had been struggling with becoming Christian long before he traveled to Damascus.

Onward to Downtown Damascus

Now, a new character appears briefly, a Christian disciple in Damascus named Ananias. Jesus speaks to him in a vision and commands that Ananias heal Saul's sight. At first, Ananias balks; he knows Saul's murderous reputation. But Jesus explains that Saul is "his instrument" for informing the Gentiles about Jesus (see Acts 9:1–16).

Ananias does what Jesus asked; he finds Saul and heals him. "So Ananias … placed his hands on him and said, 'Brother Saul, the Lord Jesus, who appeared to you on the road you were traveling, has sent me so you may regain your sight and be filled with the Holy Spirit.' At once something like scales fell from his eyes, and he regained his sight. Then he got up and was baptized …." (Acts 9:17–19 HCSB)

Walking with the Wise

Saul's vision on the road to Damascus thus equipped him with an entirely new perspective …. Israel's destiny had been summed up and achieved in Jesus the Messiah. The Age to Come had been inaugurated. Saul himself was summoned to be its agent. He was to declare to the pagan world that YHWH, the God of Israel, was the one true God of the whole world, and that in Jesus of Nazareth he had overcome evil and was creating a new world in which justice and peace would reign supreme.

—N. T. Wright, *What Saint Paul Really Said*

A Sojourn in Arabia

The Apostle tells what happened next in his letter to the Galatians: "I did not immediately consult with anyone. I did not go up to Jerusalem to those who had become apostles before me; instead I went to Arabia and came back to Damascus. Then after three years I did go up to Jerusalem to get to know Cephas [Peter] and I stayed with him 15 days." (Galatians 1:15–18, HCSB)

Biblical "Arabia" was the kingdom of the Nabateans—the region south of Damascus that today is part of Jordan. Scripture doesn't actually say that Paul spent a full three years in Arabia, although this is a common interpretation of Galatians 1:15–18.

Many scholars assume that Saul needed this time alone to think through the three "impossibilities" of his encounter with Jesus, which forced him to reconsider all that he knew and believed:

◆ Jesus Christ had been resurrected.

◆ The many blasphemous claims about Jesus had been vindicated.

◆ Jesus Christ, the promised Messiah, had been crucified by the Romans—as part of God's plan to rescue humanity through the Jewish people.

Eventually, Saul came to understand that Jesus' shameful, but atoning, death (see Chapter 6) was the price of humanity's redemption. Some scholars believe that the Apostle developed the theology that he subsequently put into his letters during this period of contemplation and reflection.

Saul's Transformation

Some Christians say that Saul's conversion should really be called a transformation that changed every aspect of his life, including his religion. Others note that Jesus didn't "convert" Saul of Tarsus on the road to Damascus; rather, Jesus urged Saul to repent and then called him to go on an evangelical mission and preach the Gospel to the Gentiles.

Simply put, Jesus converted Saul into an Apostle; Saul's "conversion" to Christianity happened later when he thought about what he'd witnessed—and its impact on his life.

Three Days in Darkness

Saul had three days to think about his predicament: "For three days he was without sight, and neither ate nor drank." (Acts 9:9, NRSV) We can safely assume that Saul was alternately thrilled and terrified during much of this period.

On the one hand, his encounter with Jesus must have given him hope. On the other hand, Saul must have recognized that blindness would effectively end every aspect of his life—including his ability to pray in the Temple in Jerusalem. Moreover, Saul must have feared revenge for his well-known persecutions.

This extraordinarily intense episode continues until Ananias comes to Saul's rescue. He lays on hands to restore Saul's sight and fill him with the Holy Spirit. And, in the words of one of Scripture's most understated sentences, "Then he got up and was baptized …." (Acts 9:18, NRSV)

A Late-Blooming Christian

Somehow, Saul thought his way beyond a lifetime of Jewish doctrine to become a Christian—while blind, hungry, thirsty, and fearful. We can only imagine his inner turmoil as he struggled to reach a new understanding about God after his wholly unexpected encounter with Jesus.

Saul might have been able to change his paradigm of faith on an empty stomach, but he couldn't have done any significant thinking with an empty mind. Specifically, if Saul was able to figure out that Christianity made sense, he must have known a great deal about Christianity prior to those crisis-filled three days.

Saul's Prior Education

Where did Saul learn the Gospel? It really isn't necessary to assume he received it in a flash of insight delivered by Jesus—although that's certainly a possibility. The simpler explanation is that Saul, a kind of prosecuting attorney, knew all the claims about Christianity made by the Jewish Christians. Not only did he know them, he understood how to refute them during trials. It's not far-fetched to say that Saul knew more about the Gospel message than most of the Christians in Jerusalem.

And Saul also understood Jewish scripture and prophecy. Acts 22:3 tells us that he studied in Jerusalem under Rabbi Gamaliel, and Acts 23:6 makes known he was a Pharisee, effectively a "doctor" of religious law. Rabbi Gamaliel I (also called Gamaliel the Elder) was reputed to be one of the greatest teachers in ancient Israel. He was known for preaching moderation and tolerance for Jewish Christians (see Acts 5:34).

As the child of a Roman citizen in Tarsus—a city located in what became modern Turkey—Saul's early education would have probably included an introduction to Greek philosophy. He would also have gained some knowledge about pagan gods, pagan religious practices, and pagan mythology.

This threefold education in Judaism, Christianity, and paganism made Saul uniquely suited to be Apostle to the Gentiles—and also to make major contributions to early Christian theology.

Another aspect of Saul's education was a trade that would enable him to work and support himself during his long journeys. Acts 18:3 reports that his trade was tent making. Historians believe that he learned the skill when he was a boy, in keeping with the Jewish custom to teach all sons a trade.

Get Wisdom

Did the Apostle ever marry? Scholars are divided on the answer. He wrote: "I say to the unmarried and to widows: It is good for them if they remain as I am." (1 Corinthians 7:8, HCSB) But not much later in the letter, he also wrote "Don't we have the right to be accompanied by a Christian wife, like the other apostles …?" (1 Corinthians 9:5, HCSB) The statements, read together, may indicate that the Apostle was a widower who'd brought his wife on early journeys.

Saul's Walk of Faith Was a Quickstep

The blind, hungry, thirsty, and fearful Saul had to reach the same conclusion that all new Christians reach: that he was a sinner who had earned God's wrath, deserved God's judgment and punishment, and needed a Savior. I don't know how many new Christians are able to understand their predicament in only three days, but it can't be many.

Saul must have done it even faster, because he needed to make a second major leap of faith. As a highly educated Pharisee, Saul had to understand that Jesus had redefined familiar expectations about the Messiah, and also had fulfilled the promises to Israel that God had made in the Hebrew Scriptures. In other words, Saul had to undo, redo, and reshape the theology he had accepted as a given during his many years as a Pharisee.

Finally, and possibly the most difficult step of all, Saul had to begin to cope with all the damage he'd done to the fledgling church in Jerusalem. He must have felt enormous guilt now that he knew his murderous mission was wrong. Many years later he described himself as a blasphemer, a persecutor, and an arrogant man—the worst of sinners (see 1 Timothy 13–15).

Universal Skepticism

Twenty-first century doubters of Saul's astonishing transformation are the latest in a long line of skeptics that spans nearly two thousand years. The story seems easy to challenge because Saul was the only witness who both saw and heard Jesus—and apparently the only person changed by the experience.

Modern naysayers question the idea of Jesus appearing to Saul in a flash of light; they prefer to explain his Damascus Road experience as a hallucination (possibly brought on by the well-deserved guilt he felt about the violence he committed on fellow Jews).

In fact, the idea that a mere hallucination transformed Saul seems much less likely than Jesus Christ making an out-of-the-blue appearance. As miracles go, that doesn't seem to stretch the laws of nature far at all. Scholars have noted that his mindset changed from industrial-strength hate to sincere love, so that in the end, the Apostle wrote about love more than the authors of the four Gospels. Many Christians believe that his "hymn of love" (see 1 Corinthians 13:1–13) is the finest of the Bible's exhortations to love.

This is why first-century disbelievers—most of them Christians—doubted that a leopard like Saul could change his spots. Ananias, as I noted, had heard of Saul's persecutions and required Jesus' personal assurances to move ahead.

The Christians in Jerusalem were equally afraid of Saul when he finally paid a visit to what was then the head office of Christianity. Acts 9:26–30 reports that no one believed Saul had become a disciple. This time Barnabas—a Greek Jewish-Christian who the other Apostles highly respected—vouched for him. Somehow Barnabas had learned the details of Saul's conversion.

Minor Mysteries Related to the Mystery

Because the story of Saul's conversion on the road to Damascus is so well known, many of the details that are not fully explained in the Bible have become minor mysteries in their own right—and the subject of much scholarly speculation.

When Did "Saul" Become "Paul"?

The first mention in Scripture that "Saul" would now be called "Paul" is in Acts 9:13, when "Saul—also called Paul—filled with the Holy Spirit" challenges a sorcerer on Cyprus, during his first missionary journey. (Acts 9:13, HCSB) Saul is a Hebrew name, while Paul is a Roman name that means "little" or "short."

Other scholars argue that Saul of Tarsus, a Jewish citizen of Rome, probably had both Hebrew and Roman names. The theory is that Saul decided to switch to Paul when he began his missionary journeys through parts of the Roman Empire.

Some scholars hold that Paul's name change is significant because all Biblical name changes were significant, for example, Abram into Abraham (see Genesis 17:5) and Simon into Peter (see Matthew 16:18). One theory is that Saul of Tarsus wanted to shed all similarities between him and the Old Testament King Saul, who persecuted David before he became King.

Why Would Saul Arrest Christians in Damascus?

Saul was based in Jerusalem, a two-to-three week journey from Damascus. Why did he care about Jewish Christians in the Roman Provence of Syria? One theory is that synagogues in Damascus and other cities in the region were under the authority of the Jewish leaders in Jerusalem. Consequently, "blasphemers" (that's how Paul viewed the early Christians) could be brought back to Jerusalem for trial and punishment.

What Happened to Paul's Companions?

Paul's companions on the road to Damascus are typically envisioned as leaders of a caravan, or possibly travelers like Paul. However, some scholars theorize that the men traveling with Paul were little more than thugs he brought along to arrest Jewish Christians in Damascus. In either case, his companions brought him into Damascus, apparently to Judah's house on Straight Street (see Acts 9:11), and went their ways.

What Was Paul's Thorn in the Flesh?

Though not directly related to his conversion, Christians continually ask, what was "the thorn in the flesh" Paul wrote about? (See 2 Corinthians 12:7) Scholars have tried to diagnose the source of Paul's "torment" for centuries. The suggestions range from epilepsy, to an obsession with sex, to vexing Christians that Paul had to deal with on a regular basis.

Perhaps the most enduring theory is some kind of eye disease that seemed repulsive to people around him. That fits with Paul's comment in Galatians 4:14–15, NRSV: "… though my condition put you to the test, you did not scorn or despise me … For I testify that, had it been possible, you would have torn out your eyes and given them to me."

When Did Paul Die?

When did Paul die? Although most Christians assume that Paul was martyred in Rome about the year 62, Scripture is silent about his fate. Acts ends abruptly and provides no clues. The most credible history of his martyrdom in Rome came from Clement, an early Church father, who described Paul's death in a letter he wrote in the year 96.

An alternative story says that Paul was released from house arrest and went on to preach in Spain. (Note Paul's optimistic words and tone in Philemon 22.)

The Least You Need to Know

- Saul of Tarsus, a committed persecutor of Jewish Christians, traveled to Damascus in the Province of Syria to arrest "blasphemers" and bring them to Jerusalem.

- On the road leading to Damascus he encountered the risen Jesus within a light flashing from Heaven that left Saul blind and shaken.

- Jesus called Saul to repent and to become his Apostle to the Gentiles.

- Saul waited three days—blind and without eating or drinking—until Ananias, sent by Jesus, restored his sight and filled him with the Holy Spirit.

- The encounter changed Saul's life (he later took the name Paul) and transformed him into an evangelist who planted churches in the Province of Asia and Macedonia.

22

The Mystery of Christianity's Amazing Growth

In This Chapter

- ◆ Jesus of Nazareth had a few dozen followers
- ◆ This insignificant messianic movement should have vanished with Jesus' death
- ◆ The world unexpectedly embraced Christianity's "foolish" message
- ◆ Christianity rapidly overthrew paganism
- ◆ Today, one third of the world's population is Christian

Most Christians take the success of Christianity for granted—we don't expend much thought wondering why roughly a third of the people in the world identify themselves as Christian. But scholars who study the origins of Christianity are endlessly curious: how could a difficult and mysterious religion based on a "foolish" Gospel have survived its infancy and become the principal faith in much of the world?

We'll explore this question in this chapter. I warn you in advance that historians and theologians have no definitive answers. The astonishing growth of Christianity has been an ongoing mystery since the first century.

Christianity: The Faith That Lived

Jesus of Nazareth was one of numerous prophets walking around the Roman Empire in the first century. When the Romans executed him as an enemy of the state, he had a few dozen followers—at most. Instead of fading away (other faith groups of the time died along with their supposed messiahs—see Chapter 13), the Jesus movement began to expand.

During the subsequent dozen years or so, the number of "Christians" (as his followers had begun to call themselves) grew to several thousand. Some were Jews who lived in Jerusalem, but most were Jews in the *Diaspora*. A small number of formerly pagan Gentiles had also joined the communities of Christians.

def•i•ni•tion

Diaspora comes from a Greek word that means "scattering" or "dispersion." It commonly refers to the descendents of Jews who never returned to Judea after their exile by the Babylonians in 586 B.C. They lived chiefly in cities that bordered the Mediterranean—most toward the eastern end.

Despite increasing persecution by the Romans—initially aimed at the leaders, and by the year 250 designed to eliminate ordinary believers—the number of Christians continued to grow throughout the Roman Empire. One scholar estimates that there were one-and-a-half million Christians, another believes there were six million—a number equivalent to 10 percent of the total population of the Roman Empire. In either case, Christianity was solidly established across the Empire.

Fast-forward to the year 1000. Christianity had become the principal religion in most of Europe and was marching deeper into Asia and Africa. The Christian church had become a major institution in its own right and countless Christians believed that the end of the first Millennia would bring Jesus' Second Coming (see Chapter 7).

Today, roughly a third of the world's population is Christian—more than two billion people. And Christianity keeps growing, especially in Asia, Africa, and Latin America. Here are some interesting statistics:

◆ China had about 1.5 million Christians in 1970; today, there are an estimated 90 million believers.

◆ Approximately 25 percent of South Korea's population is Christian—some 12 million people. This compares with only 300,000 believers on the entire Korean peninsula in 1920.

◆ The number of Christians in Africa soared from about 9 million in 1900 to approximately 400 million today.

◆ By 2025, it's estimated that approximately two thirds of the world's Christians will live in Africa, Latin America, or Asia.

Christianity *Shouldn't* Have Thrived

The success of Christianity is one of its major mysteries, because both Paganism and Judaism were moving full-speed ahead in the first century. Scholars point to two compelling reasons why this new—and often mysterious—faith should *not* have been able to make headway in the Roman Empire.

The "Foolishness" of the Cross

When the Apostle Paul wrote that "… we proclaim Christ crucified, a stumbling block to Jews and foolishness to Gentiles …" (1 Corinthians 1:23, NRSV), he touched on a fundamental problem of Christianity that is usually overlooked by contemporary Christians like you and me.

I'll guess that more than half of the Christians you know wear a cross around their necks; perhaps you do, too. The cross—in one form or another—has become the universal symbol of Christianity. Our familiarity with the cross has taken away much of its terror. Crucifixion wasn't merely a method of killing someone—it was the absolutely worst possible method of execution.

The famed Roman orator Cicero described crucifixion as "a most cruel and disgusting punishment." He also urged that the word *cross* should be "far removed not only from the person of a Roman citizen, but also from his thoughts, his eyes and ears." The first-century Jewish historian Josephus called crucifixion "the most wretched of deaths."

Crucifixion was agonizing, but it was also demeaning and intentionally humiliating. It stigmatized its victims in a way that made crucifixion a fate worse than death. This is why the Romans went to the considerable extra expense of crucifying wrongdoers who threatened the Empire.

Paul realized that crucifixion was a stumbling block to the Jews, because he had tripped over the issue himself (see Chapter 21). Jews knew that Deuteronomy 21:23 said, "For anyone hung on a tree is under God's curse." But the Messiah—a man anointed by God—can't possibly be under God's curse. Thus, many (probably most) devout Jews considered the idea of a crucified Messiah a logical impossibility—at least, at first glance.

Get Wisdom

Historians believe that the Romans routinely used three methods of execution: beheading (also called "the sword"), burning at the stake, and crucifixion. The Romans imported crucifixion from Persia, where it had been developed around 400 B.C. Crucifixion was much more complex than beheading or burning and required a squad of specially trained men. Some scholars believe that crucifixion was reserved for cases where it could have a strong deterrent effect—to punish rebels, pirates, slaves, and enemies of the state.

Paul's Gentile listeners didn't know the Hebrew Scriptures, but they were familiar with the horrors of crucifixion, especially the way it degraded and disgraced victims. And so they thought it inane—the very height of foolishness—that Jesus (or God the Father) would allow the Son of God to be publically dishonored on a cross.

Walking with the Wise

The early Christian use of the cross as a symbol was not simply a creation out of nothing. It took genius to see that the symbol which had spoken of Caesar's naked might now spoke of God's naked love. And I think that the genius in question belonged to Paul.

—N. T. Wright, *Paul*

An illustration: Celsus, a vocal opponent of Christianity who lived in the second century, argued that Jesus proved that he wasn't God by the way he responded to his crucifixion. Simply put, any self-respecting divinity would have suddenly vanished from the cross. Consequently, both Jews and Gentiles had good reasons for rejecting Paul's preaching about Christ crucified. Neither should have found comfort in a religion centered on a crucified savior.

Historians note that surviving ancient literature says almost nothing about the process of crucifixion. As a result, the accounts in the Gospels represent some of the most detailed descriptions available (see Matthew 27:32–44, Mark 15:21–32, Luke 23:26–43, John 19).

Christianity Challenged Rome

Christianity emerged among the Jews and was perceived by the Romans as yet one more form of Judaism—a religion Rome tolerated out of respect for its great antiquity.

As the Roman Empire grew, it absorbed proponents of many different pagan religions. The Romans apparently had no objections to conquered peoples worshiping their own gods as long as they also worshiped Rome's gods—including the Roman Emperor.

Pagan worship was impossible, of course, for the Jews, who believed firmly in one God. Their refusal to make sacrifices to Rome's assorted deities was tolerated by the authorities, who extended the same tolerance to the early Christians. *Toleration* is the right word, because the Romans viewed the one-God teaching of Judaism and Christianity as a dangerous kind of atheism that might arouse the ire of the Roman gods and ultimately damage Rome.

In time, however, the Romans observed that Christians did not follow Jewish practices and recognized Christianity as a distinct religion—a newfangled, fast-growing faith that refused to worship or make sacrifices to Rome's gods, without (from the Roman perspective) a good reason based on ancient traditions.

Keep in mind that Roman officials regarded universal worship and sacrifices to the gods as necessities to ensure the public good. Refusing to participate in sacrifices was seen as the equivalent to harming Rome—a disloyal and subversive act. It's no wonder that Christians were viewed with suspicion!

While we're on the topic of seeming subversive .... The core Christian message must have sounded downright rebellious to Roman ears. When first-century Christians proclaimed, "Jesus is Lord," the obvious unspoken implication was, "and Caesar is not." Christianity left no doubt that God was above the governing authorities in the Roman Empire—including Caesar. Jesus himself had said much the same thing when he was alive: "All authority in heaven and on earth has been given to me." (Matthew 28:18, NRSV)

Scripture Says

Rome might have seen *some* Christian acquiescence of Roman governance in Paul's advice: "Let every person be subject to the governing authorities; for there is no authority except from God, and those authorities that exist have been instituted by God. Therefore whoever resists authority resists what God has appointed .... Pay to all what is due them—taxes to whom taxes are due, revenue to whom revenue is due, respect to whom respect is due, honor to whom honor is due." (Romans 13:1–2, 7, NRSV)

Challenging the authority of the Emperor was hardly a wise course of action in a totalitarian Empire like Rome—a classic "go along to get along" society.

Consequently, the least likely converts to Christianity should have been people who depended on the Roman Empire for their livelihoods and security. The new faith based on radical principles might be okay for peasants, slaves, and fishermen, but why would a citizen of Rome or anyone else in a privileged position take the risk of denying that Caesar was Lord?

What About Persecution?

You might expect me to list persecution as a *dis*incentive to becoming a Christian. In fact, historians now recognize that widespread persecution of Christians was not practiced by Rome during the early years of the faith. Persecution tended to be sporadic, limited, and typically aimed at leaders of the young Christian community. Although thousands died over many years, Christianity lived on.

The first attempt at Empire-wide persecution took place in 250, during the reign of Decius. Apparently, Decius issued a decree requiring everyone to perform a public sacrifice—proof of their allegiance to the Emperor and the Empire. Some Christians were martyred when they refused, others fled the cities, and still others performed the sacrifices and then tried to rejoin their Christian communities.

Another Empire-wide persecution occurred early in the fourth century—but it was largely unenforced by officials in the western parts of the Empire. In any case, by then Christianity was so extensive and entrenched that persecution no longer threatened the growing faith.

So ... Why Did Christianity Prosper?

Most Christians will answer that God's will and the work of the Holy Spirit overcame every obstacle.

Certainly! But this would be the shortest chapter in the book if we stopped there. So, I'll give you several additional reasons proposed by historians and theologians. They're interesting and worth considering, but as I've already noted, all are possibilities rather than sure things.

The Christian Message of Hope and Love

Many scholars believe that Christianity grew so quickly because it met significant human needs, including:

- The hope of a better life to come

- The unique notion that every individual—even those with the lowest status in Roman society—is valued by God

- The idea that Sovereign God cares about—and intends to bring about—justice

- The revolutionary concept that God loves us enough to send his Son into the world to die an atoning death for humankind

Theologians also point out that Jesus himself is a key aspect of Christianity's first century message. The images drawn of Roman gods tended to look either aristocratic or nonhuman. Jesus, by contrast, was presented as a true man of the people—God with us, but in the form of an ordinary man, who became our mediator in Heaven.

Successful Jewish Mission

When Barnabas and Saul set off on what would be Saul/Paul's first missionary journey, they traveled to Salamis, Cyprus, and "proclaimed the word of God in the synagogues of the Jews." (Acts 13:5, NRSV) Scholars note that this wasn't by accident. The first Christians in the Holy Land were Jewish Christians, so it made good sense to seek converts among Jews who lived in the Diaspora's largest cities:

- Teachers from Jerusalem often visited synagogues in the Diaspora—Saul and Barnabas knew they would be welcomed.

- Diaspora Jews lived in an essentially non-Jewish culture and found the exercise of Orthodox Judaism difficult so far from Jerusalem (this became even more true after the destruction of the Jerusalem Temple in the year 70).

- Some theologians think that Jews in the Diaspora were open to new and different interpretations of Jewish Messianic expectations.

Scholars believe that the Gospel resonated among these far-from-Jerusalem Jews. They were able to see Jesus as a fulfillment of the prophecies in the Hebrew Scriptures—as a redeemer who embodied traditional Jewish hopes in an unexpected and radical way.

Paul learned to tailor his message to Jews in the Diaspora: "To the Jews I became as a Jew, in order to win Jews. To those under the law I became as one under the law (though I myself am not under the law) so that I might win those under the law." (1 Corinthians 9:20, NRSV)

Paul didn't always succeed. He reports in 2 Corinthians 11:24, NRSV, that "Five times I have received from the Jews the forty lashes minus one." Scripture doesn't explain why Paul was punished, but it's likely that some of the Diaspora synagogues he visited were violently unreceptive to his message.

But enough were receptive—to Paul and other Christian evangelists—that some historians now believe that the great majority of believers by the middle of the third century were Jewish Christians. If so, this would mean that as many as one out of five Diaspora Jews became Christians.

Christian Fellowship and Community

Some scholars claim that the ability of early Christians to build a new kind of community may have been the single most important reason for the success of Christianity. When converts became Christians they entered a community that offered a better sense of belonging—of sincere fellowship—than any other religion could offer.

Back then (as today), a new Christian joined a unique family of brothers and sisters in Christ wherein everyone was equal. To quote Paul, "As many of you as were baptized into Christ have clothed yourselves with Christ. There is no longer Jew or Greek, there is no longer slave or free, there is no longer male and female; for all of you are one in Christ Jesus." (Galatians 3:27–28, NRSV)

This kind of community was unheard of in the gender and class conscious Roman Empire. It must have astonished people who looked at Christianity from a distance. And it probably attracted many converts.

Christian Social Institutions

Christians implement agape—love that is self-sacrificing, voluntary, and unconditional. Christians care for other Christians and also for nonbelievers. Christians also create social institutions to serve community needs.

The Book of Acts describes how the first Christians sold their property and shared the proceeds: "There was not a needy person among them … for it [the proceeds] was distributed to each as any had need." (Acts 4:34–35, NRSV)

As the young church grew, Christians took care of widows, established health care facilities, supported the poor, and (at least in Rome) ensured that Christian dead would be buried. Many scholars argue that Christianity's agape-driven care networks attracted converts and contributed significantly to the growth of to the faith.

Upper-Class Early Christians

Jesus traveled with few possessions and little money during his earthly mission. This fact has helped to create the impression that Christianity grew by attracting the poorest segments of Roman society.

In fact, historians now believe that many of the believers in Rome and other large cities were from the middle and upper classes. (The poorest people in the Roman Empire lived outside the cities.) Typical first-century Christian communities were led by heads of households (the wealthiest believers) and included the dependents who lived in these households—and often each household's slaves.

Because so many Christians were among the Roman Empire's "solid citizenry," they attracted unbelievers from all social strata to *The Way*. They also had the financial resources to provide for the poor and establish the social services I talked about earlier.

That so many elite Romans became converts testifies to the power of the Gospel message. Scholars point out that these members of the establishment were people who had the most to lose by associating with "subversive" Christians.

Committed Christian Evangelists

The Apostles took Jesus' Great Commission seriously: "Go therefore and make disciples of all nations …." (Matthew 28:19, NRSV) Several reportedly traveled to the ends of the earth (see Chapter 20). Paul walked more than 6,000 miles during his missionary journeys. Imagine hiking from New York to California—and then back—on primitive roads and paths.

But besides making disciples, the Apostles *wrote*. They authored biographies of Jesus Christ, they created *how-to* guidance for recently planted churches, they fashioned the core of Christian theology, they outlined Christian ritual, and one of them produced what many Christians believe is a prophetic description of the End Times (see Chapter 7). It's hard to imagine oral tradition alone sustaining the rapid expansion of Christianity. The Gospels and epistles that became the New Testament helped to drive

Get Wisdom

Another kind of Christian writing that stimulated growth was apologetic literature. These books and essays attempted to prove that Christianity—rather than threatening the Roman Empire—actually benefited Rome. Other apologists explained the Christian faith; some tried to show that Christian teachings led to truth in ways that were compatible with Greek and Roman philosophy.

growth since the first of Paul's letters were circulated among the young churches he established in Asia.

Better Nursing

This is an especially fascinating explanation of Christianity's growth—a theory related to what I told you earlier about social institutions. Historians theorize that the elementary nursing care believers provided within their communities—which was apparently much better than the care most non-Christians received—reduced the death rate among Christians during two major plagues that struck the Roman Empire (between 165 and 180, and between 251 and 270). Each of these long epidemics—probably caused by smallpox, measles, or both—may have killed up to a third of the total population.

Because Christian communities enjoyed higher survival rates, the percentage of Christians in the Roman Empire had increased when the epidemics were finally over. It's also possible that significant numbers of unbelievers became converts because Christians had offered them help during the epidemics.

The Emperor Constantine

Historians consider the accession of Constantine I—born about 280, died in 337—to the imperial throne as a milestone in the history of Christianity, because in 313 his Edict of Milan allowed Christians to freely practice Christianity in the Roman Empire.

Get Wisdom _____

Tradition claims that Constantine became a Christian after his victory at the battle of the Milvian Bridge in 312. He saw a cross of light above the Sun, along with the words "By This, Conquer!" He told his soldiers to put Christian symbols on their shields. They did; and were victorious. In fact, Constantine never fully converted to Christianity until the end of his life (he apparently was baptized on his deathbed).

Constantine subsequently organized the first real *Ecumenical Council*—the First Council of Nicaea, in 325—that addressed the Arian heresy and clarified the doctrine of Christ's divinity.

The Least You Need to Know

◆ Christianity currently has more than two billion believers throughout the world.

◆ Christianity began as insignificant messianic movement in an obscure province of the Roman Empire.

◆ The "Jesus movement" should have vanished with Jesus' shameful death at the hands of the Romans—instead, it grew and prospered.

◆ Historians can't fully explain Christianity's spectacular growth during the past 2,000 years.

◆ Scholars have proposed many theories, including the appeal of Christianity's core message, the fellowship communities Christians build, and Christian commitment to agape love.

◆ Most Christians don't seek to explain the mystery; they credit God's will and the work of the Holy Spirit.

23

The Mystery of Christianity's Internal Squabbles

In This Chapter

◆ Jesus warned against Christians squabbling

◆ Paul worked hard to stop fights in churches he planted

◆ In-fighting spawned thousands of Christian denominations

◆ Some denominations grew from deep theological arguments

◆ Many sprang from minor disagreements

This chapter is about one the less noble aspects of Christianity—the propensity of Christians to squabble among themselves, break away from established churches, and create new communities. Like it or not, the history of the church is a 2,000-year tale of infighting, internal strife, bickering, schisms, and occasional open warfare.

Why do Christians fight? What do they fight about? And what has all the fighting accomplished? Those are some of the questions I'll try to answer in this chapter.

Jesus' Prayer for Unity

Shortly before Jesus was arrested, he prayed for the unity of the church. "I ask … that they may all be one. As you, Father, are in me and I am in you, may they also be in us … so that they may be one, as we are one, I in them and you in me, that they may become completely one …." (John 17:20–23, NRSV)

Jesus clearly foresaw that the growing cadre of Christians would often disagree about faith-related issues—but I think the disciples who heard him pray would be astonished at the vast number of different Christian *denominations* that exist around the world. One guess puts the total at 40,000; but even the most conservative count—9,000— seems extraordinary. There are more than 2,000 denominations in North America alone, each with its own spin on some aspect of Christianity or church *polity*.

This seems to be a record for diversity among the world's leading faiths—but is it a good thing or a bad thing that Christianity comes in so many flavors? As with almost everything else in Christendom, you'll find people with different opinions on the subject.

def•i•ni•tion

> A **denomination** is a group of Christian congregations, often numbering many thousands of churches, that share distinctive teachings and a specific form of organization and church government. Some denominations are international in scope, others regional or national. **Polity** comes from a Greek word meaning "government." Church polity is the form of government used by a specific church or denomination. The three most common polities in North America are episcopal (bishops lead the church), presbyterian (elders lead the church), and congregational (members lead the church).

An Explosion of Denominations

Many Christians see denominations as a practical way to deal with the inevitable conflicts that will emerge when billions of people come together in a common endeavor. The church, after all, is a community of people—and people often disagree.

Other Christians argue that Christendom's many thousands of different denominations represent a failure to achieve the unity that Jesus prayed for and which the Apostle Paul urged in the churches he planted. In other words, "denominationalism" really means conflict, confrontation, division, and separation.

Perhaps Paul was too optimistic. As a highly-educated Jewish scholar, he knew that religious conflict is an age-old problem. The Kingdom of Israel split into two parts: Israel (northern Israel) and Judea (southern Israel) over a secondary issue that eventually became a serious theological divide (see 1 Kings 12:25–33).

Scripture Says

Paul urged unity in the church at Ephesus: "I ... urge you to walk worthy of the calling you have received, with all humility and gentleness, with patience, accepting one another in love, diligently keeping the unity of the Spirit with the peace that binds us. There is one body and one Spirit ... one Lord, one faith, one baptism, one God and Father of all ...." (Ephesians 4:1–6, HCSB)

Christians Belong to a "Universal Church"

When Jesus said, "... you are Peter, and on this rock I will build my church ..." (Matthew 16:18, NRSV), he appeared to be talking about *one* church. (*Church* is the English translation of "ekklesia," a Greek word that means "a gathering of people" or "an assembly." It does not have a religious connotation in Greek.)

Consequently, theologians have long used the term "Universal Church" (or sometimes "Church Universal") to label the single body to which all Christians belong. "Universal" is actually a translation of the Greek word "katholikos."

The transliteration of "katholikos" gives us the English word "catholic" (written with a small "c"). This also means universal. When Christians who are not Roman Catholics recite the verse in the Apostles' Creed (see Appendix B) that states, "I believe in the holy catholic church," they are affirming that Jesus created a universal church, and that they belong to it.

A Christian who belongs to a church that is part of a denomination (I'm one of them) actually holds *three* memberships:

- ◆ Membership in his or her local church
- ◆ Membership in the denomination
- ◆ Membership in the Universal Church that Jesus created

Several Christian denominations use "Universal Church" or "Church Universal" as part of their name. This can be confusing until you remember that the Universal

Church created by Jesus doesn't have a building, pews, an address, or a telephone number. It encompasses all members of the Christian faith.

Bickering Christians

Although we don't know what caused Euodia and Syntyche in Philippi to disagree, we do have Paul's exhortation that they stop: "I urge Euodia and I urge Syntyche to be of the same mind in the Lord." (Philippians 4:2, NRSV)

> **Scripture Says**
>
> Here's another example of Paul encouraging unity: "Now may the God of endurance and encouragement grant you agreement with one another, according to Christ Jesus, so that you may glorify the God and Father of our Lord Jesus Christ with a united mind and voice." (Romans 15:5–6, HCSB)

And Paul also asked church members in Corinth not to cause dissent by choosing between Paul and Apollos, a gifted teacher: "For as long as there is jealousy and quarreling among you, are you not of the flesh, and behaving according to human inclinations? For when one says, 'I belong to Paul,' and another, 'I belong to Apollos,' are you not merely human?" (1 Corinthians 3:3–4, NRSV)

Conflict among Christians is hardly a new problem. Divisions within and among churches go back to the earliest established house churches in the first century.

Not All Fighting Is Destructive

Some disagreements in and among denominations can lead to improved doctrine, better governance, and the possibility of greater unity in the future. A popular metaphor for constructive disputation is found in Proverbs 27:17, NRSV: "Iron sharpens iron, and one person sharpens the wits of another."

The American Battleground

Scholars note that the United States—a free market for religious ideas—provides especially fertile ground for destructive church divisiveness. Today's newspapers are full of stories about disgruntled churches and splinter groups who threaten to break away from the mainstream denominations, chiefly over a specific denomination's response—or lack thereof—to contemporary societal issues. American churchgoers could read similar stories more than 200 years ago.

There were ongoing denominational *schisms* in the United States late in the eighteenth century and through much of the nineteenth. Opposing views on slavery drove many disputes, but theological differences played major roles.

Church historians point out that schisms rarely produce a true winner. Typically, both sides come away weakened and tattered, and the Universal Church—the body of Christ—gains no benefit. Jesus' reminder to the Pharisees also applies to religious institutions: a house divided against itself won't stand (see Matthew 12:25).

def•i•ni•tion

Schism (pronounced *siz-um* or *skis-um*) comes from a Greek word that means "to split." It means a formal breach within—or separation from—a church or religious body, usually because of a doctrinal difference.

Denominationalism: The Intended Peacemaker

You won't find the word *denomination* in the Bible. It's a manmade concept, an invention designed to prevent conflict in churches and enhance unity among Christians.

The idea of formal denominations dates back to the mid-seventeenth century—a time when Christendom was recovering from the Thirty Year's War—a long, disastrous struggle that began as a conflict between Catholics and Protestants in the Holy Roman Empire, but eventually involved most of the powers in Europe.

Religious conflicts often turned violent in the past because opposing sides each believed that their position represented the "Christian truth." People were willing to fight—and die—for their vision of the truth.

And so, scholars and theologians looked for a way to maintain Christian unity in the face of disagreements. The "philosophy of denominations" is one of the solutions they devised. It's based on four underlying principles:

1. There will always be differences in opinion about the external form of the church, because human beings can't interpret Scripture perfectly and are unable to discern divine truth with total clarity.

2. People rightly consider the differences important, even though they don't involve the core teachings of the Christian faith.

3. Because of humanity's limited knowledge of divine truth, no single form of church invented by human beings will ever be the true church of Christ.

4. The existence of different kinds of churches doesn't mean that Christians are no longer a single body; even though they worship differently, they are united in Christ.

In time, this philosophy grew into the sensible concept that separate denominations—each with its own mode of worship and form of church government—should be able to coexist peacefully as functioning parts of Christendom. Simply put, each denomination establishes its own specific teachings and practices without causing a schism in the larger Universal Church.

The original idea of denominationalism assumed that we Christians have more holding us together than pushing us apart. Consequently, a specific denomination would only be slightly different from the others. For example:

♦ A different mode of baptism or a different perspective about baptizing infants

♦ A different rule for when worshipers can partake in the Lord's Supper

♦ A distinct teaching about free will in its doctrine of Salvation

♦ A characteristic belief about the role of works in achieving Salvation

♦ Specific opinions about the Millennium and Last Things

♦ Alternative viewpoints on speaking in tongues

♦ A specific approach to church governance

♦ Distinguishing rituals, worship styles, and clergy attire

> **Get Wisdom**
>
> The use of "denomination" to label different groups of churches comes from the word "denominate," which means to "name" or "designate." The idea was that churches of various forms would each be denominated in a way that labeled their different doctrinal and governmental approaches.

Most Christians consider teachings in these areas to be important but not central tenets of the faith. They represent many of the in-house debates of Christianity and we can agree to disagree about them.

It's important to emphasize that the denominational freedom to disagree doesn't extend to the core teachings of Christianity (see Principle 2, earlier in the chapter). I'll discuss more about the core teachings later in this chapter.

Denominationalism vs. Sectarianism

We can guess that the theologians who proposed the idea assumed that a few dozen Christian denominations would emerge over the years—not tens of thousands! Denominationalism has been able to grow far beyond its initial boundaries and still be successful at keeping many open conflicts in check.

The advocates of denominationalism saw themselves opposed to sectarianism. A sect is a church group that claims it alone represents the true body of Christ. By contrast, a denomination should acknowledge that the members of other denominations are also true Christians in every sense of the term.

I say "should," because some contemporary Christian groups that are called denominations think of themselves as the sole keepers of Christian truth. Although this violates the spirit of denominationalism, we can take some comfort that today's battles in Christendom are fought with words rather than weapons.

Even so, the words can be harsh.

What About False Prophets and Teachers?

When one group of Christians seeks to discredit another group, one of the most popular techniques is to call the leaders on the other side "false prophets" or "false teachers."

The New Testament warns about false prophets and teachers. For example, Jesus said, "Beware of false prophets who come to you in sheep's clothing but inwardly are ravaging wolves. You'll recognize them by their fruit." (Matthew 7:15–16, HCSB)

Peter counseled, "... because of these [false] teachers the way of truth will be maligned." (2 Peter 2:2, NRSV)

And Paul cautioned the Church in Galatia, "I am astonished that you are so quickly deserting the one who called you in the grace of Christ and are turning to a different gospel—not that there is another gospel, but there are some who are confusing you and want to pervert the gospel of Christ." (Galatians 1:6–7, NRSV)

The bottom line: False prophets and false teachers have suddenly appeared at the helm of strange new Christian sects in recent years—and caused well-publicized tragedies, including group suicides by the members of Jim Jones's "People's Temple" in 1978 and the members of Heaven's Gate in 1997. We do have to keep watch. On the other hand, it's wrong to label a fellow Christian a false teacher merely because he or she advocates an unusual nonessential teaching or church polity.

How Do You Spot a False Prophet?

As theologians have long pointed out, one Christian's truth can be another Christian's heresy. That's one of the reasons it can be difficult to identify a genuinely false prophet. A good guide seems to be the essential teachings of Christianity, because as Peter warns, "… They [false teachers] will secretly introduce destructive heresies, even denying the sovereign Lord who bought them [paid the penalty for their sin] …." (2 Peter 2:1, NIV)

In fact, adherence to the core doctrines of Christianity is an indispensable test of the validity of any Christian denomination. Remember Principle 2 from earlier in the chapter: all denominations should agree on the basics of Christianity.

Most Christians include the Trinity, discussed in Chapter 3, among Christianity's most central core doctrines. However, there are Christian denominations that deny the Trinity, which raises the question: can one deny the Trinity (and presumably the deity of Jesus Christ) and still be considered Christian?

Clearly the members of these groups say, Yes! Believers belonging to many long-established Christian denominations insist that the answer is, No!

"Essentials" and "Non-Essentials"

"In essentials unity, in non-essentials liberty, in all things love." This oft-seen motto, used by many churches, has been traditionally attributed to Augustine of Hippo.

def•i•ni•tion

Orthodox is a Greek word that means, "right belief." An orthodox teaching is a correct teaching. Theologically speaking, an orthodox teaching passed muster at one of the Ecumenical Church Councils. Note that "orthodox" is used in the denominational names of many eastern churches. This can lead to confusion; all truly Christian churches teach orthodoxy.

Historians now believe it was written early in the seventeenth century by a German theologian (probably during the height of the Thirty Year's War).

Whoever wrote them, the words beautifully sum up the central idea that all Christians—no matter the denomination they chose—should accept the "essentials" of Christianity. Reasonable Christians may disagree about "non-essential" doctrines, but we are one unified church as far as the core doctrines are concerned. These are the *orthodox* teachings that represent the foundation of the faith.

Hold it! What's the definition of a non-essential doctrine? And who gets to decide if a specific teaching is non-essential?

Happily, the major skirmishes in that battle were fought more than 1,500 years ago. The beliefs expressed in the Apostles' Creed—with the exception of the statement that Christ descended into hell—are accepted by the great majority of the world's Christians.

Every Sunday, the Creed is recited in hundreds of thousands of churches, of many denominations. Moreover, most of the denominations that reject the use of creeds acknowledge that the Apostles' Creed accurately summarizes the core teachings of Christianity.

The Apostles' Creed compresses an astonishing amount of theology in 110 words (not counting the final Amen). But, surprisingly to many, it says nothing about the authority of the Old and New Testaments. Nor does it mention baptism. Both of these topics are often included in well-rounded statements of faith published by specific churches. The Creed, though, focuses on the teachings that the great majority of Christians accept.

> **Get Wisdom**
>
> Few Christians understand the Creedal phrase "I believe in the … communion of saints" when they speak it. This is widely—but not universally—held to be an affirmation of Paul's statement that all Christians are members of one body (see 1 Corinthians 12:12).

The Least You Need to Know

◆ Although Jesus and the Apostle Paul both urged unity among Christians, believers have bickered since the earliest days of Christianity.

◆ Fighting about doctrine and governance inside Christendom has led to the creation of tens of thousands of different denominations.

◆ Denominationalism was originally proposed as a way to ensure that Christians remained united about the essential teachings of the faith.

◆ Some self-styled "Christian denominations" reject essential teachings, such as the Trinity.

◆ The Apostles' Creed is a widely accepted summary of Christianity's orthodox doctrines that makes a good starting point for identifying the essential teachings.

24

The Mysteries of Pain and Evil

In This Chapter

- ◆ The "problem of pain" is a famed Christian mystery
- ◆ Why is the world full of pain and evil?
- ◆ Should a good and omnipotent God prevent suffering and evil?
- ◆ How skeptics challenge the existence of God

Why does a caring God allow suffering and evil to exist? Every thinking Christian has pondered this question at one time or another.

Why does God allow all this pain and evil? Why doesn't he act to prevent it? These are ancient questions that have puzzled theologians for hundreds of years. We'll look at the problem of pain in this final chapter.

The "Problem of Pain" in a Nutshell

We watch TV news and see daily reports of senseless violence, horrific natural disasters, wars that kill millions of people, widespread famine, and deadly epidemics.

We look closer to home and see bad things happening to the good people we know: illness, disability, accidents, crime, financial woes, all manner of abuse—the list of miseries we may experience goes on and on.

The evidence is all around us, but Christians seem to ignore an "obvious" contradiction. On the one hand, we acknowledge that the world is full of evil and suffering that appear to be pointless. (I'll talk more about supposedly pointless evil and pain later in this chapter.) On the other hand, we claim that God is omnipotent, omniscient, and completely good in all ways. These statements don't seem to fit together:

- An omniscient God would know that pointless evil and pain exist.

- An omnipotent God would have the power to prevent pointless evil and pain.

- A perfectly good (and benevolent) God would act to prevent his creatures from suffering pointless evil and pain.

Therefore … God is not omniscient, or not omnipotent, or not benevolent—or worse yet, doesn't even exist!

Enter Epicurus

About than 2,300 years ago, the Greek philosopher Epicurus (the founder of Epicureanism, a popular school of thought) came up with what scholars call "The Riddle of Epicurus":

> Either God wants to abolish evil, and cannot; or he can, but does not want to. If he wants to, but cannot, he is impotent. If he can, but does not want to, he is wicked. If God can abolish evil, and God really wants to do it, why is there evil in the world?

This riddle remains popular among atheists who routinely use the reality of evil and suffering to "prove" that the God of the Old and New Testaments can't possibly exist.

Many nonbelievers see this as a strong argument against the existence of a God who knows everything, is all-powerful, and loves humankind. At the very least, they say, the obvious existence of pain and evil it makes it foolish to rely on a God who knowingly allows people to suffer.

If God Doesn't Exist ...

If you truly believe that God doesn't exist, it becomes impossible to even ask the question, "Why is there evil in the world?" This is because God provides the external moral yardstick that enables us to identify something as evil.

Without God, evil is simply whatever you don't like. And who says what you don't like is evil?

It's a Really Hard Mystery!

Some Christians ponder the problem of pain for a while, then throw their hands up and give the answer you first saw in Chapter 1. They acknowledge that the existence of pain and evil in our world poses a genuine problem—but also remind the questioner that this is one of the thorniest Christian mysteries.

So don't expect a solution!

Well, I can't deny that humankind will never fully understand why God allows his creatures to suffer. But it's also true that Christian theologians have thought about the problem of pain for many centuries. They've sought a convincing *theodicy* that would explain why God tolerates pain and evil in his creation.

def•i•ni•tion

Theodicy comes from two Greek words that literally mean "God's justice." A theodicy is an attempt to vindicate God's justice in tolerating the evil and suffering in the world. A theodicy is created by thought alone; it is not based on revelation or faith. The purpose of a theodicy is to provide compelling reasons why an omnipotent, omniscient, and perfectly good God permits pointless evil and suffering to exist.

While no scholar has come up with a definitive explanation of why God arranged things to allow pain and evil, there are several proposed answers that offer interesting insights and are worth your consideration. At the very least, they'll give your thinking muscles a good workout.

Six Popular Theodicies

I've outlined six proposed answers to the problem of pain in this section. Keep in mind that each of them ...

- Guesses at what God has in mind.

- Starts with specific assumptions that not all Christians agree with.

- Is based on thought rather than Scriptural witness.

- Has its own scholarly proponents and opponents (this is an unsettled area of theology).

We Don't Understand God's Plan

Some theologians assert that everything that happens is a part of God's divine plan—a vast scheme that is inherently good, but which involves suffering that people mistakenly see as evil.

Simply put, the limitations of our minds and knowledge make it impossible for us to understand the good that God is working to accomplish, or to appreciate the unusual tools (including pain and evil) he works with to achieve his purpose.

> **Take Warning!**
>
> While it can be interesting to read—and think—about the reasons why God allows so much pain and evil in his creation, please keep in mind that a theodicy is rarely comforting to someone who is suffering. That person needs a caring friend or pastoral care, not a speculative explanation of why God allowed him or her to suffer.

Consider this simple analogy: Imagine a woman—I'll call her Mrs. Smith—who is the mother of a three-year-old daughter named Jane. One day, Mrs. Smith allows a total stranger to stab her defenseless child with several sharp, steel needles. Jane finds the experience extremely painful and responds with screams and tears. Jane knows she has suffered, but she doesn't understand why.

Years later, Mrs. Smith reminisces with Jane about her childhood. Jane partially remembers a day filled with fear and pain. "I remember that day, too," Mrs. Smith says. She goes on to explain how she once took Jane to a far-away pediatrician for a series of blood tests and injections to diagnose and cure a serious illness.

The advocates of the *we-don't-understand* solution argue that we're in the same position as Jane when we classify all suffering as evil. Like Jane, we'd probably feel differently if our heavenly parent explained his purpose and we understood the good our pain accomplished.

But all pain isn't for good, of course. Although pain may be justified in many situations, few of us believe that *all* pain and evil ultimately serve good purposes? Frankly, much (perhaps most) of the evil and suffering we see in the world seems pointless. Does God really have a big-picture purpose in mind when millions of people die of starvation during an African famine caused by a senseless war? And what possible purpose does the suffering of animals fulfill?

"We can't understand" doesn't seem a satisfactory answer to these questions. After all, the God we follow has told us that, "Even though I walk through the darkest valley, I fear no evil; for you are with me; your rod and your staff—they comfort me. You prepare a table before me in the presence of my enemies; you anoint my head with oil; my cup overflows. Surely goodness and mercy shall follow me all the days of my life, and I shall dwell in the house of the LORD my whole life long." (Psalms 23:4–6, NRSV)

Suffering Helps Bring Sinners to Jesus

Another frequently heard possibility is that God allows evil and pain to exist because suffering encourages people to become Christians and helps in the ongoing process of sanctification. Specifically, suffering …

- ◆ Changes humankind's perspective—eliminating self-satisfaction and encouraging humility.

- ◆ Persuades people that we're fragile, that our time on Earth is short, and that we need to be reconciled to God.

- ◆ Encourages us to turn our attention away from worldly things and toward on our eternal destinies.

This explanation has much in common with the theodicy I wrote about in the previous section—and has a similar problem. While *some* suffering might goad unbelievers toward Christ, we seem to have an unnecessary abundance of pain and evil. We can certainly ask why God hasn't cut back suffering to a more appropriate level.

Pain and Suffering Are Short-Lived

Another theory argues that a beneficent God allows pain and evil in this world because the short time we spend in it—compared to our eternal futures and glorified bodies that will not experience pain—makes our suffering today relatively unimportant.

To quote the Apostle Paul: "For I consider that the sufferings of this present time are not worth comparing with the glory that is going to be revealed to us." (Romans 8:18, HCSB)

Some Christians argue that a certain amount of short-lived suffering may actually be worthwhile. James said, "Consider it a great joy, my brothers, whenever you experience various trials, knowing that the testing of your faith produces endurance." (James 1:2–3, HCSB)

This explanation really doesn't explain why God tolerates pain and evil in his creation—even for a relatively short time. Quite the contrary, it makes him seem almost indifferent to the widespread suffering on Earth.

And as for the notion that unpleasant trials can teach valuable lessons …. While this may be true, the tuition can be very high—and people who can't afford the payments are often forced to make them. In the end, we're left to wonder what God had in mind when more than 200,000 people are killed by a sudden tsunami.

Pain and Suffering Are Humanity's Fault

Some scholars resolve the mystery by putting the blame for evil on fallen humanity. The world is full of evil because humankind's sinful nature gives people the propensity to do morally wrong things. Evil will exist until Jesus' Second Coming (see Chapter 7). Those resurrected to eternal life will not have the capacity to do evil.

This theory also holds that the curse God put on creation, as part of his punishment for rebellious humankind's disobedience (see Genesis 3:17), is responsible for the suffering caused by illness and natural disasters. When God restores the creation and establishes New Earth, this kind of suffering will no longer be a problem.

This explanation—like the one before it—doesn't explain why a beneficent God would allow so much suffering to exist, or why he arranged things in a way that brings more suffering to some people than to others.

God Knows … We Shouldn't Pry

A few theologians claim that it's wholly inappropriate for mere creatures like us to search for theodicies that justify God's actions. For starters, we don't have any basis for deciding which of God's decisions are beneficent and which aren't. We also don't know how much evil and suffering God may have prevented, so we can't evaluate how much is left on Earth. The bottom line: we imagine that the problem of pain exists, but there really isn't one.

And another thing … God is so superior to humankind that we have no right to decide what is benevolent, or to otherwise judge him. Moreover, it's nothing but arrogance on our part to tell the all-powerful God what he should or should not do. We have to let God do what God decides to do.

In many ways, this is the lesson taught by the Old Testament Book of Job. Job is a righteous man who suffers a bewildering series of grievous losses. He's sure that he hasn't done anything to deserve what happened to him. And so he asks God. Why me? God chastises Job for even asking the question: "Then the LORD answered Job from the whirlwind: Get ready to answer Me like a man; When I question you, you will inform Me. Would you really challenge My justice? Would you declare Me guilty to justify yourself?" (Job 40:6–8, HCSB)

God went on to remind Job that he was not God's equal and that God had no need to explain his actions to Job. Job ultimately comes to terms with the reality that his relationship with God was more important than his understanding of God's purpose for allowing him to suffer.

The Answer to Evil Lies in Free Will

One of the most popular explanations for the widespread existence of evil begins with a key assumption: God decided to give humankind genuinely free will—the freedom to perform an action *and* the freedom not to perform an action.

Consider an action as simple as telling a lie. You can decide to speak a falsehood, or you can decide to be wholly truthful. The decision is yours alone. Scholars call this "morally responsible free will," because people have the freedom to act (or not act) in ways that have moral significance— they can be good or they can be evil. Many people argue that this is the only kind of free will worth having.

Alas, there's the rub: sinful human nature means that people left to their own devices will sometimes chose to do seriously evil things. We have the freedom to lie, cheat, steal, murder, deceive, blaspheme, start wars, be cruel, be selfish—you get the idea.

> **Get Wisdom**
>
> This explanation of the problem of pain is a "defense" rather than a theodicy. The difference is subtle to those of us who aren't philosophers. A defense shows that it's possible for a good God to tolerate evil; a theodicy actually explains *why* God decided to allow evil in his creation.

Let me emphasize four important points to keep in mind here:

- ◆ The best kind of free will includes the ability to do evil as well as good.

- ◆ If God had chosen to prevent humanity from doing anything evil—if he had chosen to oversee all of our actions—this would have represented a major *weakening* of our free will.

- ◆ Fallen humanity—*not* God—is responsible for evil in the world. People make the decision on their own to perform evil acts. God never requires people to do evil, he merely makes it possible by giving humankind free will.

- ◆ Mankind is fully accountable for the evil we do. The fact that God gave people free will doesn't shift the blame for doing wrong to him, nor does it mean that evil people don't deserve to be judged by God and punished.

The free-will defense explains why God seems to tolerate evil. I say *seems to tolerate* because God did not make a specific decision to incorporate evil in his creation. Rather, he gave humankind the ability to do things that *may* include evil.

Because people are the source of evil in the world, this raised the possibility that human beings might sometimes do evil things. There was also a possibility—albeit much smaller—that people would always choose to do good.

The only way for God to absolutely eliminate evil would be to take away humanity's free will. But that would have represented a fundamental change in the rules of his creation. The problem of evil would disappear, but so would humankind's sense of freedom.

The theologians who champion this explanation don't try to explain why God decided to give people this open-ended kind of free will—other than to say that God believed his decision had great value, and that morally responsible free will somehow represents a greater good that outweighs the evil humankind might do.

Walking with the Wise

C. S. Lewis proposed a more complete answer in *Mere Christianity:* "Why, then, did God give them [people] free will? Because free will, though it makes evil possible, is also the only thing that makes possible any love or goodness or joy worth having. A world of automata—of creatures that worked like machines—would hardly be worth creating. The happiness which God designs for His higher creatures is the happiness of being freely, voluntarily united to Him and to each other .... And for that they must be free. Of course, God knew what would happen if they used their freedom the wrong way: apparently He thought it worth the risk."

Other scholars add that true free will—the freedom to choose or reject both good and evil—is a prerequisite for developing a moral compass. A person who isn't allowed to make bad choices never develops the desire to make good choices. Looked at the other way around, a person can only become good if he or she lives in world where doing evil is a genuine option.

The Least You Need to Know

- One of Christianity's greatest mysteries is why an omnipotent, omniscient God who is completely good in all ways would allow pain and evil to exist in his creation.

- This so-called problem of pain is one of the most difficult Christian mysteries to contemplate.

- Skeptics "solve" the problem by claiming either God doesn't know people suffer (and is not omniscient), or he can't do anything about it (and is not omnipotent), or he doesn't care (and is not completely good).

- Atheists use the problem of pain to "prove" that the God of the Bible doesn't exist.

- Christians invent theodicies that try to reconcile God with the existence of evil and pain—they try to explain why God does nothing to eliminate suffering from his creation.

- A popular explanation of why God tolerates evil is that he gave humankind the best kind of free will—consequently people have the ability to do evil as well as good.

Glossary

adoptionism   An early Christological heresy that claims that Jesus, an exemplary human, was not born with a divine nature but rather became the Son of God when God the Father adopted Jesus at the time of his baptism.

agape   Love that is self-sacrificing, voluntary, and unconditional in the sense that it is not based on feelings or an expectation of being loved in return. Although the Greek word "agape" is translated as "love" in most modern Bibles, it was translated as "charity" in the King James Version—better capturing the concept that agape seeks to do what is in the recipient's best interest, no matter the cost to the giver. *See also* eros, philios, and storge.

allegory   A literary narrative that presents abstract ideas as symbolic events and characters. Traditionally used to teach religious principles.

analogy   A comparison drawn between a familiar thing and an unfamiliar thing to build understanding about the unfamiliar thing, often expressed as a figure of speech. For example, the first line a of well-known hymn written by Martin Luther asserts, "A mighty fortress is our God, a bulwark never failing." God is not really a fortress or a bulwark, but the comparison—the analogy—communicates that God is strong, enduring, and protective.

Annunciation   The announcement to Mary by the angel Gabriel that she would become pregnant with Jesus. The Annunciation is reported in Luke 1:26–38.

antichrist   An adversary of Christ written about by John (See for example 1 John 2:18–22) who teaches false doctrine. This false teacher has come to be identified with the lawless man Paul wrote about in 2 Thessalonians 2 and different evil figures in Revelation.

apocalypse   From a Greek word that means "unveiling." Any of several writings in the Bible or apocryphal books that claim to reveal how the world will end. For example, the canonical Book of Revelation is alternately called "The Apocalypse of John." Apocalyptic writing is characterized by strong symbolic imagery (difficult to understand or interpret thousands of years after it was written) and a belief that God will overcome the powers of evil that currently rule the world.

Apocrypha   From a Greek word that means "hidden." A collection of ancient Jewish writings that are considered part of the Biblical canon by some, but not all, Christian denominations. Many of these documents were written during the 400 years before Jesus was born. Consequently, this period is called the "intertestamental period" because it begins after the writing of the Hebrew Scriptures (Old Testament) and before the writing of the Christian Scriptures (New Testament).

apocryphal   Pertaining to the writings known as the Apocrypha.

Apollinarism   The heresy championed by Apollinarius (born 310), that Jesus' mind was not a human mind, but rather the divine mind of God the Son, the second Person of the Trinity. This meant that Jesus was not fully human.

apologetics   From an ancient Greek word for the speech a defendant made at trial. The branch of theology that uses intellectual techniques to defend the Christian faith. Apologetics is sometimes described as the opposite of polemics, in that apologetics attempts to win people to Christ, while polemics attempts to drive them away from other belief systems.

apologist   A person who give speeches or prepares writings that explain or defend the Christian faith. C. S. Lewis is a well-known twentieth-century apologist. Lee Strobel is a popular contemporary apologist.

apostasy   The intentional abandonment of the beliefs of a faith group. *See also* apostate.

apostate   A person who was once a member of a faith group, but has since "fallen away" and left the group. It has been said that most converts to Christianity are viewed as apostates by their former faith groups.

apostle   From a Greek word meaning "a person sent on a special mission." An apostle is a kind of ambassador, often charged with delivering a message. In first-century Christianity, Apostle specifically referred to the disciples Jesus chose to travel and preach the Gospel message.

Apostles' Creed   One of the earliest known Christian creeds, a summary of the core Christian teachings. Although the Apostles' Creed contains the main teachings of the Apostles, few scholars believe it was written by the Apostles themselves. Some parts were written as early as the year 150 and reflect the baptismal confessions of the early Church. The present Creed was probably completed during the fourth century.

Apostolic age   The years of the first century when the Apostles preached the Gospel message and the New Testament was written.

appropriation   The doctrine that Father, Son, and Holy Spirit are involved in everything God does, but that it's convenient to associate specific activities with one Person of the Trinity. Thus, we associate the Father with the creation of the universe, the Son with redemption of humankind, and the Holy Spirit with sanctification—although all three persons take part in all of these activities.

Aramaic   The ancient Semitic language that Jesus spoke. Aramaic was used throughout the ancient Near East and appears sparingly in the Hebrew Scriptures (parts of Ezra and Daniel) and the New Testament (for example, abba means father in Aramaic).

Arianism   A major Christological heresy, which taught that Jesus is less than divine, although the most supreme of God's creations. Arianism was the teaching of Arius (died 336), a priest in the Alexandrian church. Two church councils condemned Arianism—The Council of Nicea in 325 and the Council of Constantinople in 381.

asceticism   An attempt to achieve spiritual perfection by intense self-discipline or self-denial. The advocates of asceticism usually view the material world as evil. By contrast, Christianity teaches that self-discipline, purity, and simplicity can be appropriate aspects of Christian discipleship, but not means to self-perfection.

aseity   From a Latin word meaning "of oneself." God's power of self-being or self-existence. God is not dependent on any other force to continue forever unchanged; that is part of his essential nature.

Asia   During the first century, "Asia" was the Roman province that comprised most of modern-day Turkey.

Athanasius   (c. 293–373) A Christian cleric and church leader who opposed Arianism at the Council of Nicea and later. His writings played a crucial role in solidifying the doctrine that Jesus is fully divine as well as fully human.

atheism   From a Greek adjective meaning "godless." The absence of belief in God, a supreme being of any kind, or any deities. As many have pointed out, atheism is a belief in its own right.

atonement   A term coined by William Tyndale, the sixteenth-century scholar who created the first significant English bible translation. He was seeking a word to translate the Latin term *reconciliatio*. Tyndale settled on "at-one-ment"—that which reconciles, or makes "at one." Atonement has since come to mean the work done by Christ to reconcile God and the world. *See also* soteriology.

attribute, communicable   An attribute of God that has a parallel in human nature. For example, God thinks and loves. Humankind can also do both.

attribute, incommunicable   An attribute of God that has no corresponding parallel in human nature. For example, God is omniscient and omnipotent, but humankind is neither.

baptism   From a Greek word meaning to "immerse." The ancient Christian initiation rite in which immersion symbolizes the participant's spiritual rebirth and cleansing from sins. Some Christian denominations baptize only those old enough to profess faith in Jesus Christ. Others baptize children of believing parents as well as adult converts to Christianity. Baptism is seen as a sacrament by some denominations, and as an ordinance by others. The modes of baptism at various denominations include immersion, pouring, and sprinkling.

baptism of the Holy Spirit   A term interpreted differently by different Christian denominations. Some see the baptism of the Holy Spirit as the empowering presence of the Holy Spirit that a believer attains when he or she becomes a Christian. Others see it as a secondary, later demonstration of God's Grace, wherein a believer receives spiritual gifts, such as the ability to "speak in tongues" (utterances in languages unknown to the speaker and typically to listeners).

belief   The assent (and faithfulness) to a religious teaching or principle; holding the teaching or principle as true, often without absolute knowledge or certainty.

Bible   From a Greek word that means "books." The collection of writings held sacred in Christianity and Judaism. The specific set of books that make up the Biblical canon varies among different denominations. The word "Bible" was coined by John Wycliffe, the fourteenth-century theologian who created the first English translation of Scripture. The Christian Bible consists of 66 books (39 in the Old Testament; 27 in the New) agreed upon by all denominations, plus the Apocrypha.

blasphemy   From two Greek words that mean "to injure" and "reputation." Blasphemy is to speak words (or commit deeds) of insult, contempt, irreverence, or scorn against God or other sacred things.

canon   From a Greek word that means "measuring rod." The set of writings chosen from Hebrew Scriptures, Christian gospels, and various epistles, to create the Bible. Some denominations also accept the validity and authority of a collection of writings commonly called the Apocrypha.

canonical   Referring to the canon of a specific denomination—the books of Scripture it accepts as valid and authoritative.

catholic   From a Latin word meaning "universal." Catholic means universal when lowercased (as it is the Apostle's Creed). When capitalized, it is often used in lieu of "Roman Catholic."

Chalcedonian Definition (Formulation)   The formal declaration by the Council of Chalcedon—a meeting, in 451, of more than 500 bishops—that affirmed that Jesus Christ was truly man and truly God without confusion, mixture, or separation of his dual natures. Moreover, each of the dual natures—divine and human—retains its own attributes. The Chalcedonian Definition countered the heresies of Monophysitism and Nestorianism.

charism   From a Greek word that means "gift." A charism is a spiritual gift of the Holy Spirit.

Christ   From a Greek word that means "rubbing with oil." Christ is the Greek translation of the Hebrew word *moshiyach* (*messiah* in English) which means "one anointed by God." The term is used in the Old Testament to describe kings, priests, prophets—and even Cyrus the Great of Persia. When the Hebrew Scriptures were translated into Greek, *moshiyach* became *Christos*, which soon transliterated into the Latin word *Christ*. Many people mistakenly think of Christ as Jesus of Nazareth's last name. It is actually a title. A more appropriate usage is "Jesus the Christ."

Christendom   The totality of the Christian world.

Christian   A follower of Jesus Christ, although the meaning is difficult to define because many denominations establish their own definitions. Generally, a Christian believes in Jesus and professes the religion based on Jesus' life and teachings. The name first applied to the disciples of Jesus living in the city of Antioch.

Christological   Pertaining to Christology.

Christology   The branch of Christian theology that studies the Person and work of Jesus Christ, and the relationship of his human and divine natures.

church fathers   Early church leaders (mostly bishops) who refined and shaped Christian teachings during the first five or six centuries after the New Testament was complete.

creed   From a Latin word that means "I believe." A summary of the Christian faith broad enough to satisfy most believers. The most widely accepted creeds are the Apostles' Creed and the Nicene Creed.

cult   A religious sect that has its own, possibly heterodox, system of religious beliefs and rites. Because cult has become a pejorative term in our culture, it should be applied carefully.

decalogue   The Greek word for the Ten Commandments.

deism   The belief that the universe was created by a supreme being who chooses to remain distant and disconnected from his creation. A familiar deist analogy equates with God with a watchmaker who fashioned creation, wound it up, and now lets it operate without his guidance or providence.

denomination   A group of Christian congregations, often numbering many thousands of churches, that share distinctive teachings and a specific form of organization and church government. Some denominations are international in scope, others regional or national.

Diaspora   From a Greek word "diasporá" that means "scattering" or "dispersion." Refers to the descendents of Jews who never returned to Judea after their exile by the Babylonians in 586 B.C.

disciple   From the Latin word "discipulus," which is the translation of a New Testament Greek word that meant the "pupil, follower, or apprentice of a specific teacher."

docetism   From a Greek word that means "to seem." An early Christological heresy that claimed that Jesus' physical body merely seemed real, that it was actually an illusion, that Jesus was a pure spirit who could not die (hence his crucifixion and death were also illusions). Docetism rejects the teaching that Jesus is fully God, fully man.

doctrine   The formal definition of a belief or a principle of faith—for example, the doctrine of the Trinity. Christians are defined by their adherence to specific doctrines about God, Scripture, and humankind, to list three key areas.

dualism   The belief that two competing principles of equal power—one good, the other evil—are in continuous opposition to each other throughout the universe. The good principle is often seen as pure spirit, the bad principle as somehow related to matter. Note that the common Christian belief that Satan opposes God is not an example of dualism because Satan was created by God, thus is not a "competing principle of equal power."

ecclesiology   The branch of Christian theology that studies, and creates, doctrine about the church.

eisegesis   The process of "reading meaning into" a Biblical passage. Eisegesis "finds" meanings that were *not* present in the passage—meanings that reflect the biases, suppositions, and preferences of the person performing the study. "Proof texting" (using brief passages taken out of context to prove a point) is one common example of eisegesis. *See also* exegesis.

Enlightenment, Age of   The term that contemporary philosophers in Europe and North America gave to much of the eighteenth century prior to the French Revolution. Many leading thinkers of the day believed that reason and science provided truth, as opposed to "outmoded" religious doctrines and trust in God.

eros   Love of what is lovable, or desirable; a longing for what is prized. The Greek word "eros" was a root of the English word erotic; it appears twice in the Septuagint, but not at all in New Testament. *See also* agape, philios, and storge.

eschatology   From a Greek word that means "the last things." The branch of Christian theology that deals with the Second Coming, the Final Judgment, hell, eternal life, other "last things."

eschaton   The end of the age. (For example, most Christians believe the Great Judgment will occur at the eschaton.)

Eutychianism   The view (named for Eutyches, a fifth-century advocate of the teaching) that Jesus did not have a dual nature—that his divinity was merely clothed in humanity, that all his other human aspects (his will, his mind, his human soul) had been absorbed by his divinity. This single-nature doctrine, also called Monophysitism, was condemned as a heresy at the Council of Chalcedon in 451.

ex nihilo   A Latin term that means "out of nothing." Christians claim that God created the world ex nihilo, without using materials that previously existed.

exegesis   The process of interpreting a Biblical passage to unpack all that it contains. The specific techniques employed in the exegesis of Scripture are usually labeled hermeneutics.

exorcism   The undertaking of casting out (removing from a person) a demon or evil spirit. An exorcism is usually accomplished by prayer that invokes the power of God. Jesus apparently had the power to cast out demons himself.

general revelation   *See* revelation, general.

Gnosticism   From a Greek word that means "knowledge." A movement that taught that specific secret knowledge known to its adherents is the key to salvation—not faith in Jesus Christ. Gnosticism emphasized the differences between the so-called material and spiritual realms, and considered the material realm evil. Many Gnostic ideas are challenged throughout the New Testament. For example, scholars believe that Colossians 3:20–23 is an attack on Gnostic asceticism.

Godhead   Deity or divinity—the unity comprised of God the Father, God the Son (Jesus Christ), and God the Holy Spirit.

Gospel   A transliteration of Godspell, an Old English word that means, "good news."

Grace   God's *unmerited* favor of humankind that is ultimately demonstrated in the undeserved gift of salvation through Jesus Christ to humanity.

heresy   A doctrine or teaching that attempts to deny or refute an orthodox Christian teaching. Theologically speaking, "heresy" applies only to doctrines and beliefs that were declared false by one of the seven ecumenical (worldwide) church councils held during the first eight centuries after Jesus' death and Resurrection.

hermeneutics   From a Greek word that means "intepretation." The principles that underlie how a Scriptural text will be interpreted. Thus, hermeneutics establish the rules of exegesis.

heterodox   From a Greek word that means "different teaching." A heterodox teaching contains an error that is contrary to established orthodox doctrine.

homoousion   From a Greek word that means "of the same substance." Homoousion became a vital word during the fourth century when it was used extensively to explain the mainstream Christological belief that Jesus Christ was "of one and the same substance as God." Some opponents argued that Christ was homoiousion ("of similar substance") to God. Thus, some scholars note tongue in cheek that the battle over Jesus' full divinity involved a fight over a diphthong (two vowels pronounced as one syllable): o or oi.

hypostasis   From a Greek word meaning to "stand beneath." The term that early Greek theologians used to label the three "somethings" in the Godhead. Thus, there are three hypostases ("Persons") of God in one divine being. *See also* Trinity.

hypostatic union   The Christological doctrine adopted at the Council of Chalcedon which teaches that Jesus' divine and human natures are unified in one hypostasis (Person) without change or confusion.

icthus   The Greek word that means "fish." In Greek, icthus is an acronym for "Jesus Christ, Savior, Son of God." Consequently, an outline of a fish became an early symbol for Christianity.

immanent   From a Latin word that means "to dwell within." To say that God is immanent implies that he is pervasively present in all creation and accessible to mankind. *Contrast with* transcendent. Note: Don't confuse immanent with imminent, which means likely to happen without delay.

immutable   Unchangeable.

impassible   Incapable of suffering or of being changed by external forces.

impeccable   From a Latin word that means "not liable to sin." Incapable of sinning. Often used to describe Jesus.

Incarnation   The Christian teaching that the second Person of the Trinity took on flesh and became Jesus of Nazareth. Jesus is fully God and fully man.

indirect (circumstantial) evidence   Provides a basis for inferring the truth or falsity of the fact in dispute. For example, wet pavement is indirect evidence of recent rain.

justification   A key step in the reconciliation between God and humanity achieved through the atoning death of Jesus Christ. When an person is justified, he or she is considered righteous (free from sin) and is reconciled to God.

legalism   A fixation on the letter of the law that ousts mercy and charitable behavior, often causes more damage than good, and ultimately offends (rather than pleases) God.

mediator   From a Greek word that means "go-between" or "reconciler." Christianity teaches that only Jesus—both fully God and fully human—is able to reconcile the differences between God and man.

messiah   Literally, the "anointed one," which can refer either to a prophet, a priest, ordinary Jewish king, or to the promised Messiah. *See also* Christ.

millennium   From two Latin words meaning "thousand" and "years." The 1,000-year reign of Christ mentioned in Revelation 20, when Jesus and his faithful followers rule on earth.

miracle   From a Latin word meaning "something wonderful." An event that can't be explained by the laws of nature and consequently is held to be supernatural and/or an act of God.

Modalism   A popular heresy, alive and well today, that teaches that the One God sometimes plays the role of the Father, sometimes plays the role of the Son (as when Jesus was alive on Earth), and sometimes plays the role of the Holy Spirit. Thus, God reveals different modes of the Godhead to achieve different purposes or at different times in history. Modalism remains popular because it seems to explain the Trinity in easily understood terms.

Monophysitism   *See* Eutychianism.

monotheism   The teaching that there is only one God.

myth   A tale that while not literally true, may convey significant spiritual truths.

Nestorianism   An inappropriate teaching attributed (possibly falsely) to Nestorius, a fifth-century patriarch of Constantinople, that claims that Jesus was not a unified person, put rather two separate individuals sharing a single human body: Jesus the man, a human being with a fully human nature; and the Son of God—the second Person of the Trinity—who has a fully divine nature—and who dwelt inside Jesus' body. The Chalcedonian Definition countered Nestorianism.

Nicene Creed   A widely accepted creed based in part on early Christian baptismal affirmations plus writings from the church council at Nicea in 325 and the church council of Constantinople in 381.

numinous   The essentially mysterious sense that God is present.

omnipotence   From a Latin word meaning "power to do all." Having unlimited power.

omniscience   From a Latin word meaning "all knowing." Having unlimited knowledge.

ordinance   An order Jesus issued to his disciples. There are two major ordinances in the New Testament: Baptism (see Matthew 28:18–19) and the Lord's Supper (see Luke 22:19).

orthodox   From a Greek word that means "true teaching." An orthodox teaching conveys the true and accepted doctrine of the Christian faith.

Parousia   From a Greek word that means "to be present." The Second Coming, when Jesus Christ is expected to return from Heaven to Earth and accomplish the resurrection of the dead, perform the final judgment of both the living and the dead, and establish the Kingdom of God on Earth.

Pentateuch   From two Greek words that mean "five" and "scrolls or books." The first five books of the Old Testament, including Genesis, Exodus, Leviticus, Numbers, and Deuteronomy.

perichoresis   The theological concept that the three Persons of the Trinity are mutually indwelling and share in each other's life. Consequently, the Trinity acts as a single being, not as some kind of divine team. Somehow, Father, Son, and Holy Spirit function together as one force and jointly participate in everything that God does. Also referred to by the Latin term *circumincession*.

philios   Simple love that is characterized by affection or personal attachment, as a matter of sentiment or feeling, but which rarely reaches the deepest levels of personal commitment. *See also* agape, eros, and storge.

pneumatology   From the Greek word *pneuma*, meaning air, spirit, or breath. The branch of Christian theology dealing with doctrines and teachings about the Holy Spirit.

polemics   From a Greek word that means "warlike." The art of arguing strongly against what someone else believes. Contrast with *apologetics*.

polity   From the Greek word "politeia," which means government. The form of government used to govern and operate a church or denomination.

revelation, general   God's Revelation of Himself and His divine attributes in His creation, our moral compasses, and some aspects of history. Looking around and pondering the wonder of creation is sufficient to convince people that God exists, but doesn't provide enough specific information to take advantage of God's provisions for salvation.

revelation, special   God's Revelation of Himself, His divine attributes, and His plan for salvation in the Holy Scriptures and in the person of Jesus Christ.

schism   A split or division in a church over a doctrinal difference that may lead to a formal separation.

Second Coming   *See* Parousia.

Septuagint   The translation of the Hebrew Scriptures into everyday Greek, begun in the third century B.C., completed in the first century B.C. Theologians often use the abbreviation LXX (70 expressed in Roman numerals) to refer to the Septuagint. The name reflects the legend of how the Septuagint came to be: Ptolemy, who ruled Egypt from 285–246 B.C., sent a request to Jerusalem for a delegation of six men from each of the tribes to make a Greek translation of the Hebrew Scriptures. These 72 men supposedly translated the Pentateuch (the first 5 books) in 72 days.

sinners prayer   A short prayer that acknowledges past sin and invites Jesus into one's life as Lord and Savior.

soteriology   From a Greek word that means "savior." The branch of Christian theology that deals with the *doctrines* of salvation, including the atoning death of Jesus that reconciled God and humankind. Many theologians use this term instead of the older phrase, "theories of atonement."

special revelation   *See* revelation, special.

storge   Familial love; like the love between mother and child. Storge also involves the expectation of being loved in return. *See also* agape, eros, and philios.

Synoptic Gospels   From a Greek word that means "to see together." The first three Gospels in the New Testament (Matthew, Mark, and Luke). The Synoptic Gospels provide similar views of the life, death, and resurrection of Jesus Christ. Many details about Jesus are covered in all three Gospels.

theodicy   From two Greek words that mean "God" and "justice." An attempt to justify goodness of God despite the presence of evil in the world. Often described as "an explanation of why a good God allows bad things to happen."

theologoumenon   An alternative history (not based on the truth) that conveys a theological truth. Some skeptics consider the story of the Virgin Birth to be a theologoumenon, a convenient explanation of how Jesus can be both fully God and fully man.

theology   From two Greek words that mean "God" and "study." The study of the nature of God and man's relationship to God.

theophany   From two Greek words that mean "God" and "show." An appearance or manifestation of God to people. A well-known example of a theophany is the burning bush that God used to talk to Moses.

transcendent   Existing apart from the material universe. To say that God is transcendent implies that he is a spirit beyond time, space, and our conception, and that he is in no way limited by the material universe. *See also* immanent.

Tribulation   The period of great distress mentioned in Matthew 24:21, NIV: "For then there will be great distress, unequaled from the beginning of the world until now—and never to be equaled again." Christians differ on how long the Tribulation will last (many say seven years), whether it has already occurred, and what will happen when it occurs.

Trinity   A word coined by Tertullian, a late third-century theologian to express tri-unity, the concept of three in one. The Trinity is the distinctively Christian teaching that the Godhead consists of three divine Persons: Father, Son, and Holy Spirit. Although the Father is God, the Son is God, and the Holy Spirit is God, there only one God.

Trinitarian   Pertaining to the Christian doctrine of the Trinity.

Trinitarianism   Belief in the doctrine of the Trinity.

tritheism   An understanding of the doctrine of the Trinity that asserts there are three separate gods in the Godhead.

Vulgate   The fifth-century translation of the Bible into Latin, largely done by Jerome. He used Hebrew Scripture rather than the Greek Septuagint as source material. He included much of the so-called apocrypha, a term for noncanonical books that he invented.

YHWH   Called the Tetragrammaton (from a Greek word that means "four-letter word"), YHWH is a transliteration of the proper name of the God of Israel, as it appears in Hebrew Scriptures. Because the four letters are all consonants, and was never spoken aloud by Jews, scholars can only guess at how YHWH was pronounced. "YAHWEH" is commonly seen; so is "Jehovah," which is known to be incorrect.

zealot   A member of the first-century Jewish revolutionary group in ancient Israel that advocated the violent expulsion of the Roman occupiers and the overthrow of the king installed by Rome.

Resources

Books

As the author of Ecclesiastes so wisely noted, "… be warned: there is no end to the making of many books, and much study wearies the body." This seems especially true of books about Christian theology and Christian apologetics. Here's a list of books that will help you delve more deeply into the mysteries I covered in this volume:

Brown, Raymond E. *An Introduction to New Testament Christology*. Mahwah, NJ: Paulist Press, 1994.

Grudem, Wayne. *Systematic Theology: An Introduction to Biblical Doctrine*. Grand Rapids, MI: Zondervan Publishing House, 1995.

Horton, David (Editor). *The Portable Seminary*. Grand Rapids, MI: Bethany House Publishers, 2006.

Lewis, C. S. (Author), and Walter Hooper (Editor). *God in the Dock: Essays on Theology and Ethics*. Grand Rapids, MI: Eerdmans Publishing Company, 1994.

Lewis, C. S. *Mere Christianity*. New York: HarperCollins Publishers, 2001.

McGrath, Alister E. *Christian Theology: An Introduction*. Hoboken, NJ: Wiley-Blackwell, 2006.

Migliore, Daniel L. *Faith Seeking Understanding: An Introduction to Christian Theology.* Grand Rapids, MI: Eerdmans Publishing Company, 2004.

Vanhoozer, Kevin J. (Editor). *Dictionary for Theological Interpretation of the Bible.* Grand Rapids, MI: Baker Academic, 2005.

Online Spiritual Gift Tests

Several online spiritual gift tests are available that use web-based forms. Other sites allow you to download test instruments. You'll find several if you search for the keywords "spiritual gift test." Two sites that I have visited and used to gauge my spiritual gifts are www.churchgrowth.org/teamministry and http://buildingchurch. net/g2s-i.htm.

Using Online Theological Resources

I have not provided a list of online theological resources for two reasons. First, many espouse specific denominational teachings that may or may not match your beliefs. Second, although there are countless online resources, few of them are carefully edited or validated. Consequently, seeking information about Christianity on the Internet can be chancy. Much of what you'll find on the Internet is presented as "gospel," but I advise you to take downloaded doctrine with a proverbial grain of salt.

The best way to tap online resources is to use a search engine. I recently searched for "Jesus' Virgin Birth" and found more than 10,000 sites that discussed the mystery. I visited a few dozen and found that many were owned by organizations that challenge or oppose Christianity.

Leading Christian Creeds

I've provided the Apostles' Creed, the Nicene Creed, and the Athanasian Creed in this appendix for your reference. The Creeds are acknowledged—and used—by many Christian denominations as summary statements of Christianity's chief teachings. The Apostles' Creed is probably the best known, but the Athanasian Creed is the most comprehensive statement of Christian doctrine. You'll find more information about both Creeds in *Systematic Theology: An Introduction to Biblical Doctrine*, a book referenced earlier in this appendix.

Apostles' Creed

I believe in God, the Father Almighty, the Creator of heaven and earth, and in Jesus Christ, His only Son, our Lord:

Who was conceived of the Holy Spirit, born of the Virgin Mary, suffered under Pontius Pilate, was crucified, died, and was buried. He descended into hell. The third day He arose again from the dead.

He ascended into heaven and sits at the right hand of God the Father Almighty, whence He shall come to judge the living and the dead.

I believe in the Holy Spirit, the holy catholic [universal] church, the communion of saints, the forgiveness of sins, the resurrection of the body, and life everlasting. Amen.

Nicene Creed

I believe in one God, the Father Almighty, Maker of heaven and earth, and of all things visible and invisible.

And in one Lord Jesus Christ, the only-begotten Son of God, begotten of the Father before all worlds; God of God, Light of Light, very God of very God; begotten, not made, being of one substance with the Father, by whom all things were made.

Who, for us men and for our salvation, came down from heaven, and was incarnate by the Holy Spirit of the virgin Mary, and was made man; and was crucified also for us under Pontius Pilate; He suffered and was buried; and the third day He rose again, according to the Scriptures; and ascended into heaven, and sits on the right hand of the Father; and He shall come again, with glory, to judge the quick and the dead; whose kingdom shall have no end.

And I believe in the Holy Ghost, the Lord and Giver of Life; who proceeds from the Father and the Son; who with the Father and the Son together is worshipped and glorified; who spoke by the prophets.

And I believe one holy catholic [universal] and apostolic Church. I acknowledge one baptism for the remission of sins; and I look for the resurrection of the dead, and the life of the world to come. Amen.

Athanasian Creed

Whoever desires to be saved should above all hold to the catholic [universal] faith. Anyone who does not keep it whole and unbroken will doubtless perish eternally.

Now this is the catholic faith:

That we worship one God in trinity and the trinity in unity, neither blending their persons nor dividing their essence.

For the person of the Father is a distinct person, the person of the Son is another, and that of the Holy Spirit still another. But the divinity of the Father, Son, and Holy Spirit is one, their glory equal, their majesty coeternal.

What quality the Father has, the Son has, and the Holy Spirit has. The Father is uncreated, the Son is uncreated, the Holy Spirit is uncreated. The Father is immeasurable, the Son is immeasurable, the Holy Spirit is immeasurable. The Father is eternal, the Son is eternal, the Holy Spirit is eternal.

And yet there are not three eternal beings; there is but one eternal being. So too there are not three uncreated or immeasurable beings; there is but one uncreated and immeasurable being.

Similarly, the Father is almighty, the Son is almighty, the Holy Spirit is almighty.

Yet there are not three almighty beings; there is but one almighty being.

Thus the Father is God, the Son is God, the Holy Spirit is God. Yet there are not three gods; there is but one God. Thus the Father is Lord, the Son is Lord, the Holy Spirit is Lord.

Yet there are not three lords; there is but one Lord. Just as Christian truth compels us to confess each person individually as both God and Lord, so catholic religion forbids us to say that there are three gods or lords.

The Father was neither made nor created nor begotten from anyone. The Son was neither made nor created; he was begotten from the Father alone. The Holy Spirit was neither made nor created nor begotten; he proceeds from the Father and the Son.

Accordingly there is one Father, not three fathers; there is one Son, not three sons; there is one Holy Spirit, not three holy spirits.

Nothing in this trinity is before or after, nothing is greater or smaller; in their entirety the three persons are coeternal and coequal with each other. So in everything, as was said earlier, we must worship their trinity in their unity and their unity in their trinity.

Anyone then who desires to be saved should think thus about the trinity. But it is necessary for eternal salvation that one also believe in the incarnation of our Lord Jesus Christ faithfully.

Now this is the true faith:

That we believe and confess that our Lord Jesus Christ, God's Son, is both God and human, equally. He is God from the essence of the Father, begotten before time; and he is human from the essence of his mother, born in time; completely God, completely human, with a rational soul and human flesh; equal to the Father as regards divinity, less than the Father as regards humanity.

Although he is God and human, yet Christ is not two, but one. He is one, however, not by his divinity being turned into flesh, but by God's taking humanity to himself. He is one, certainly not by the blending of his essence, but by the unity of his person. For just as one human is both rational soul and flesh, so too the one Christ is both God and human.

He suffered for our salvation; he descended to hell; he arose from the dead; he ascended to heaven; he is seated at the Father's right hand; from there he will come to judge the living and the dead.

At his coming all people will arise bodily and give an accounting of their own deeds. Those who have done good will enter eternal life, and those who have done evil will enter eternal fire.

This is the catholic faith: one cannot be saved without believing it firmly and faithfully.

Index

M

R

S